THE CASE OF THE
KILLER
ROBOT

THE CASE OF THE
KILLER
ROBOT

Stories about
the Professional, Ethical, and Societal
Dimensions of Computing

RICHARD G. EPSTEIN
West Chester University of Pennsylvania

JOHN WILEY & SONS, INC.
New York • Chichester • Brisbane • Toronto • Singapore

ACQUISITIONS EDITOR   Regina Brooks
MARKETING MANAGER   Jay Kirsch
PRODUCTION MANAGER   Lucille Buonocore
SENIOR PRODUCTION EDITOR   Tracey Kuehn
TEXT DESIGNER   Helen Iranyi
COVER DESIGNER   Michael Jung
COVER PHOTO © The Stock Market / Al Francekevich
MANUFACTURING MANAGER   Marsheela Evans

This book was set in Optima and Palatino by Publication Services and
printed and bound by Courier/Westford. The cover was printed by Phoenix Color.

The Case of the Killer Robot is a work of fiction. Except for the individuals and institutions listed in
the appendix, the people, places, and situations described in the case are products of the Author's
imagination. Any resemblance between them and real persons, places, and situations is purely
coincidental.

ISBN 0-471-13823-1

Printed in the United States of America
10 9 8 7 6 5 4 3 2

Dedicated to the blessed memory of
Professor Herbert Jehle

PREFACE

Nature of This Book

This book consists of twenty-nine stories about the professional, ethical, and societal dimensions of computing. The stories also contain a strong software engineering component. One major theme in the book is the interaction between computer ethics and software engineering. Another theme is the impact of computers both upon society and upon those who develop software systems. The basic question that drove the composition of these stories was, What do students of computer science and technology need to know about the professional and ethical dimensions of computing? I was especially interested in communicating important information that the computer science or technology professional might need in his or her career—information that might not get covered in the usual undergraduate curriculum.

Each of the twenty-nine stories has three components:

- The story itself
- The endnotes and references for the story
- The discussion questions for the story

The endnotes give credit to those authors who have influenced me in my thinking. They also provide references to papers in the literature and to books that provide additional information about the topics being discussed.

The discussion questions are an important part of each story. For one thing, they bring out the concepts that I had in mind in writing the story. Beyond that, they introduce some thematic threads that lend greater coherence to the book. I am grateful to one of my reviewers who insisted that the questions be included as part of the book. These questions enabled me to bring out the profound issues that the stories are raising.

The stories take a variety of forms, but each story is a complete fiction except for the factual knowledge that the story tries to impart. These are the various literary genres that are employed: newspaper reports and human feature stories, magazine interviews, radio and television talk show transcripts, and a televised lecture transcript. Thus, all stories are intended to be factual stories within the fictitious world of the killer robot incident.

As noted in the previous paragraph, all of the stories give factual informa-tion about at least one of the following topics: software engineering, computer ethics, legal issues, policy issues (e.g., data privacy policies), repetitive strain injuries, stress in the workplace, stress and health, the ethics of speech, and computer applications. The knowledge is often placed in the mouths of experts, and like any responsible author of fiction I have tried to make the knowledge that they reveal as accurate as possible. For example, one charac-ter talks about stress in the workplace. I am not an expert on this subject, but I have made an effort to give high-quality information about this subject and to refer the reader (in the endnotes) to additional sources of information about the issue of stress and the quality of one's work life.

The Outer Book versus the Inner Book

This volume consists of a book within a book. The outer book is called *The Case of the Killer Robot,* and it is completely factual. The inner book is called *The Killer Robot Papers,* and it contains the twenty-nine stories that constitute the killer robot scenario. The inner book is a work of fiction, although it refers to real people and institutions. In addition, it strives to be accurate in its depic-tion of technical knowledge. The outer book uses Roman numerals (i, ii, iii, . . .) for page numbering, and the inner book uses Arabic numerals (1, 2, 3, . . .) for page numbering. Thus, if you see an Arabic numeral at the bottom of the page, you know you are in the fictional part of the book.

The outer book is a necessary shell for the inner book. The outer book is completely factual. It contains the dedication to my college physics professor, Herbert Jehle, this preface, and three appendices. The appendices are found at the very end of this volume (after the inner book). Richard Epstein (that's me) is the author of the outer book.

The inner book is entitled *The Killer Robot Papers.* It consists of the twenty-nine stories that have been alluded to. The author of the inner book is a fictitious character whose name is Pam Pulitzer. Pam is a reporter with the *Sil-icon Valley Sentinel-Observer,* a fictitious newspaper. *In the world of the killer robot, in the fictitious world where the killer robot is reality, the inner book is an actual book that is being sold at Barnes and Noble, Waldenbooks, and Dal-ton's.* Please reread the previous sentence until you've got it, because it is important to this entire enterprise. In the fictitious world of the killer robot Pam Pulitzer is a newspaper reporter who covered the killer robot incident. She collected articles about the killer robot and about the social impact of comput-ing, and she published them as a book, *The Killer Robot Papers.* Pam Pulitzer does not acknowledge Richard Epstein in her book (that's gratitude for you!).

Pam Pulitzer's book has its own cover, its own preface, and its own table of contents. However, I did not include a dedication in Pam's book for fear of diminishing the profound sense of respect that I have for Professor Herbert Jehle, to whom this whole enterprise is dedicated. In addition, Pam's book does not contain any appendices.

From Pam Pulitzer's perspective, the killer robot incident was a real event. Randy Samuels, Bart Matthews, Silicon Techchronics, CyberWidgets, and so on are all real people and institutions. She works for the *Silicon Valley Sentinel-Observer,* a real newspaper. From our perspective, these are all fictitious people and institutions. However, as previously mentioned, the information that is provided about software engineering, computer ethics, professionalism, the healthy workplace, and the social impact of computing is intended to be factual and realistic.

As is often the case with a work of fiction, Pam Pulitzer's book refers to real people, institutions, and places. This is because Pam Pulitzer is working in the same world of computing that you and I work in. When one of my colleagues (George Atkins) told me that one of his students, after reading *The Killer Robot Papers,* did not realize that the ACM was a real organization, I realized that I had the obligation to inform readers that institutions such as the ACM are real. There are dozens of fictitious characters in this book, but there are several dozen real characters and institutions that are mentioned, such as SEI, Ben Shneiderman, and Bertrand Meyer. I decided that I could not assume that all readers would know that Ben Shneiderman and Bertrand Meyer are real people or that SEI is a part of the real world of computing. Thus, I have included an appendix (Appendix A of the outer book) that lists all real people and institutions that are part of the cultural landscape of computing that are mentioned in Pam Pulitzer's inner book. This appendix includes explanations of actual institutions and people such as ACM, SEI, IEEE Computer Society, Jim Foley, Ben Shneiderman, and Bertrand Meyer.

Appendix B presents endnotes and references for each story. Professors can use the references given here to create "course packs" of readings depending on which articles in *The Killer Robot Papers* they intend to use. I believe that some truly creative and innovative courses with diverse titles such as software engineering, computer ethics, computers and society, and social impact of technology can be created in this way. Appendix B also includes the sample contents for a "computers and society" course pack that uses some of the references that are given. Finally, Appendix C presents discussion questions for each story or group of stories. I believe that the use of the discussion questions, even for the lone reader, will greatly enhance the value of the twenty-nine stories in the inner book.

Insofar as the detailed content of the inner book is concerned, I will allow Pam Pulitzer to explain her book in her own words. Again, remember that the inner book is an actual book that you could buy in a bookstore if you lived in the fictitious world of the killer robot. Humor me.

Dedication

This book is dedicated to the memory of Professor Herbert Jehle. Herb was my physics professor when I was a student at George Washington University. He was an accomplished physicist, and he is acknowledged in Richard Feynmann's Nobel Prize lecture. But I remember Herb more as a spiritual mentor than as a physics professor. He had a profound impact upon the course that my life has taken; I am eternally grateful to him, and he holds a special place in my heart. He was deeply religious in the only true sense: His life expressed the love and justice of God. He shared with me some of his essays about God and also a book on "perennial philosophy." A German from an influential Prussian family, Herb refused to serve in Hitler's armaments industry and was sent to a concentration camp in southern France. He was literally a barracks-mate of the well-known German Christian resistance leader, Deitrich Bonhoeffer. Herb was nearly beaten to death by prison camp guards, but he was eventually allowed to leave Europe for the United States.

Herb was a member of the Society of Friends, and his life proved his profound commitment to peace and justice. Out of respect for Herbert Jehle and for the other men and women of God who have influenced my life, I am donating all royalties for this book to charities that help the needy and the homeless: So Others Might Eat, in Washington, D.C.; the Bethesda Project and the Committee to End Homelessness, in Philadelphia; the Salvation Army of Philadelphia; and the Salvation Army of Chester County, Pennsylvania.

Acknowledgments

I would like to acknowledge Jesus Chahin, who wrote me an encouraging letter; Gary Ford, David Bellin, Bruce Jawer, and Keith Pierce for encouraging me to disseminate this material more widely; Bob Aiken and David Bellin for stressing that this material had book potential; Bruce Barnes and Julian Epstein for their support and enthusiasm; and the reviewers of the first draft of this book who provided excellent criticisms. Indeed, I feel that the final form that this book has taken owes much to their thoughtful and insightful comments. These reviewers were Bruce Barnes (National Science Foundation), David Bellin (North Carolina A & T State University), Keith Pierce (University of Minnesota, Duluth), Ron Anderson (University of Minnesota, Minneapolis), and Gerald Ourada (U.S. Air Force). I would also like to thank Steve Elliot and Regina Brooks, my editors at John Wiley. I would like to thank George Adams, George Atkins, Joseph Kizza, and many others for their kind words and encouragement. I would like to thank Lem Mason for doing such an excellent job of printing early versions of *The Killer Robot Papers* for class testing. I would like to thank Rabbi David Glanzberg-Krainin for teaching me how to read from the Torah scrolls, John and Margaret Weaver for being good friends over many years, and my neighbors, Don and Jane Rice. I would also like to thank Allen Tucker, Jim Bradley, Robert Cupper, and Charles Kelemen for their help and encouragement. I would also like to thank my students in many courses who have offered helpful suggestions.

Richard Epstein
West Chester, Pennsylvania
January 7, 1996

GENERAL CONTENTS

THE KILLER ROBOT PAPERS

Edited and with an Introduction by
PAM PULITZER
Silicon Valley Sentinel-Observer
Silicon Valley, USA

ABOUT THE AUTHOR

Pam Pulitzer is a reporter for the Silicon Valley *Sentinel-Observer*. A native of Silicon Valley, Ms. Pulitzer is a graduate of Smith College. She earned an M.A. degree at the Silicon Valley University School of Journalism. She joined the staff of the *Sentinel-Observer* in 1981. Her coverage of the case of the killer robot won her the prestigious prize that is named after her great-great-grandfather, Ralph Meltzer. Ralph Meltzer was cofounder of the Silicon Valley *Sentinel* in the 1880s. He sketched the original design for the sentinel figure that stands guard over the front page of the *Sentinel-Observer* to this day. In awarding the Meltzer Prize to Pam Pulitzer, the awards committee cited her success in "bringing to the public's attention an issue of great import that might otherwise have been overlooked."

This is Pam Pulitzer's first book. Her husband, Sam, is a sports reporter for the *Sentinel-Observer*. They live in Silicon Heights with their two sons, McNeil and Lehrer.

INTRODUCTION

This book is a collection of papers that relate to the case of the killer robot. My intention is to show the widespread impact of the killer robot on our consciousness. The killer robot has had an impact on the print and the broadcast media. This book is a collection of articles, papers, and radio and television broadcast transcripts. All these diverse materials have something to do with the case of the killer robot and with the public's reaction to that unfortunate incident.

The impact of the killer robot is much greater than my own award-winning newspaper stories could possibly communicate. My stories serve as a means of communicating the basic facts in the case. In addition to my stories, this book includes stories and interviews by my colleagues at the *Sentinel-Observer*, including such accomplished reporters as Bob Franklin and Frank Kafka. The *Sentinel-Observer* Sunday magazine section also carried several human interest stories that related to the killer robot and to the future of computer technology. These contributions from the Sunday magazine include an article by Turina Babbage, the president of the ACM. Her article describes the ACM's code of ethics. These stories and interviews are collected in Part I of this book.

Beyond the pages of the *Sentinel-Observer*, the killer robot was discussed on radio talk shows and on televised public affairs programs. Transcripts of five of these programs are included in Part II of this book.

Let me then review for the reader the contents of this book. Part I consists of factual material that originally appeared in print, including the newspaper stories that reported the basic killer robot scenario. In addition, there is one article from a scholarly journal (about user interfaces), an interview from the Sunday magazine, and many human interest stories covering such topics as software maintenance, the future of computing, the healthy workplace, and the social impact of the World Wide Web.

Part II presents materials from radio and television programs, including the celebrated "Fresh Talk" radio program that explored teamwork and the ethics of speech as well as two episodes of my own "Roundtable" public affairs television program. The "Roundtable" discussions looked at expert systems and at data privacy and security. There is an excellent "Close-Up" interview concerning the ethics of computer systems themselves and an episode of "Candid Professor" in which a computer ethics class taught by Professor Yoder is broadcast live from the Silicon Valley University campus. Of course, Professor Yoder had no advance warning that his lecture would be televised. That's why the show is called "Candid Professor."

This book covers a wide range of issues in the field of software engineering, including the following:

The software life cycle

Software process models

Programmer psychology

Programmer teams

Analysis, design, and CASE tools

User interfaces

Requirements

Software testing

Programming paradigms

Professionalism and codes of ethics

Software reliability

Quality assurance

Process maturity

Software maintenance

Software reuse

Megaprogramming

Futuristic programming environments

The book covers many issues in computer ethics and social implications of computing, including:

Intellectual property and software theft

Software reliability

Hacking

Information quality and the Web

Data privacy

Military use of computers

Applications of AI

Are computers "intelligent"?

Honesty and trust

Ethics of speech

Ethical implications of stealing

Ethical laws for computer systems

Ethical analysis of computer systems

Codes of ethics in computing

Tests of ethical behavior

Educating computing professionals

Avoiding doing harm

Accountability and responsibility

The nature of creativity: its use and misuse

Cost of not doing it right the first time

Databases and database security

Injuries due to work with computers

Stress, work, and happiness

I hope that the reader will find this collection both stimulating and educational. If there are any shortcomings in the selection of articles, the fault is entirely mine. If you have any quarrel with a particular article, please contact the author of that article.

This book would not have been possible without the help of many people. I want to thank my publisher, Ben Bentley, for being the crusty old curmudgeon that he is. It's hard for me to imagine a good newspaper without a crusty old curmudgeon at its helm, and Ben fulfills that expectation for me. Seriously, however, Ben's help has been constant, and I cannot thank him enough. I would also like to thank Regina Brooks, my editor at John Wiley & Sons, for recognizing the public's urgent need to read about the killer robot incident in a cheaply produced book. Robert Franklin, my closest friend on the *Sentinel-Observer*, gave me useful criticism of the first draft of this book; perhaps because of the paradoxical nature of his criticisms, I was forced to do some deep thinking, and the result has been a better book. Professor Harry Yoder of Silicon Valley University is a wonderful gentleman who guided me around campus when the story first broke. Thanks to him I was able to meet some of the world's leading experts on software engineering and computer ethics. I would also like to thank my husband and my two sons, who frequently pulled me away from the computer so I could clean house or prepare dinner.

Pam Pulitzer
Silicon Valley, USA
New Year's Day, 1996
(It's not easy being an author.)

CONTENTS

PART I

PRINT MEDIA

Factual stories, articles, and interviews about the
killer robot that appeared in the print media. The
focus is on Silicon Techchronics, the company
that produced the killer robot.

NEW GENERATION OF ROBOTS DELIVERED TO CYBERWIDGETS, INC.

Robbie CX30 Employs New AI Technologies

by Ralph Forrest

Sentinel-Observer Business Reporter

One dozen Robbie CX30 robots were delivered to CyberWidgets, Inc., last week. CyberWidgets CEO Christopher Jenkins called the robots "revolutionary tools for improving productivity on the shop floor." CyberWidgets has made ambitious efforts in recent years to improve its market share in the area of machine tool parts and widget manufacture.

"If we are going to compete with the Japanese," Jenkins said with an angry scowl, "then we will have to master the technologies of tomorrow."

The Robbie CX30 is the latest version of the Robbie CX series of robots produced by Silicon Techchronics. Silicon Techchronics has placed increasing emphasis on the use of artificial intelligence throughout the corporation. Silicon Techchronics Robotics Division Chief Ray Johnson praised the Robbie CX30 and its development team. He participated in the dedication ceremony for the robots at CyberWidgets, Inc.

"We have the highest quality people at Silicon Techchronics," Johnson said. "When we give them something to do, they do it, and nothing can get in their way." He especially praised Robbie CX30 project director George Cuzzins, "who took extraordinary measures to ensure that Robbie CX30 would be ready for today's ceremonies."

Reporters were taken on a tour of the CyberWidgets shop floor. Several robot operators demonstrated the extraordinary abilities of the new robot. The robot has taken over several dangerous responsibilities from human laborers. Bart Matthews, a resident of East Silicon Valley, was one of the robot operators that spoke to this reporter. "I trust this robot," Mr. Matthews told the reporters as he demonstrated how Robbie CX30 could detect a certain kind of widget on a conveyor belt and could place that widget in an acid bath. He showed this reporter a scar from a severe acid burn on one of his arms. "No more acid burns for this widget handler!" he exclaimed.

The Robbie CX30 robot uses sophisticated visual processing techniques to classify, identify, and "see" widgets so that they can be processed in an appropriate way. The robot removes operators from dangerous shop floor areas and relegates them to the operation of the robot from the operator console.

One reporter asked Mr. Matthews whether there was anything he did not like about the robot. "Well, yes, the user. . ."

At this point, Mr. Johnson interrupted Bart Matthews and said, "This is a bad time to bring up negative comments. We're celebrating the installation of these wonderful new robots. Look, no technology is 100 percent perfect."

ROBOT KILLS OPERATOR IN GRISLY ACCIDENT

Operator Had Filed Complaints about User Interface

This late-breaking story was filed by
Yvette Jones, Richard Norton, and **Pam Pulitzer**

A Robbie CX30 robot killed its operator today at CyberWidgets, Inc., in what police are calling an "unbelievable scene of blood and gore." "I have covered a lot of murders, but nothing like this," said Silicon Valley Chief of Police Jack Ripkin. In an unusual move that has been protested by the *Sentinel-Observer*, reporters and photographers were barred from the scene of the accident. "There is just too much blood and tissue splashed all around, and we don't want the press making it sound any worse than it already is."

Before getting into the details, here are the facts: At about 10:30 this morning a Robbie CX30 robot literally attacked its operator on the shop floor at CyberWidgets. The operator is identified as Bart Matthews, who is reported to have been married and the father of several children. Bart Matthews was working alone with the robot in the widget cleaning and processing area of the assembly line.

Apparently the robot's arm motion became extremely violent, and the robot arm struck Mr. Matthews with great velocity. It is not clear whether Mr. Matthews had any means of defending himself against the advancing robot.

When asked whether the robot had an on-off switch, one CyberWidgets official said, "We are looking into that." An insider at Silicon Techchronics told one of our reporters that an on-off switch was considered an unnecessary expense by the system designers. "There were at least ten ways to turn off the robot using system menus," this programmer said, requesting anonymity.

Mr. Matthews, who attained brief notoriety back in the 1970s with a hit rock single, "You Push All the Right Buttons!", had complained to his foreman at CyberWidgets about the robot operator console. Although the shop foreman, Will Addley, refused to comment, one CyberWidgets employee who wished to remain anonymous stated that the robot user interface was difficult to use.

Several experts have told the *Sentinel-Observer* that the user interface could have contributed to this incident. "But it's much too early to say," said Silicon Valley University professor Horace Gritty. "Computer systems are very complex."

One reporter asked Police Chief Ripkin whether this incident was being treated as a crime. "Not at all," he replied. "I am here to keep you folks at bay. This is private property. There is no indication that a crime has been committed here."

The man on the street does not necessarily agree with Chief Ripkin. We interviewed several people at the Silicon Valley Mall. Sally Winters of South Silicon Valley was of the opinion that this should be treated as a crime. "Someone has to be held accountable for what happened. The robot did not act out of its own free will." Jamie Winters, her eleven-year-old son, agreed. "Someone could have programmed the robot to ice that guy!"

CyberWidgets has suspended use of the Robbie CX30 until the cause of the tragedy can be tracked down. A CyberWidgets spokesperson moved to qualm investor fears that CyberWidgets would be hurt by this suspension. "We anticipate only a brief suspension of robot operations due to this incident," the spokesperson said. "We will be prudent in weighing the risks to our employees against the financial cost of not getting our product out to our customers."

Silicon Techchronics CEO Michael Waterson refused to appear before reporters. He issued the following statement: "The Silicon Techchronics family feels the pain of the Matthews family, and it would be tasteless for us to comment on the robot and its problems at this point."

The killer robot incident has had a chilling effect throughout the valley. This is the first known case of a robot operator being killed in the valley, although a robot operator was killed in Japan in the 1980s. People in the valley are quite sophisticated when it comes to understanding computer systems, and many feel that it will not be easy to assign blame in this incident.

Special to the *Silicon Valley Sentinel-Observer*, Silicon Valley, USA

McMURDOCK PROMISES JUSTICE IN "KILLER ROBOT" CASE

At Issue Is Accountability for Software Developers

by Pam Pulitzer

Just one month after Bart Matthews was brutally slain in the "killer robot" incident, Silicon Valley Prosecuting Attorney Jane McMurdock announced that she would launch an investigation into the case on the grounds that the robot's behavior was possibly the result of criminal negligence.

"If I do not enter this case," Ms. McMurdock told a news conference early this morning, "then no one will be held responsible for the death of Bart Matthews. The only recourse to the immediate victims in this case and to society at large would be to file suit under strict liability. That does not bode well for the full disclosure of all factors that led to this tragedy. Only a criminal investigation will be able to uncover the whole truth."

One reporter asked Ms. McMurdock whether she had any specific leads that suggest criminal behavior on someone's part. "Yes, I do!" she exclaimed. "However, it would compromise our investigation if I were to say anything further at this point. Let me just say that a bug was found in the software."

In the month since the accident, the press has been able to determine almost nothing about its causes. CyberWidgets and Silicon Techchronics have both placed a tight lid of secrecy over the Robbie CX30 project. Because there has been no criminal investigation, Silicon Techchronics has been able to hide most details of Robbie CX30 hardware and software from public scrutiny. A terse statement issued several weeks ago by Silicon Techchronics stated, "All software components made at Silicon Techchronics are proprietary and shall not be placed in the public domain."

Sally Matthews, widow of Bart Matthews, has told reporters that she is not thinking about a lawsuit at this time because "I am still in a period of mourning and grief. If I sue CyberWidgets or Silicon Techchronics, it will not be to alleviate the grief but to satisfy a sense of justice."

Silicon Techchronics and CyberWidgets have placed an especially tight lid upon the issue of the robot user interface. It was reported that Bart Matthews had complained about the user interface to his foreman at CyberWidgets. That foreman has since been relocated to the CyberWidgets Canada plant in Yarmouth, Nova Scotia.

One reporter asked Jane McMurdock what kind of legal theory she would apply to support a criminal indictment in the case of the killer robot.

"I think that if someone was substandard in performance of their duties, for example, if they made an unusual programming error, then that would be a basis for prosecution. I am going to go much further in pursuing this than any of my detractors ever thought possible. I am not talking negligence here. I think it is more like operating a vehicle in a reckless and dangerous manner."

One reporter pointed out that this approach would be without legal precedent. McMurdock replied, "I am trying to establish a legal precedent that will force software developers to think twice before they release a product as dangerous as the killer robot."

Shoppers at Silicon Valley Mall seemed to support McMurdock in her quest to hold someone criminally responsible for the incident. Sally Winters, who once again had kept her son Jamie out of school in order to get some shopping done, said, "All I know is that when innocent blood is shed, there's got to be some kind of accounting for it." Jamie said that his classmates at school thought that the killer robot was "real cool." He showed this reporter a sketch he had made of the killer robot using coarse paper and crayons. It was a graphic portrayal of a violent death to say the least.

Special to the *Silicon Valley Sentinel-Observer*, Silicon Valley, USA

SILICON VALLEY PROGRAMMER INDICTED FOR MANSLAUGHTER

Program Error Caused Death of Robot Operator

by Pam Pulitzer

Jane McMurdock, Prosecuting Attorney for the city of Silicon Valley, announced today the indictment of Randy Samuels on charges of manslaughter. Samuels is employed as a programmer at Silicon Techchronics, Inc. The charge involves the death of Bart Matthews, who was killed last May by an assembly line robot.

Matthews, who worked as a robot operator at CyberWidgets, Inc., in Silicon Heights, was crushed to death when the robot he was operating malfunctioned and started to wave its arm violently. The robot arm struck Matthews, throwing him against a wall and crushing his skull. Matthews died almost instantly in a case that shocked and angered many in Silicon Valley. According to the indictment, Samuels wrote the particular piece of computer program that was responsible for the robot malfunction.

"There's a smoking gun!" McMurdock announced triumphantly at a press conference held in the Hall of Justice.

"We have the handwritten formula, provided by the project physicist, which Samuels was supposed to program. But he recklessly misinterpreted the formula, leading to this gruesome death. Society must protect itself against programmers who make careless mistakes, or else no one will be safe, least of all our families and our children," she said.

The *Sentinel-Observer* has been able to obtain a copy of the handwritten formula in question. There are actually three similar formulas, scrawled on a piece of yellow legal-pad paper. Each formula describes the motion of the robot arm in one direction: east-west, north-south, and up-down.

The *Sentinel-Observer* showed the formulas to Bill Park, a professor of physics at Silicon Valley University. He confirmed that these equations could be used to describe the motion of a robot arm.

The *Sentinel-Observer* then showed Professor Park the program code, written by the accused in the C programming language. This reporter asked Professor Park, who is fluent in C and several other languages, whether the program code was correct for the given robot arm formulas.

Professor Park's response was immediate. "By Jove! It looks like he misinterpreted the y-dots in the formulas as y-bars, and he made the same mistake for the x's and the z's. He was supposed to use the derivatives, but he took the averages instead! He's guilty as hell, if you ask me."

The *Sentinel-Observer* was unable to contact Samuels for comment. "He is deeply depressed about all this," his live-in girlfriend told us over the phone. "But Randy believes the charges will be dropped when he gets a chance to tell his side of the story."

Jane McMurdock reiterated the theme that she first stated four months ago when she announced her intention to investigate the possibility of criminal negligence in this case. "At issue is whether a programmer who commits a gross mistake, such as Mr. Samuels did, will remain free from any kind of accountability. I am determined to pursue this case through all necessary courts until it is established that a careless programmer should be held accountable for his or her errors just as someone who accidentally shoots someone with a firearm. I do not see that the Robbie CX30 robot is much different from a firearm."

Jane McMurdock has become very unpopular among software developers. One Silicon Valley software developer, who requested anonymity, charged that McMurdock used misleading metaphors over and over again. "Frankly, I cannot see any commonality between a sophisticated robot and a firearm. It's a ludicrous comparison. When a gun is fired, someone pulled the trigger. When a robot accidentally kills someone, how does the trigger analogy apply at all? I think existing liability laws are adequate to protect consumers against software and hardware failures."

Special to the *Silicon Valley Sentinel-Observer,* Silicon Valley, USA

"KILLER ROBOT" DEVELOPERS WORKED UNDER ENORMOUS STRESS

by Pam Pulitzer

The *Sentinel-Observer* learned today that Randy Samuels and others who worked on the "killer robot" project at Silicon Techchronics were under tremendous pressure to finish the robot software by January 1 of this year. According to an informed source, top-level management warned killer robot project staffers that "heads would roll" if the January 1 deadline was not met.

Randy Samuels, a Silicon Techchronics programmer, was indicted last week on charges of manslaughter in the now famous "killer robot case." Samuels wrote the flawed software that caused a Silicon Techchronics Robbie CX30 industrial robot to fatally crush its operator, Bart Matthews. Matthews was a robot operator at CyberWidgets, Inc. According to Silicon Valley Prosecuting Attorney Jane McMurdock, Samuels misinterpreted a mathematical formula, "turning harmless Robbie into a savage killer."

Our informed source, who wishes to remain anonymous and whom we shall call "Martha," has intimate knowledge of all aspects of the Robbie CX30 project. Martha told the *Sentinel-Observer* that there was an enormous amount of friction between Robotics Division Chief Ray Johnson and the Robbie CX30 project manager George Cuzzins. "They hated each other's guts," Martha told the *Sentinel-Observer* in an exclusive interview.

"By June of last year the robot project had fallen six months behind schedule, and Johnson went through the roof. There were rumors that the entire Robotics Division, which he headed, would be terminated if Robbie [the CX30 robot] didn't prove a commercial success. He [Johnson] called George [Cuzzins] into his office, and he really chewed George out. I mean, you could hear the yelling all the way down the hall. Johnson told George to finish Robbie by the first of January or 'heads would roll.'

"I'm not saying that Johnson was ordering George to cut corners," Martha added. "I think the idea of cutting corners was implicit. The message was, 'cut corners if you want to keep your job.'"

According to documents that Martha provided the *Sentinel-Observer*, twenty new programmers were added to the Robbie CX30 project on June 12 of last year. This was just several days after the stormy meeting between Johnson and Cuzzins that Martha recounted.

According to Martha, the new hires were a disaster. "Johnson unilaterally arranged for these new hires, presumably by shifting resources from other aspects of the Robbie [CX30] project. George was vehemently opposed to this. Johnson only knew about manufacturing hardware. That was his background. He couldn't understand the difficulties that we were having with the robotics software. You can't speed up a software project by adding more people. It's not like an assembly line."

According to Martha and other sources inside the project, the hiring of twenty new programmers led to a staff meeting attended by Johnson, Cuzzins, and all members of the Robbie CX30 software project. "This time it was George who went through the roof. He complained that the project didn't need more people. He argued that the main problem was that Johnson and other management people did not understand that Robbie CX30 was fundamentally different from earlier versions of the robot."

These sources told the *Sentinel-Observer* that the new hires were not fully integrated into the project, even six months later, when several dozen Robbie CX30 robots, including the robot that killed Bart Matthews, were shipped out. According to Martha, "George just wanted to keep things as simple as possible. He didn't want the new people to complicate matters. They spent six months reading manuals. Most of the new hires didn't know diddly about robots, and George wasn't about to waste his time trying to teach them."

According to Martha, the June 12 meeting has become famous in Silicon Techchronics corporate lore because it was at that meeting that Ray Johnson announced his "Ivory Snow theory" of software development. According to Martha, "Ray [Johnson] gave us a big multimedia presentation, with slides and everything. The gist of his 'Ivory Snow theory' is simply that Ivory Snow is 99 and 44/100 percent pure, and there was no reason why robotics software has to be any purer than that. He stated repeatedly that 'perfect software is an oxymoron.'"

Martha and the other insiders who came forward with information consistently portrayed Johnson as a manager in desperate need of a successful project. Earlier versions of Robbie, the CX10 and the CX20, were experimental in nature, and no one expected them to be commercial successes. In fact, the Robotics Division of Silicon Techchronics had been operating heavily in the red since its inception six years ago. Either CX30 would succeed, or Silicon Techchronics would be out of the industrial robotics business altogether.

"The earlier Robbie robots got a lot of press, especially here in Silicon Valley," said another source, who also wishes to remain anonymous. "Robbie CX30 was going to capitalize on the good publicity generated by the earlier projects. The problem was that Robbie CX30 was more revolutionary than Johnson wanted to admit. CX30 represented a gigantic step forward in terms of sophistication. There were a lot of questions about the industrial settings that the CX30 would be working in. Much of what we had to do was entirely new, but Johnson couldn't bring himself to understand that. He just saw us as unyielding perfectionists. One of his favorite quotes was, 'Perfection is the enemy of the good.'"

Special to the *Silicon Valley Sentinel-Observer*, Silicon Valley, USA

"KILLER ROBOT" PROGRAMMER WAS PRIMA DONNA, CO-WORKERS CLAIM

by Pam Pulitzer

A well-known computer scientist, Dr. Hiram Milton of Silicon Valley University, conducted a study of the inner workings of the "killer robot" software development team, it was revealed today. In a news conference held at the university, Dr. Milton revealed that Randy Samuels, the former Silicon Techchronics programmer who was indicted for manslaughter in the gruesome killer robot incident, had a personality type that predisposed him to reject criticism.

Dr. Milton said, "Randy Samuels had little patience for criticism. He loved his work, the problem-solving aspect of his work, to the extent that his own personal identity became completely wrapped up in the programming code that he produced. Thus, he never achieved the kind of objectivity and egolessness that a true team effort requires."

Dr. Milton and his graduate students videotaped actual team meetings that took place during the early stages of the development of the killer robot software. They also taped interviews with individual programmers, during which they asked the programmers to discuss their perceptions of one another. These interviews reveal that Randy Samuels was viewed as a troublesome team member long before a Robbie CX30 robot slew its operator, Bart Matthews, at CyberWidgets last May. In one interview that Dr. Milton played at the news conference, a team member, whose face was covered by a blue dot, called Randy Samuels a "prima donna." She recounted several incidents in which Randy Samuels displayed extreme sensitivity to criticism of his work.

A male team member also called Randy Samuels a prima donna. This second team member, whose identity was also concealed, said that Randy Samuels had been inflexible to the point of being "downright ornery" when it came to the issue of choosing a programming language for the killer robot project. "We had all come to a consensus that C was the way to go, but Randy stuck to the idea that we should be using C++. We wasted a considerable amount of time trying to get him to change his mind. I find Randy a very difficult person to work with. He's extremely dogmatic about things."

Dr. Milton gave his interpretation of these remarks during the news conference. "Randy Samuels is a fairly typical software developer. He has what we call a task-oriented personality, although his personality borders on being self-oriented. I base this assessment not on the use of any psychological instrument nor solely on the basis of these interviews, but on the basis of my own observation of Mr. Samuels during team meetings. I taped every meeting that the 'killer robot' team held for a period of one month. Of course, they weren't known as the 'killer robot' team back then."

Dr. Milton explained that software psychologists, those researchers who study psychological factors in software development and use, classify programmers into three broad personality types: interaction-oriented, task-oriented, and self-oriented. The interaction-oriented individual is motivated by the desire to interact with others and to facilitate interaction among team members. The task-oriented individual focuses on the problem that needs to be solved. The self-oriented individual focuses on his or her own objectives as opposed to team objectives.

Dr. Milton explained that Randy Samuels, like most programmers, was task-oriented. "Randy loved to solve problems. He was more interested in programming and less interested in the formal aspects of design and developing specifications. However, my observations reveal Randy as probably being more self-oriented than most programmers, and this focus on his own private agenda probably caused his co-workers to view him as a 'prima donna.'"

Dr. Milton went on to describe the kinds of personalities that might emerge during a team effort. "A prima donna is a person who cannot accept criticism, who feels that his or her work is beyond reproach. A sniper is a person who disrupts team unity with thinly veiled sarcastic remarks. A tyrant is a person who tries to dominate the entire team, imposing his or her will upon everyone else. On several occasions, according to his fellow team members, Randy Samuels reacted to criticism in a manner that was inappropriate. This gave rise to the perception that he was a prima donna. According to his co-workers, he stormed out of several quality review meetings. He never stormed out of a meeting that I had taped."

A quality review meeting involves peer review of work. One kind of quality review meeting is called a code review. At a code review, program code that a programmer develops is reviewed by a small committee of code readers, who attempt to identify errors in the code and to suggest improvements that might be made. Randy Samuels stormed out of at least one code review meeting that was held during the development of the killer robot software. One such meeting was held several months after Dr. Milton did his taping. One of the killer robot team members described this incident in an interview with this reporter.

"The code review meeting in question included Samuels, myself, and two other readers of a software module that he had designed and coded," this team member told this reporter, seeking anonymity. "One of my colleagues pointed out that Samuels had used an inefficient method for achieving a certain result, and Samuels turned beet red. He yelled a stream of obscenities and then stormed out of the meeting. He never returned. We later sent him a memo about the faster algorithm, and he eventually did use the more efficient method in his code."

The software module in the quality assurance incident was the very one that was found to be at fault in the killer robot incident. However, this co-worker was quick to point out that the efficiency of the algorithm was not an issue in the malfunctioning of the robot. "I do wonder, though," she added, "whether his volatility inhibited our committee from examining his code with the kind of critical eye that was really required."

At his news conference, Dr. Milton remarked that young, talented people like Randy Samuels may have volatile personalities. "This implies that the manager of a programming project must act to bring out the best in each team member.

"Somehow, the team leader needs to communicate the ethic of 'egoless programming' to the task-oriented or self-oriented team member," Dr. Milton added. "The idea behind egoless programming is that a software product belongs to the team and not to the individual programmers. The idea is to be open to criticism and to be less attached to one's work. Code reviews are certainly consistent with this overall philosophy. A self-centered attitude needs to be replaced by a team-centered attitude, which views the quality of the product and the success of the team as being of greater value than one's own cherished ideas."

Dr. Milton noted that studies of team dynamics have shown that a successful team contains a variety of personality types. "A heterogeneous team with a variety of personality types—interaction-oriented, self-oriented, and task-oriented—is going to be more successful than a team that is homogeneous. For example, a team of exclusively task-oriented people is not going to be as successful as a team that has at least one interaction-oriented personality. The interaction-oriented team member can help the team to manage and even to take advantage of the inevitable conflicts that will arise."

During his news conference, Dr. Milton suggested that George Cuzzins, the project leader, was not an effective leader, especially from the point of view of managing conflict and guiding a talented young programmer like Randy Samuels. "George Cuzzins had a background in data processing," Dr. Milton told the news conference. "He knew how to manage a team, but because of his lack of domain expertise [in robotics], his role on the killer robot project was mostly administrative. The killer robot team functioned as a democratic team. In other words, decisions were made by consensus, and all team members had equal input into the decision-making process. George Cuzzins did not impose his leadership. He depended heavily, however, on the technical expertise of one particular team member. He depended upon that person because he lacked expertise in robotics."

One co-worker told this reporter that Randy Samuels loved to tackle problems that had been assigned to some other team member. She told this reporter about one such incident: "Randy hated meetings, but he was pretty good one on one. He was always eager to help. I remember one time when I ran into a serious roadblock, and instead of just pointing me in the right direction, he took over the problem and solved it himself. He spent nearly five entire days on my problem, even through he had pressing responsibilities of his own.

"In retrospect, it might have been better for poor Mr. Matthews and his family if Randy Samuels had stuck to his own assigned tasks instead of taking it upon himself to solve other people's problems," she added.

Special to the *Silicon Valley Sentinel-Observer*, Silicon Valley, USA

"KILLER ROBOT" PROJECT MIRED IN CONTROVERSY RIGHT FROM START

Warring Factions Fought Over How Project Should Proceed

by Pam Pulitzer

Two groups committed to different software development philosophies nearly came to blows during the initial planning meetings for Robbie CX30, the Silicon Techchronics robot that killed an assembly line worker last May. At issue was whether the Robbie CX30 project should proceed according to the "waterfall model" or the "prototyping model."

The waterfall model and the prototyping model are two common methods for organizing a software project. In the waterfall model, a software project goes through definite stages of development. The first stage is requirements analysis and specification, during which an attempt is made to arrive at an agreement concerning the detailed functionality of the system. As the project passes from one stage to the next, there are limited opportunities for going back and changing earlier decisions. One drawback of this approach is that potential users do not get a chance to interact with the system until very late in the system's life cycle.

In the prototyping model, great emphasis is placed on producing a working model or prototype early in the life cycle of a system. The prototype is built for the purpose of arriving at a final specification of the functionality of the proposed system. Potential users interact with the prototype early and often until the requirements are agreed upon. This approach affords potential users the opportunity to interact with a prototype system early during the development cycle and long before the final system is designed, coded, and delivered.

In a memo dated December 11 of the year before last, Jan Anderson, a member of the original Robbie CX30 project team, bitterly attacked the decision of the project manager, George Cuzzins, to employ the waterfall model. The *Sentinel-Observer* has obtained a copy of Anderson's memo, which is addressed to Cuzzins, and Anderson verified the authenticity of the memo for this reporter.

Cuzzins fired Anderson late on the afternoon of December 24, just two weeks after she wrote the memo.

The Anderson memo refers to an earlier meeting at which an angry exchange occurred relating to software development philosophy. Anderson underlined the following passage in her memo:

> *I did not intend to impugn your competence at our meeting yesterday, but I must protest most vehemently against the idea that we complete the Robbie CX30 software following the waterfall model that you have used in previous projects. I need not remind you that those were data processing projects involving the processing of business transactions. The Robbie CX30 project will involve a high degree of interaction, both between robot components and between the robot and the operator. Since operator interaction with the robot is so important, the interface cannot be designed as an afterthought.*

Randy Samuels, who has been charged with manslaughter in the death of robot operator Bart Matthews, father of three, was in attendance at the December 11 meeting.

Anderson said that Samuels did not have much to say about the waterfall-prototyping controversy, but she did state that she would give her "eye teeth" to have Samuels exonerated.

"The project was doomed long before Samuels misinterpreted those formulas," Anderson stated emphatically in the living room of her suburban townhouse.

In her conversation with this reporter, Anderson did her best to explain the waterfall-prototyping controversy in lay terms. "The main issue was really whether we could agree on the system requirements without allowing actual robot operators to get a feel for what we had in mind. Cuzzins has been in the data processing business for three decades, and he's good in that domain, but he never should have been made manager of this project."

According to records obtained by the *Sentinel-Observer*, Silicon Techchronics moved George Cuzzins from the Data Processing Division, which took care of inventory and payroll, to the Robotics Division just three weeks before the December 11 meeting alluded to in Anderson's memo.

Cuzzins was moved to the Robotics Division by Silicon Techchronics president Michael Waterson. Cuzzins replaced John Cramer, who managed the earlier Robbie CX projects, the CX10 and the CX20. Cramer was placed in charge of Robbie CX30, but he died unexpectedly in a skydiving accident. Our sources tell us that in placing Cuzzins in charge of the CX30 project, Waterson was going against the advice of Ray Johnson, Robotics Division chief.

According to these sources, Johnson strongly opposed Waterson's choice of Cuzzins to head the Robbie CX30 project. These sources tell the *Sentinel-Observer* that Waterson's decision was purely a cost-saving measure. It was cheaper to move Cuzzins to the Robotics Division than to hire a new project leader from outside the corporation.

The anonymous source that the *Sentinel-Observer* calls "Martha" described the situation in this way: "Waterson thought it would be cheaper to move Cuzzins to Robotics rather than try to find a new manager for the Robbie project from outside. Also, Waterson tends to be suspicious of people from the outside. He often sends down memos about how long it takes people to master 'the Silicon Techchronics way of doing things.' In Waterson's view, Cuzzins was a manager, and he was moved to his new position in Robotics as a manager and not as a technical expert. Clearly Cuzzins saw himself as both a manager and a technical expert. *Cuzzins was not aware of his own technical limitations.*"

According to Martha, Cuzzins was very reluctant to manage a project that would not use the waterfall model that had served him so well in data processing. He attacked prototyping as a "fad" at the meeting on December 11 and after a few verbal exchanges things got pretty personal.

"Anderson was especially vocal," Martha recalled. "She had lots of experience with user interfaces, and from her perspective the operator-robot interface was critical to the success of CX30, since operator intervention would be frequent and at times critical."

In her interview with the *Sentinel-Observer*, Jan Anderson commented on this aspect of the December 11 meeting: "Cuzzins was vehemently opposed to 'wasting time'—to use his words—on any kind of formal analysis of the user interface and its human factors properties. To him user interfaces were a peripheral issue.

"Anything new was a 'fad' to him [Cuzzins]," Anderson added. "Computer interfaces were a fad, object-oriented design was a fad, formal specification and verification techniques were a fad, and, most of all, prototyping was a fad."

Exactly one week after the December 11 meeting, the Robbie group received a memo from George Cuzzins concerning the project plan for the Robbie CX30 project.

"It was the waterfall model, right out of a textbook," Anderson told this reporter as she reviewed a copy of the project plan memo. "Requirements analysis and specification, then architectural design and detailed design, coding, testing, delivery and maintenance. In Cuzzins's view of things, there was no need to have any user interaction with the system until very, very late in the process."

In a great irony, the *Silicon Techchronics Annual Report for Shareholders*, published last March, has a picture of a smiling Bart Matthews on its glossy front cover. Matthews, the killer robot's victim and one of the first operators ever to use a Robbie CX30 robot on the assembly line, is shown operating the very same Robbie CX30 robot that crushed him to death barely two months after the photograph was taken. Beneath the picture is a quote that Mr. Matthews gave to this newspaper: "I trust this robot."

Special to the *Silicon Valley Sentinel-Observer*, Silicon Valley, USA

FALLEN PROJECT DIRECTOR ACCUSED OF CONFLICT OF INTEREST IN KILLER ROBOT CASE

Cramer Was Major Investor in Local Firm that Provided Software Development Tools for Robbie CX30 Project

Human Interest Story
by Pam Pulitzer

"I can still remember the last time that I saw him," David Tabriz said nervously in his book-lined cubicle at Silicon Techchronics. He was talking about John Cramer, the original project director for the Robbie CX30 robot project at Silicon Techchronics. "We were in the middle of yet another stormy meeting concerning where he was leading us on the CX30 project when he looked at his watch and exclaimed, 'Gotta go!' It was time for skydiving! He grabbed his black leather pilot's jacket and turned to us just as he got to the door of the conference room. 'We'll settle all of this when I get back.'"

Tabriz took a sip of coffee from a mug decorated with a *Far Side* cartoon. "Well, as you know, he never did come back, and I never did get to see him again because there was a closed casket at his funeral."

Cramer was killed in a skydiving accident that ended his controversial leadership of the killer robot project.

Tabriz was just one of nearly a dozen members of the killer robot development team who spoke to this reporter concerning John Cramer and his role in the killer robot catastrophe. Most of those interviewed requested anonymity. What emerged from our discussion with team members was a disturbing picture of John Cramer as a reckless leader with serious personal problems.

The *Sentinel-Observer* has also established that John Cramer was guilty of a gross conflict of interest. He was a major investor in a local software firm that provided software tools for the CX30 project. Apparently no one at Silicon Techchronics was aware of this conflict.

Here are some additional details in this still unfolding story: John Cramer had been project director for the Robbie CX10 and CX20 robot projects. Ray Johnson, Robotics Division chief, named Cramer to head the new CX30 project about five months before his death. The CX30 robot eventually became the infamous killer robot.

"Cramer had been on leave for three months before he was put in charge of the CX30 project," one of the development team members told us. She requested anonymity. "He had been through a really difficult divorce, and he requested some time for himself. He came back like a roaring bull, full of ideas and energy, a totally different person. He had been a very deliberate and considerate manager, soft-spoken in his mannerisms, but now he seemed strangely reckless, aggressive, and inconsiderate of others. He used to listen to our suggestions, but now he could not accept opposing points of view. He talked about two things incessantly: OOPS and skydiving—not that I'm trying to draw a comparison between them."

OOPS is computer jargon for *object-oriented programming and systems*. It refers more generally to a new paradigm for software development: the object-oriented paradigm. Software development goes through the stages of analysis, design, and implementation. There are different methodologies for accomplishing analysis and design, and different programming languages for doing the actual implementation (i.e., the programming).

Object-oriented analysis (or OOA) involves arriving at a description of system functionality that can serve as the system requirements using the terminology of the object-oriented paradigm. That terminology includes the object concept. An object is often an attempt to model a real world entity, but objects are also used to model more abstract concepts. Fundamentally, an object contains data and exhibits certain behavior.

Object-oriented design (or OOD) involves using some notation, usually diagrammatic or graphical, to specify the overall system architecture, much as one would use a blueprint in standard building architecture. Again, this is an object-oriented methodology because the basic concepts of the object-oriented paradigm are employed.

Many vendors are marketing special software products, called CASE tools, for doing OOA and OOD. CASE stands for *computer-aided software engineering*. These tools help analysts and developers to develop and document decisions concerning system functionality and design. The result is a set of discrete "deliverables" that provide specific information about the objects in an analysis or in a design and about the relationships among those objects. The best CASE tools are based upon a coherent notational system for representing the basic constructs in the object-oriented view of things.

Once a design has been developed, it can be implemented using one of the available programming languages. Languages that support object-oriented concepts are called object-oriented languages. Popular object-oriented languages include C++, Smalltalk, and Eiffel. However, an implementation of an object-oriented design can be attempted using a language that is not object-oriented, such as C.

The *Silicon Valley Sentinel-Observer* has learned through our interviews with members of the killer robot development team that John Cramer was militantly in favor of using the object-oriented paradigm as soon as he returned from his leave of absence to head the killer robot project. Neither the CX10 nor CX20 robot had been developed using object technology. The software for these robots was developed using well-established "structured" techniques for real-time systems analysis and design.

David Tabriz remembers the initial meeting between Cramer and the development team in this way: "John looked around the table with this funny gleam in his eye, acknowledging us but not permitting any discussion, as if the first words had to be his. Then with total seriousness he said, 'Skydiving teaches you one thing about life: Grab every opportunity when it comes your way, and don't let it pass you by. Gentlemen—and, oh yes, ladies—we are going to use OOPS on this project from day one right down to the bitter end. Any questions?'"

Tabriz got up to pour another mug of coffee, offering some to this reporter. "I had a question, but when I tried to ask my question, he scowled. 'My question was rhetorical, Tabriz! I'm not interested in questions. I want answers! People who ask a lot of questions slow things down. If there is anything I cannot tolerate it's people who slow things down. In fact, the greatest experience I have ever known is speeding up, speeding up, speeding up, at the relentless rate of 9.8 meters per second squared.'"

There was a noticeable tremor in Tabriz's hand as he took another gulp of coffee. "At that precise moment Cramer flipped over a sheet on an easel board, and there, for the first time, we saw the fateful words:

SHEOL: Shell Object Language

The new OOA/OOD CASE tool from

Lucrative Object and Object Technologies, Inc.

Is your object technology project going all to hell?

Then head for SHEOL instead.

"Lucrative Object and Object Technologies—or Lucrative, as we came to call them—was going to provide us with a CASE tool that would help us to do OOA and OOD for the robot project. This was at a point in time when almost no one on the team knew anything about OOPS. None of us had ever heard anything about Lucrative or its CASE tool, SHEOL. More importantly, none of us knew that Lucrative had anything to do with Cramer, let alone that Lucrative was Cramer's own company! We didn't find that out until after the guy was dead and buried."

In fact, Cramer was a major investor in Lucrative, one of only five major investors in a venture that had nearly half a million dollars in investment capital. The *Sentinel-Observer* has obtained the papers of incorporation and other documents that show that Cramer was indeed a major investor although not an officer in the corporation. We have sworn affidavits that show that Cramer was one of the founders of Lucrative and that he planned all along to return to Silicon Techchronics with the intention of forging a deal between Silicon Techchronics and Lucrative for the use of Lucrative products in CX30 software development.

In playing a key role in negotiating the contract between Silicon Techchronics and Lucrative, Cramer was in effect lining his own pockets. That $350,000 contract stipulated that Lucrative would provide Silicon Techchronics with the SHEOL CASE tool, customer support for use of that tool, and extensive training in OOPS, OOA, and OOD and in the use of the SHEOL CASE tool. The contract included a disclaimer stating that Lucrative could not be held liable for the failure of Silicon Techchronics to make effective use of the SHEOL CASE tool.

David Tabriz became emotional when he discussed the implications of the disclaimer. "Can you believe it? How can such a disclaimer be legal? Here they [Lucrative] sold us software that was totally useless and totally untested, and we signed a contract that protected them from any responsibility for the quality of their product? In my opinion SHEOL was totally inadequate for a real-time systems project such as a robot. It might be applicable to a small business database system project, but I am skeptical even about that. Surely John [Cramer] understood the limitations of SHEOL, or did he?"

The team members that we spoke to were unanimous in their condemnation of Lucrative's SHEOL product and of the training in object technology that Lucrative provided. One team member, requesting anonymity, had this to say: "It's irresponsible to bet the success of a multimillion dollar project on untested technology. To some extent OOPS itself is still young, and much needs to be learned about doing large-scale software projects using the object paradigm. However, it is being done, and there have been successes. What was indefensible, in my opinion, was tying us in to this untested CASE tool. Whenever we discussed how this CASE tool related to our particular concerns, developing a robot running in real-time, all we got from John [Cramer] and from Lucrative was a lot of hand-waving."

Another troubling aspect of John Cramer's leadership of the killer robot project was his insistence that he serve as the project librarian. David Tabriz explained, "All important documentation relating to the project was held by him in his office. All OOA and OOD deliverables were kept by him in his office."

Another team member, Edna Barsky, told the *Sentinel-Observer*, "On many occasions I asked Cramer if there was a central repository where all important group decisions were stored, including minutes of meetings, analysis of deliverables, and so on. I couldn't believe his answer. He tapped his forehead and said, 'It's all up here.'"

Barsky painted a portrait of a boss who drank heavily and had a desperate need to feel indispensable. "He used to come into my office to chat quite a bit. I think he was lonely. He desperately needed to know that he would not be discarded, the way that his ex-wife had discarded him. She literally threw him out the front door of their house—physically. These feelings probably led him to drink. He did not drink at all as far as I can recall from our days together on the CX10 and CX20 projects.

"As you know, after his death, we did not find clear documentation about where the project was and where it was headed. It was total chaos. He was not a very good project librarian, which is really what he had become, more and more. The project documentation and records were a complete mess. It was especially hard to trace things chronologically. Which version came first? Which second?"

Just weeks before John Cramer died so tragically, the CX30 development team assigned Edna Barsky the unenviable task of speaking to Ray Johnson about Cramer's drinking and his strange behavior. Barsky described her encounter with Johnson as follows: "Johnson was a heavy smoker and he had this thing about 'do-gooders' trying to tell other people what to do. He was still bitter about the no-smoking regulations imposed in the cafeteria years ago. So he did not take kindly to my report about Cramer's alcoholism. In a voice dripping with sarcasm he said, 'What will it take to get you people to stop? You can't stand it if someone enjoys a little pleasure. Give the guy a break. He just went through a tough divorce. I especially resent your coming here because John has a proven track record over many years with this company. Tell your colleagues down there on the CX30 project to buckle down and learn the new technology that John wants you to learn! I think that's what this is really about. You people are dragging your feet about making a commitment to new technologies.'"

As our interview drew to a close, David Tabriz started to make another carafe of coffee, carefully scooping coffee grounds into a paper coffee filter. "I didn't use to drink this much coffee, but it helps me to keep up with all of the change going on around here. Things change so fast. After Cramer died and Cuzzins came in, we were totally demoralized. We started over from scratch. We did not have a useful analysis product to work with and certainly no preliminary ideas concerning a design. Everything that smelled of SHEOL was tossed out the window. I think the trouble—you know, this whole thing with the death of that robot operator—started here, with the incompetent leadership of Cramer and management's unwillingness to give us some more time to complete the robot."

Tabriz turned on the switch to start the coffee maker. "Cramer sure left behind quite a mess."

Silicon Techchronics issued a brief statement from the office of its president, Michael Waterson, concerning John Cramer's apparent conflict of interest. "John Cramer was in violation of corporate ethical guidelines. These require that an employee who has a vested interest in a potential client or supplier and who is in a position to make a recommendation concerning a sale or a purchase by this company must reveal the extent of his or her investment with that potential client or supplier. No one at Silicon Techchronics was informed of John Cramer's involvement with Lucrative Object and Object Technologies, Inc."

Lucrative Object and Object Technologies, Inc., declared bankruptcy and went out of business last month.

Special to the *Silicon Valley Sentinel-Observer*, Silicon Valley, USA

THE "KILLER ROBOT" INTERFACE

Dr. Horace Gritty

*Department of Computer Science
and Related Concerns,
Silicon Valley University,
Silicon Valley, USA*

Abstract: *The Robbie CX30 industrial robot was supposed to set a new standard for industrial robot intelligence. Unfortunately, one of the first Robbie CX30 robots killed an assembly line worker, leading to the indictment of one of the robot's software developers, Randy Samuels. This paper propounds the theory that it was the operator-robot interface designer who should be on trial in this case. The Robbie CX30 robot violates nearly every rule of interface design. This paper focuses on how the Robbie CX30 interface violated every one of Shneiderman's "Eight Golden Rules."*

INTRODUCTION

Two years ago on May 3, a Silicon Techchronics Robbie CX30 industrial robot killed its operator, Bart Matthews, at CyberWidgets, Inc., in Silicon Heights, a suburb of Silicon Valley. An investigation into the cause of the accident led authorities to the conclusion that a software module written and developed by Randy Samuels, a Silicon Techchronics programmer, was responsible for the erratic and violent robot behavior that led to the death by decapitation of Bart Matthews.[1]

As an expert in the area of user interfaces (1, 2, 3) I was asked to help police reconstruct the accident. In order to accomplish this Silicon Techchronics was asked to provide me with a Robbie CX30 simulator, which included the complete robot operator console. This allowed me to investigate the robot's behavior without actually risking serious harm. Because of my extensive understanding of user interfaces and human factors, I was able to reconstruct the accident with uncanny accuracy. On the basis of this reconstruction, I came to the conclusion that it was the interface design and

---

[1]The media were misled to believe that Bart Matthews was crushed by the robot, but the photographic evidence given to this author shows otherwise. Perhaps authorities were attempting to protect public sensibilities.

not the admittedly flawed software that should be viewed as the culprit in this case.

Despite my finding, Prosecuting Attorney Jane McMurdock insisted on pursuing the case against Randy Samuels. I believe that any competent computer scientist, given an opportunity to interact with the Robbie CX30 simulator, would also conclude that the interface designer and not the programmer should be charged with negligence, if not manslaughter.

SHNEIDERMAN'S EIGHT GOLDEN RULES

My evaluation of the Robbie CX30 user interface is based on Shneiderman's eight golden rules (4). I also used other techniques to evaluate the interface, but those will be published in separate papers. In this section I offer a brief review of Shneiderman's eight golden rules, a subject that would be more familiar to computer interface experts such as myself than to the robot hackers who read this obscure journal.

The eight golden rules are as follows:

1. **Strive for consistency.** As we shall see later, it is important for a user interface to be consistent on many levels. For example, screen layouts should be consistent from one screen to another. In an environment using a graphical user interface (GUI) this also implies consistency from one application to another.
2. **Enable frequent users to use shortcuts.** Frequent users (or power users) may be turned off by overly tedious procedures. Allow those users a less tedious procedure for accomplishing a given task.
3. **Offer informative feedback.** Users need to see the consequences of their actions. If a user enters a command but the computer does not show that it is either processing or has processed that command, this can leave the user confused and disoriented.
4. **Design dialogues to yield closure.** Interacting with a computer is somewhat like a dialogue or conversation. Every task should have a beginning, a middle, and an end. It is important for the user to know when a task is at its end. The user needs to have the feeling that a task has reached closure.
5. **Offer simple error handling.** User errors should be designed into the system. Another way of stating this is that no user action should be considered an error that is beyond the ability of the system to manage. If the user makes a mistake, the user should receive useful, concise, and clear information about the nature of the mistake. It should be easy for the user to undo his or her mistake.
6. **Permit easy reversal of actions.** More generally, users must be permitted to undo what they have done, whether it is in the nature of an error or not.
7. **Support internal locus of control.** User satisfaction is high when the user feels that he or she is in control, and user satisfaction is low when the user

feels that the computer is in control. Design interfaces to reinforce the feeling that the user is the locus of control in the human-computer interaction.

8. **Reduce short-term memory load.** Human short-term memory is remarkably limited. Psychologists often quote Miller's law to the effect that short-term memory is limited to seven discrete pieces of information. Do everything possible to free the user's memory burden. For example, instead of asking the user to type in the name of a file that is going to be retrieved, present the user with a list of files currently available.

ROBOT CONSOLE OVERVIEW

The Robbie CX30 operator interface violated each and every one of Shneiderman's rules. Several of these violations were directly responsible for the accident that ended in the death of the robot operator.

The robot console was an IBM PS/2 model 55SX with an 80386 processor and an EGA color monitor with 640 × 480 resolution. The console had a keyboard but no mouse. The console was embedded in a workstation that included shelves for manuals and an area for taking notes and for reading manuals. However, the reading/writing area was quite a distance from the computer screen, so that it was quite awkward and tiresome for the operator to manage any task that required looking something up in the manual and then acting quickly at the console keyboard. The operator's chair was poorly designed and much too high relative to the console and the reading/writing area. This placed much strain on the operator's back and also caused excessive eye strain.

I cannot understand why a sophisticated system such as this would not include a better device for input. One can only conclude that Silicon Techchronics did not have much experience with user interface technology. The requirements document (5) specified a menu-driven system, which was a reasonable choice. However, in an application where speed was of the essence, especially when operator safety was at issue, the use of a keyboard for all menu selection tasks was an extremely poor choice, requiring many keystrokes to achieve the same effect that could be achieved almost instantaneously with a mouse. [See the paper by Foley et al. (6). Actually, I had most of these ideas before Foley published them, but he beat me to the punch.]

The robot operator could interact with the robot and thus affect its behavior by making choices in a menu system. The main menu consisted of twenty items, too many in my opinion, and each main menu item had a pull-down submenu associated with it. Some of the submenus contained as many as twenty items—again, too many. Furthermore, there seemed to be little rhyme or reason as to why the menu items were listed in the order in which they were listed. A functional or alphabetical organization would have been better.

Some items in the pull-down submenus had up to four pop-up menus associated with them. These would appear in sequence as submenu choices were made. Occasionally, a submenu choice would cause a dialogue box to appear at the screen. A dialogue box requires some kind of interaction between the operator and the system to resolve some issue, such as the diameter of the widgets being lowered into the acid bath.

The menu system presented a strict hierarchy of menu choices. The operator could backtrack up the hierarchy by pressing the escape key. The escape key could also terminate any dialogue.

The use of color in the interface was very unprofessional. There were too many colors in too small a space. The contrasts were glaring and the result, for this reviewer, was severe eye strain in just fifteen minutes. There was excessive use of flashing and of silly musical effects when erroneous choices or erroneous inputs were made.

One has to wonder why Silicon Techchronics did not attempt a more sophisticated approach to the interface design. After a careful study of the Robbie CX30 applications domain, I have come to the conclusion that a direct manipulation interface, which literally would display the robot at the operator console, would have been ideal. The very visual domain within which the robot operated would lend itself naturally to the design of appropriate screen metaphors for that environment, metaphors that the operator could easily understand. This would allow the operator to manipulate the robot by manipulating the graphical representation of the robot in its environment at the computer console. I have asked one of my doctoral students, Susan Farnsworth, to give up her personal life for the better part of a decade in order to investigate this possibility a bit further.

HOW THE ROBBIE CX30 INTERFACE VIOLATED THE EIGHT GOLDEN RULES

The Robbie CX30 user interface violated every golden rule in multitudinous ways. I shall only discuss a few instances of rule violation in this paper, leaving a more detailed discussion of these violations for future articles and my forthcoming book.[2] I will emphasize those violations that were relevant to this particular accident.

Strive for Consistency

There were many violations of consistency in the Robbie CX30 user interface. Error messages could appear in almost any color and could be accompanied by almost any kind of musical effect. Error messages could appear almost anywhere at the screen.

---

[2]*Codependency: How Computer Users Enable Poor User Interfaces,* New York: Angst Press. This book presents a radical new theory concerning the relationship between people and their machines. Essentially, some people need a poor interface in order to avoid some unresolved psychological problems in their lives.

When Bart Matthews saw the error message for the exceptional condition that occurred, an exceptional condition that required operator intervention, it was probably the first time he had seen that particular message. In addition, the error message appeared in a green box, without any audio effects. This is the only error message in the entire system that appears in green and without some kind of orchestral accompaniment.

Enable Frequent Users to Use Shortcuts

This principle was not implemented in any way in the entire interface design. For example, it would have been a good idea to allow frequent users to enter the first letter of a submenu or menu choice in lieu of requiring the use of the cursor keys and the enter key to effect a menu choice. The menu selection mechanism in this system must have been quite a mental strain on the operator.

Furthermore, some form of type-ahead should have been supported, which would have allowed a frequent user to enter a sequence of menu choices without having to wait for the actual menus to appear.

Offer Informative Feedback

In many cases the user has no idea whether a command that was entered is being processed. This problem is exaggerated by inconsistencies in the user interface design. In some cases the operator is given detailed feedback concerning what the robot is doing. In other cases the system is mysteriously silent. In general, the user is led to expect feedback and consequently becomes confused when no feedback is given. There is no visual representation of the robot and its environment at the screen, and the operator's view of the robot is sometimes obstructed.

Design Dialogues to Yield Closure

There are many cases in which a given sequence of keystrokes represents one holistic idea, one complete task, but the operator is left without the kind of feedback that would confirm that the task has been completed. For example, a fairly complicated dialogue is necessary in order to remove a widget from the acid bath. However, upon completion of this dialogue the user is led into a new, unrelated dialogue without being informed that the widget removal dialogue has been completed.

Offer Simple Error Handling

The system seems to be designed to make the user regret any erroneous input. Not only does the system allow numerous opportunities for error, but when an error actually occurs, it is something that is not likely to be repeated for some time. This is because the user interface makes recovery from an error a tedious, frustrating, and at times infuriating ordeal. Some of the error messages were downright offensive and condescending.

Permit Easy Reversal of Actions

As mentioned in the previous paragraph, the user interface makes it very difficult to recover from erroneous inputs. In general, the menu system does allow easy reversal of actions, but this philosophy is not carried through to the design of dialogue boxes and to the handling of exceptional conditions. From a practical (as opposed to theoretical) point of view, most actions are irreversible when the system is in an exceptional state, and this contributed to the killer robot tragedy.

Support Internal Locus of Control

Many of the deficiencies discussed in the previous paragraphs diminish the feeling of *internal locus of control*. For example, not offering feedback, not bringing interactions to closure, and not allowing easy reversal of actions when exceptions arise all act to diminish the user's feeling of being in control of the robot. There are many features of this interface that make the operator feel that there is an enormous gap between the operator console and the robot itself, whereas a good interface design would have made the user interface transparent and would have given the robot operator a feeling of being in direct contact with the robot. In one case, I commanded the robot to move a widget from the acid bath to the drying chamber, and it took twenty seconds before the robot seemed to respond. Thus, I did not feel like I was controlling the robot. The robot's delayed response along with the lack of informative feedback at the computer screen made me feel that the robot was an autonomous agent—an unsettling feeling to say the least.

Reduce Short-Term Memory Load

A menu-driven system is generally good in terms of the memory burden it places upon users. However, there is great variation among particular implementations of menu systems regarding memory burden. The Robbie CX30 user interface has very large menus without any obvious internal organization. These place a great burden upon the operator in terms of memory and also in terms of scan time, the time it takes the operator to locate a particular menu choice.

Many dialogue boxes require the user to enter part numbers, file names, and other information from the keyboard. The system could easily have been designed to present the user with these part numbers and so forth without requiring the user to recall these things from his or her own memory. This requirement greatly increases the memory burden on the user.

Finally—and this is really unforgivable, incredible as it may seem—there is no on-line, context-sensitive help facility! Although I was taken through the training course offered by Silicon Techchronics, I often found myself leafing through the reference manuals in order to find the answer to even the most basic questions, such as, "What does this menu choice mean? What will happen if I make this choice?"

A RECONSTRUCTION OF THE "KILLER ROBOT" TRAGEDY

Police photographs of the accident scene are not a pleasant sight. The operator console was splattered with a considerable amount of blood. However, the photographs are of exceptional quality, and using blow-up techniques I was able to ascertain the following important facts about the moment when Bart Matthews was decapitated.

1. *The NUM LOCK light was not lit, but it should have been.* The IBM keyboard contains a calculator pad that can operate in two modes. When the NUM LOCK light is on, it behaves like a calculator. Otherwise the keys can be used to move the cursor at the screen. I found that although the cursor keys were in calculator mode at the time of the accident, the NUM LOCK light was not lit. In other words, the NUM LOCK light was not functioning properly.
2. *Blood was smeared on the calculator pad.* Bloody fingerprints indicate that Bart Matthews was using the calculator pad when he was struck and killed.
3. *A green error message was flashing.* This tells us the error situation in effect when the tragedy occurred. The error message said, "ROBOT DYNAMICS INTEGRITY ERROR—45."
4. *A reference manual was open and laid flat in the workstation reading/writing area.* One volume of the four-volume reference manual was open to the index page that contained the entry "Errors/Messages."
5. *A message giving operator instructions was also showing on the screen.* This message was displayed in yellow at the bottom of the screen. This message read, "PLEASE ENTER DYNAMICAL ERROR ROBOT ABORT COMMAND SEQUENCE PROMPTLY!!!"

On the basis of this physical evidence, other evidence contained in the system log, and the nature of the error that occurred (robot dynamics integrity error 45, the error that was caused by Randy Samuels's program), I have concluded that the following sequence of events occurred on the fateful morning of the killer robot tragedy.

10:22.30. "ROBOT DYNAMICS INTEGRITY ERROR—45" appears on the screen. Bart Matthews does not notice this because there is no beep or audio effect such as occurs with every other error situation. Also, the error message appears in green, which in all other contexts means that some process is proceeding normally.

10:24.00. Robot enters a state violent enough for Bart Matthews to notice.

10:24.05. Bart Matthews notices error message, does not know what it means, and does not know what to do. He tries "emergency abort" sub-menu, a general-purpose submenu for turning off the robot. This involves *six* separate menu choices, but Mr. Matthews does not notice that the NUM LOCK light is not functioning properly. Thus, the menu choices aren't registering because the cursor keys are operating as calculator keys even though the NUM LOCK light is not lit.

10:24.45. Robot turns from acid bath and begins sweeping toward operator console, its jagged robot arms flailing wildly. No one anticipated that the operator might have to flee a runaway robot, so Bart Matthews is cornered in his work area by the advancing robot. At about this time, Bart Matthews retrieves the reference manual and starts looking for a reference to robot dynamics integrity error 45 in the index. He successfully locates a reference to error messages in the index.

10:25.00. Robot enters the operator area. Bart Matthews gives up trying to find the operator procedure for the robot dynamics integrity error. Instead, he tries once again to enter the emergency abort sequence from the calculator keypad, when he is struck.

SUMMARY AND CONCLUSIONS

While the software module written by Randy Samuels did cause the Robbie CX30 robot to oscillate out of control and attack its human operator, a good interface design would have allowed the operator to terminate the erratic robot behavior. Based on an analysis of the robot-user interface using Shneiderman's eight golden rules, this interface design expert has come to the conclusion that the interface design and not the programmer was the more guilty party in this unfortunate fiasco.

REFERENCES

1. Gritty, Horace (1990). *The Only User Interface Book You'll Ever Need.* Oshkosh, WI: Vanity Press. 212 pp.

2. Gritty, Horace (1992). "What We Can Learn from the Killer Robot," invited talk given at the Silicon Valley University International Symposium on Robot Safety and User Interfaces, March 1991. Also to appear in Silicon Valley University Alumni Notes.

3. Gritty, Horace (expected 1997). *Codependency: How Computer Users Enable Poor User Interfaces.* New York: Angst Press. 321 pp.

4. Shneiderman, Ben (1987). *Designing the User Interface.* Reading, MA: Addison-Wesley. 448 pp.

5. *Robbie CX30 Intelligent Industrial Robot Requirements Document: CyberWidgets Inc. Version.* Technical Document Number 91-0023XA. Silicon Valley, USA: Silicon Techchronics Corporation. 1245 pp.

6. Foley, J. P., Wallace, V. L., and Chan, P. (1984). "The Human Factors of Computer Graphics Interaction Techniques." *IEEE Computer Graphics and Applications,* 4(11):13–48.

Reprinted with permission of *Robotics World,* the premiere journal of *Robotics and Robotics Applications.*

SILICON TECHCHRONICS PROMISED TO DELIVER A SAFE ROBOT

Quality of Operator Training Questioned

by Pam Pulitzer

At a news conference this afternoon, a ragtag group of programmers who call themselves the "Justice for Randy Samuels Committee" distributed documents showing that Silicon Techchronics had obligated itself to deliver robots that would "cause no bodily injury to the human operator." Randy Samuels is the programmer who has been charged with manslaughter in the infamous "killer robot" case.

"We cannot understand how the prosecuting attorney could charge Randy with manslaughter when in fact Silicon Techchronics was legally bound to deliver a safe robot to CyberWidgets," said committee spokesperson Ruth Witherspoon. "We believe that there is a cover-up going on and that there is some kind of collusion between SiliTech [Silicon Techchronics] management and the prosecuting attorney's office. Michael Waterson was a major contributor to Ms. McMurdock's reelection campaign last year."

Michael Waterson is president and CEO of Silicon Techchronics. Jane McMurdock is the Prosecuting Attorney for the city of Silicon Valley. The *Sentinel-Observer* has confirmed that Waterson made several large contributions to the McMurdock reelection campaign last fall.

"Randy is being made the scapegoat for a company that had lax quality control standards, and we are not going to stand for it!" Witherspoon shouted in an emotional statement to reporters. "We believe that politics has entered this case."

The documents that were distributed by the Justice for Randy Samuels Committee were portions of what is called a "requirements document." According to Ruth Witherspoon and other committee members, this document proves that Samuels was not legally responsible for the death of Bart Matthews, the unfortunate robot operator who was killed by a Silicon Techchronics robot at CyberWidgets in Silicon Heights last May.

The requirements document amounts to a contract between Silicon Techchronics and CyberWidgets. The requirements document spells out in complete detail the functionality of the Robbie CX30 robot that Silicon Techchronics promised to deliver to CyberWidgets.

According to Witherspoon, the Robbie CX30 robot was designed to be an "intelligent" robot that would be capable of operating in a variety of industrial settings. Separate requirements documents were required for each corporate customer, since Robbie CX30 was not an "off-the-shelf" robot, but a robot that needed to be programmed differently for each application.

However, all requirements documents that were agreed upon under the auspices of the Robbie CX30 project, including the agreement between Silicon Techchronics and CyberWidgets, contain the following important statements:

> *The robot will be safe to operate, and even under exceptional conditions (see Section 5.2) the robot will cause no bodily injury to the human operator.*

> *In the event of the exceptional conditions that potentially contain the risk of bodily injury (see Section 5.2.4 and all of its subsections), the human operator will be able to enter a sequence of command codes, as described in the relevant sections of the functional specification (see Section 3.5.2), which will arrest robot motion long before bodily injury can actually occur.*

"Exceptional conditions" include unusual events such as bizarre data from the robot sensors, erratic or violent robot motion, and operator error. It was just such an exceptional condition that led to the death of Bart Matthews.

These paragraphs were extracted from the portion of the requirements document that dealt with "nonfunctional requirements." The nonfunctional requirements state in complete detail the constraints under which the robot would be operating. For example, the requirement that the robot be incapable of harming its human operator is a constraint, and according to Ruth Witherspoon, Silicon Techchronics was legally obligated to satisfy this constraint.

"The significance of the requirements document as a contract is that it provides CyberWidgets with grounds for a lawsuit based on breach of contract," Ruth Witherspoon explained.

The functional requirements portion of the requirements document covers (again in complete detail) the behavior of the robot and its interaction with its environment and with its human operator. In particular, the functional requirements specified the behavior of the robot under every anticipated exceptional condition.

In her statement to reporters at the news conference, Witherspoon explained that Bart Matthews was killed when exceptional condition 5.2.4.26 arose. This involved an exceptionally violent and unpredictable robot arm motion. This condition required operator intervention, namely, the entering of the command codes mentioned in the document, but apparently Bart Matthews became confused and could not enter the codes successfully.

"Although Randy Samuels's program was in error—he did misinterpret the robot dynamics formulas, as reported in the media—exceptional condition 5.2.4.26 was designed to protect against just this sort of contingency," Witherspoon told reporters. "The robot motion values generated by Randy's program correctly set off this exceptional condition, and the robot operator received due warning that something was wrong."

Witherspoon claimed that she has a signed affidavit from another CyberWidgets robot operator to the effect that the training sessions offered by Silicon Techchronics never mentioned this and many other exceptional conditions. According to Witherspoon, the robot operator has sworn that neither she nor any other robot operator was ever told that the robot arm could oscillate violently. Witherspoon quoted the affidavit at the news conference. "Neither I nor Bart Matthews was ever trained to handle this sort of exceptional condition. I doubt that Bart Matthews had any idea what he was supposed to do when the computer screen started flashing the error message."

Exceptional conditions requiring operator intervention cause an error message to be generated at the operator console. Silicon Valley police confirm that when Bart Matthews was killed, the reference manual at his console was opened to the page of the index that contained entries for errors.

Witherspoon then quoted sections of the requirements document that obligated Silicon Techchronics (the vendor) to adequately train robot operators:

The vendor shall provide forty (40) hours of operator training. This training shall cover all aspects of robot operation, including exhaustive coverage of the safety procedures that must be followed in the case of exceptional conditions that potentially contain the risk of bodily injury.

The vendor shall provide and administer appropriate test instruments, which shall be used to certify sufficient operator understanding of robot console operations and safety procedures. Only employees of the customer who have passed this test shall be allowed to operate the Robbie CX30 robot in an actual industrial setting.

> *The reference manual shall provide clear instructions for operator interven-*
> *tion in all exceptional situations, especially and including those that poten-*
> *tially contain the risk of bodily injury.*

According to Witherspoon, sworn affidavits from several robot operators at CyberWidgets, Inc., state that only one work day (approximately
eight hours) was spent in operator training. Furthermore, almost no time
was spent discussing potentially dangerous exceptional conditions.

"The written test developed by Silicon Techchronics to certify a robot
operator was considered a 'joke' by CyberWidgets employees," Witherspoon asserted. "Silicon Techchronics obviously did not give much thought
to the training and testing procedures mandated by the requirements document according to the evidence in our possession."

Special to the *Silicon Valley Sentinel-Observer*, Silicon Valley, USA

SOFTWARE ENGINEER CHALLENGES AUTHENTICITY OF "KILLER ROBOT" SOFTWARE TESTS

SVU Professor's Inquiry Raises Serious Legal and Ethical Issues

by Pam Pulitzer

The "killer robot" case took a significant turn yesterday when a Silicon Valley
University professor issued a report questioning the authenticity of software
tests that were purportedly performed on the robot software by Silicon Techchronics. Professor Wesley Silber, professor of software engineering, told a
packed news conference held at the university that the test results reflected
in Silicon Techchronics internal documents were not consistent with test
results obtained when he and his associates tested the actual robot software.

Silicon Valley is still reacting to Professor Silber's announcement, which
could play an important role in the trial of Randy Samuels, the Silicon Tech-

chronics programmer who has been charged with manslaughter in the now infamous "killer robot" incident.

Pressed for her reaction to Professor Silber's report, Prosecuting Attorney Jane McMurdock reiterated her confidence that a jury will find Randy Samuels guilty. McMurdock shocked reporters, however, when she added, "But this does raise the possibility of new indictments."

Ruth Witherspoon, spokesperson for the "Justice for Randy Samuels Committee," was exultant when she spoke to this reporter. "McMurdock cannot have it both ways. Either the programmer is responsible for this tragedy, or management must be held responsible. We believe that the Silber report exonerates our friend and colleague, Randy Samuels."

Silicon Techchronics CEO Michael Waterson issued a terse statement concerning the Silber report:

Soon after the indictment of Randy Samuels was announced, I personally asked the esteemed software engineer Dr. Wesley Silber to conduct an impartial inquiry into quality-assurance procedures at Silicon Techchronics. As the chief executive of this corporation, I have always insisted on quality first, despite what you might have read in the press.

I asked Professor Silber to conduct an impartial inquiry into all aspects of quality-assurance at Silicon Techchronics. I promised Professor Silber that he would have access to all information relevant to this unfortunate situation. I told him in a face-to-face meeting in my office that he should pursue his investigation wherever it might lead, regardless of the implications.

It never occurred to me, based upon the information that I was getting from my managers, that there might be a problem in which software quality-assurance procedures were either lax or deliberately circumvented. I want the public to be reassured that the person or persons who were responsible for the failure of software quality assurance within the Robotics Division of Silicon Techchronics will be asked to find employment elsewhere.

Sally Matthews, widow of Bart Matthews, the robot operator who was killed in the incident, spoke to the *Sentinel-Observer* by telephone from her home. "I still want to see Mr. Samuels punished for what he did to my husband. I don't understand what all the commotion is about. The man who murdered my husband should have tested his own software!"

The *Sentinel-Observer* interviewed Professor Silber in his office shortly after his news conference. On his office wall were numerous awards he has received because of his work in the field of software engineering and software quality assurance. This reporter began the interview by asking Professor Silber to explain why software is sometimes unreliable. He answered the question by citing the enormous complexity of software.

"Large computer programs are arguably the most complex artifacts ever fashioned by the human mind," Professor Silber explained, seated in front of a large computer monitor. "At any point in time, a computer program is in one of an extremely large number of possible states, and it is a practical impossibility to ensure that the program will behave properly in each of those states. We do not have enough time to do that kind of exhaustive testing. Thus, we use testing strategies, or heuristics, that are very likely to find bugs if they exist."

Professor Silber has published numerous papers on software engineering. He made headlines last year when he published his list of "Airlines to Avoid as if Your Life Depended on It." That list named domestic airlines that he deemed irresponsible because of their purchase of airplanes that are almost completely controlled by computer software.

Soon after Randy Samuels was indicted in the "killer robot" case, the CEO of Silicon Techchronics, Michael Waterson, asked Professor Silber to conduct an impartial review of quality-assurance procedures at Silicon Techchronics. Waterson acted to counter the bad publicity generated for his company after the Samuels indictment.

"Quality assurance" refers to those methods a software developer uses to ensure that the software is reliable, correct, and robust. These methods are applied throughout the development life cycle of the software product. At each stage appropriate quality-assurance methods are applied. For example, when a programmer writes code, one quality-assurance measure is to test the code by actually running it using test data. Another method is to run special programs, called static analyzers, against the new code. A static analyzer is a program that looks for suspicious patterns in programs—patterns that might indicate an error or bug. These two forms of quality assurance are called dynamic testing and static testing, respectively.

Software consists of discrete components or units that are eventually combined to create larger systems. The individual units themselves must be tested, and this process is called unit testing. When the units are combined, the integrated subsystems must be tested, and this process is called integration testing.

Professor Silber told the *Sentinel-Observer* about his work at Silicon Techchronics: "Mike [Waterson] told me to go in there [into the company] and conduct an impartial review of his software testing procedures and to make my findings public. Mike seemed confident, perhaps because of what his managers had told him, that I would find nothing wrong with quality assurance at Silicon Techchronics."

Soon after arriving at Silicon Techchronics, Professor Silber focused his attention on procedures for dynamically testing software at the high-tech company.

Assisted by a cadre of graduate students, Professor Silber discovered a discrepancy between the actual behavior of the section of program code (written by Randy Samuels) that caused the Robbie CX30 robot to kill its operator and the behavior recorded in test documentation at Silicon Techchronics. This discovery was actually made by Sandra Henderson, a graduate student in software engineering who is completing her doctorate under Professor Silber. We interviewed Ms. Henderson in one of the graduate computer laboratories at Silicon Valley University.

"We found a problem with the unit testing," Ms. Henderson explained. "Here are the test results given to us by Mr. Waterson at Silicon Techchronics, which are purported to be for the C [programming language] code that Randy Samuels wrote. This is the code that is known to have caused the killer robot tragedy. As you can see, everything is clearly documented and organized. There are two test suites: one based on white-box testing and another based on black-box testing. Based on our own standards for testing software, these test suites are well designed, complete, and rigorous."

Black-box testing involves viewing the software unit (or component) as a black box that has formally specified input and output behaviors. If the component's behavior satisfies the specifications for all inputs in the test suite, it passes the test. Test suites are designed to cover all "interesting" behaviors that the unit might exhibit without any knowledge of the structure of the actual code.

White-box testing involves covering all possible paths through the unit. Thus, white-box testing is done with thorough knowledge of the unit's structure. In white-box testing the test suite must cause each program statement to execute at least once so that no program statement escapes execution.

Sandra Henderson went on to explain the significance of software testing: "Neither black-box nor white-box testing 'proves' that a program is correct. However, software testers, such as those employed at Silicon Techchronics, can become quite skillful at designing test cases so as to discover new bugs in the software. The proper attitude is that a test succeeds when a bug is found.

"Basically, the tester is given a set of specifications and does his or her best to show that the code being tested does not satisfy its specifications," Ms. Henderson explained.

Ms. Henderson then showed this reporter the test results that she actually obtained when she ran the critical killer robot code using the company's test suites for white-box and black-box testing. In many cases the outputs recorded in the company's test documents were not the same as those generated by the actual killer robot code.

During his interview with the *Sentinel-Observer* yesterday, Professor Silber discussed the discrepancy: "You see, the software that was actually delivered with the Robbie CX30 robot was not the same as the software that was tested—at least according to these documents! This suggests several possibilities. First, the software testing process, at least for this critical part of the software, might have been deliberately faked. We all know that there was enormous pressure to get this robot out the door by a certain date. A second possibility is that there was some kind of version management difficulty at Silicon Techchronics, so that correct code was written and successfully tested, but the wrong code was inserted into the delivered product."

We asked Professor Silber to explain what he meant by "version man-agement." "In a given project, a given software component might have sev-eral versions: version 1, version 2, and so forth. These reflect the evolution of that component as the project progresses. Some kind of mechanism needs to be in place to keep track of versions of software components in a project as complex as this one. Perhaps the software testers tested a correct version of the robot dynamics code, but an incorrect version was actually delivered. However, this raises the question as to what happened to the correct code, that is, the code that generated the correct test results. We have not been able to track down the correct code anywhere at Silicon Techchronics."

Professor Silber sat back in his chair and sighed. "This really is a great tragedy. If the 'killer code' had gone through the testing process in an honest manner, the robot would never have killed Bart Matthews. So the question becomes, What was going on at Silicon Techchronics that prevented the honest testing of the robot software?"

The *Sentinel-Observer* asked Professor Silber whether he agreed with the notion that the user interface was the ultimate culprit in this case. "I don't buy the argument being put forth by my colleague Horace Gritty that all of the culpability in this case belongs to the user interface designer or design-ers. I agree with some of what he says, but not all of it. On the other hand, I do have to ask myself whether Silicon Techchronics was placing too much emphasis on the user interface as a last line of defense against disaster. That is, they knew there was a problem, but they felt that the user interface could allow the operator to handle that problem."

The *Sentinel-Observer* then asked Professor Silber about the charge that he should never have accepted Waterson's appointment to conduct an impartial investigation into the accident. Critics point out that Silicon Valley University, and Professor Silber in particular, have many business ties with Silicon Techchronics, including research grants and purchasing agreements. These critics charge that Professor Silber could not be counted upon to con-duct an impartial investigation.

"I think my report speaks for itself," Professor Silber replied, visibly angered by our question. "I have told you reporters over and over again that this was not a government investigation but a corporate investigation, so I believe that Silicon Techchronics had the right to choose whomever they desired. I believe I was known to them as a person of integrity."

Late yesterday, George Cuzzins, the Robbie CX30 project manager, hired an attorney, Valerie Thomas. Ms. Thomas issued this statement on behalf of her client:

My client is shocked that someone at Silicon Techchronics has misled Profes-sor Silber concerning the software tests for the Robbie CX30 robot. My client asserts that the software was tested and that he and others were well aware of the fact that there was something wrong with the robot dynamics software. However, Mr. Ray Johnson, my client's immediate superior at Silicon Tech-

chronics, decided that the robot could be delivered to CyberWidgets, Inc., based on Mr. Johnson's "Ivory Snow theory." According to that theory, the software was nearly bug free and thus could be released. According to Mr. Johnson, the risk of failure was very small, and the cost of further delaying delivery of the robot was very great.

According to my client, Mr. Johnson felt that the environmental conditions that could trigger erratic and violent robot behavior were extremely unlikely to occur. Furthermore, Mr. Johnson felt that the robot operator would not be in danger because the user interface was designed to permit the operator to stop the robot dead in its tracks in the case of any life-threatening robot motion."

Mr. Johnson, Robotics Division chief at Silicon Techchronics, could not be reached for comment.

Randy Samuels will be placed on trial next month at the Silicon Valley Courthouse. When contacted by phone, Samuels referred all questions to his attorney, Alex Allendale.

Allendale had this to say concerning Professor Silber's findings: "My client submitted the software in question in the usual way, with the usual documentation, and with the usual expectation that his code would be thoroughly tested. He was not aware until Professor Silber's report came out that the code involved in this terrible tragedy had not been tested properly or that the test results might have been faked.

"Mr. Samuels wants to express again the great sorrow he feels about this accident. He, more than anyone else, wants to see justice done in this case. Mr. Samuels once again extends his heartfelt condolences to Mrs. Matthews and her children."

Special to the *Silicon Valley Sentinel-Observer*, Silicon Valley, USA

SILICON TECHCHRONICS EMPLOYEE ADMITS FAKING SOFTWARE TESTS

Electronic Mail Messages Reveal New Details in "Killer Robot" Case

Professional Association Launches Investigation into Ethics Code Violations

by Pam Pulitzer

Cindy Yardley, a software tester at Silicon Techchronics, admitted today that she was the person who created the fraudulent "killer robot" software tests. The fraudulent tests were revealed earlier this week by Professor Wesley Silber in what has come to be known as the "Silber Report." Professor Silber is professor of software engineering at Silicon Valley University.

At issue are quality-assurance procedures that were performed on the program code written by Randy Samuels, the programmer charged with manslaughter in the killer robot incident. The Silber Report asserted that the official test results given in internal Silicon Techchronics documentation were inconsistent with the test results that he obtained when he ran the actual killer robot software.

In a startling development at noontime yesterday, Max Worthington, chief security officer for Silicon Techchronics, announced his resignation at a packed news conference that was broadcast live by CNN and other news organizations.

Worthington stunned the assembled reporters when he began his news conference with the announcement, "I am Martha."

Worthington described his responsibilities at Silicon Techchronics in this way: "My job was to protect Silicon Techchronics from all enemies—domestic and foreign. By foreign I mean adversaries from outside the corporation. My role was mostly managerial. Those working under me had many responsibilities, including protecting the physical plant and watching out for industrial spying and sabotage. I was also responsible for keeping an eye out for employees who might be abusing drugs or who might be disloyal in some way to Silicon Techchronics. For example, I went to Ray Johnson with information about Cramer's drinking and reckless behavior, but nothing was done about it."

50

Worthington then pointed to a stack of bound volumes on a table to the left of the speaker's rostrum. "These volumes represent just some of the electronic surveillance of employees that I conducted over the years for my superior, Michael Waterson. These are printouts of electronic mail messages that Silicon Techchronics employees sent to one another and to persons at other sites. I can assert with certainty that no employee was ever told that this kind of electronic surveillance was being conducted. However, I think the evidence shows that some employees suspected that this might be going on."

A reporter shouted a question asking who at Silicon Techchronics knew about the electronic surveillance.

Worthington replied, "No one knew about this except Mr. Waterson, myself, and one of my assistants, who was responsible for conducting the actual monitoring. My assistant produced a special report, summarizing e-mail [electronic mail] activity once a week, and that report was for Waterson's eyes and my eyes only. Upon request, my assistant could produce a more detailed accounting of electronic communications."

Worthington explained that he was making the electronic mail transcripts available to the press because he wanted the whole truth to come out concerning Silicon Techchronics and the killer robot incident.

The electronic mail messages that Worthington made available to the press indeed revealed new facets of the case. They revealed that Cindy Yardley was the employee who generated the fraudulent software tests. An e-mail message from Cindy Yardley to Robotics Division chief Ray Johnson indicates that she faked the test results at his request. Here is the text of that message:

To: ray.johnson
From: cindy.yardley
Re: Samuels software

I have finished creating the software test results for that troublesome robot software, per your idea of using a simulation rather than the actual software. Attached you will find the modified test document showing the successful simulation.

Should we tell Cuzzins about this?

—Cindy

Johnson's response to Yardley's message suggests that he suspected that electronic mail might not be secure:

In-reply-to: cindy.yardley
From: ray.johnson
Re: Samuels software

I knew I could count on you! I am sure that your devotion to Silicon Techchronics will be repaid in full.

Please use a more secure form of communication in the future when discussing this matter. I assure you that the way we handled this was completely above board, but I have my enemies here at good ol' SiliTech.

Do not tell George Cuzzins about this because his attitudes are, to put it bluntly, a bit old-fashioned.
—*Ray*

Another e-mail message shows Johnson pushing Cuzzins aside so that Johnson would be the point man for CyberWidgets' acceptance of the robot. At issue in Johnson's meeting with CyberWidgets would be whether Robbie CX30 was fulfilling all the requirements that were agreed upon. Here is that message from Johnson to Cuzzins:

To: george.cuzzins
From: ray.johnson
Re: CyberWidgets sign-off

George:
For the sake of expediency I am taking things out of your hands for the purpose of getting CyberWidgets and the others to sign off on Robbie CX30. I want to manage the acceptance testing myself and I have enlisted the help of Cindy Yardley in this regard. She is the person most familiar with the software tests.

Rest assured that I will provide CyberWidgets and the other customers with all of the information that they could possibly need in order to decide whether Robbie CX30 is ready to go to work.
—*Ray*

These communications were exchanged just a few weeks before the Robbie CX30 robot was shipped out to CyberWidgets, Inc. This fact is important because the fake software tests were not part of a cover-up of the killer robot incident. These messages seem to indicate that the purpose of the fake tests was to make sure that CyberWidgets and other customers would accept delivery of the Robbie CX30 robots.

The electronic mail transcripts also reveal repeated messages from Ray Johnson to various people to the effect that the Robotics Division would definitely be closed down if the Robbie CX30 project was not completed on time. In one message, sent about one month prior to the aforementioned message from Johnson to Cuzzins, Ray Johnson lectures George Cuzzins on the infamous "Ivory Snow theory": 99.44% perfect.

To: george.cuzzins
From: ray.johnson
Re: don't be a perfectionist!

George:
You and I have had our differences, but everyone knows that I like you personally. Please understand that everything I am doing is for the purpose of SAVING YOUR JOB AND

THE JOB OF EVERYONE IN THIS DIVISION. I view you and all of the people who work with me in the Robotics Division as my family.

Waterson has made it clear that he wants the robot project completed on time. That's the bottom line. Thus, we have no recourse but "Ivory Snow." You know what I mean by that. It doesn't have to be perfect. The user interface is our fallback if we cannot get rid of all known bugs. The robot operator will be safe because the operator will be able to abort any robot motion at any time from the robot console.

I agree with you that the nonfunctional requirements are too vague in places, but that is water under the bridge. If this weren't crunch time, I would be among the first to suggest that we quantify the amount of time it would take the operator to stop the robot in case of an accident. However, we cannot afford to negotiate these requirements over again just so that you can have peace of mind. Nor do we have time to design and implement new tests for new nonfunctional requirements.

I cannot emphasize enough that this is crunch time. It's no sweat off Waterson's back if he lops off the entire Robotics Division. His Wall Street friends will just say, "Congratulations!" You see, to Waterson, we are not a family, we are just corporate fat. And that's not the only rumor I've heard from my superiors. Did you ever consider the implications of a hostile takeover if our profits go down?
—Ray

In this message, Ray Johnson seems to be less concerned with the security of communicating by electronic mail.

The *Sentinel-Observer* interviewed Cindy Yardley at her home yesterday evening. Neither Ray Johnson nor George Cuzzins could be reached for comment.

Ms. Yardley was obviously upset that her private electronic mail messages had been released to the press. "I am relieved in some ways. I felt tremendous guilt when that guy was killed by a robot that I helped to produce. Tremendous guilt." Ms. Yardley's arms were crossed in front of her and her long fingernails dug into the flesh of her forearms.

The *Sentinel-Observer* asked Ms. Yardley whether she felt that she had made an ethical choice in agreeing to fake the software test results. She responded with great emotion: "Nothing, nothing in my experience or background prepared me for something like this. I studied computer science at a major university, and they taught me about software testing, but they never told me that someone with power over me might ask me to produce a fake software test!"

"When Johnson asked me to do this, he called me to his office, as if to show me the trappings of power. I had never been in a division chief's office before. It was impressive. You see, someday I would like to be in a managerial position. I sat down in his office, and he came right out and said, 'I want you to fake the test results on that Samuels software. I don't want Cuzzins to know anything about this.'"

Ms. Yardley is currently pursuing an M.B.A. degree at night at Silicon Valley University.

Yardley fought back tears. "He assured me that no one would ever see the test results because the robot was perfectly safe. It was just an internal matter, a matter of cleanliness, to make sure that our customers would accept the Robbie CX30. I asked him whether he was sure about the robot being safe and all that, and he said, 'It's safe! Look, hon. If there's one thing I care about, it's safety! The user interface is our line of defense. In about six months we can issue a second version of the robotics software and by then this Samuels problem will be solved.'"

Yardley paused to catch her breath. "At this point he opened his desk drawer, and he took out this plaque, some kind of award, and he flashed it by me. He said, 'If I didn't care about safety I wouldn't have won this award from the Robot Manufacturers' Safety Association.' He didn't let me read the inscription on the plaque. Before I could read anything, it was back in his desk drawer."

Yardley leaned forward in her chair as if her next remark needed special emphasis. "He then told me that if I did not fake the software tests, everyone in the Robotics Division would lose their job. He said something about a hostile takeover, I think. On that basis I decided to fake the test results—I was trying to protect my job and the jobs of my co-workers."

The *Sentinel-Observer* then asked Ms. Yardley whether she still felt that she had made an ethical decision, in view of the death of Bart Matthews. "I think I was misled by Ray Johnson. He told me that the robot was safe. I'm only a software tester. I'm not one of the big players."

Another revelation contained in the released electronic mail transcripts was the fact that Randy Samuels stole some of the software that he used in the killer robot project. This fact was revealed in a message Samuels sent to Yardley when she first tested his software and it gave erroneous results:

In-reply-to: cindy.yardley
From: randy.samuels
Re: damned if I know

I cannot for the life of me figure out what is wrong with this function, swing_arm(). I've checked the robot dynamics formula over and over again, and it seems to be implemented correctly. As you know, swing_arm() calls 14 different functions. I lifted five of those from the PACKSTAT 1-2-3 statistical package verbatim. Please don't tell a soul! Those couldn't be the problem, could they?
—Randy

Experts tell the *Sentinel-Observer* that lifting software from a commercial software package like PACKSTAT 1-2-3 is a violation of the law. Software such as the immensely popular PACKSTAT 1-2-3 is protected by the same kind of copyright that protects printed materials.

Michael Waterson, CEO of Silicon Techchronics, issued an angry statement concerning Max Worthington's release of "confidential" electronic mail transcripts. Waterson's statement said, in part, "I have asked our attorneys to look into this matter. We consider those transcripts the exclusive property of Silicon Techchronics. We intend to press charges against Mr. Worthington."

In reaction to yesterday's developments in the killer robot case, the Association for Computing Machinery (ACM) announced its intention to investigate whether any ACM members at Silicon Techchronics have violated the ACM Code of Ethics. The ACM is an international association of computer scientists with 85,000 members.

Dr. Turina Babbage, ACM president, issued a statement from the ACM's Computer Science Conference, which is held every winter and which is being held this winter in Duluth, Minnesota.

An excerpt from Dr. Babbage's statement follows:

All members of the ACM are bound by the ACM Code of Ethics and Professional Conduct. This code states, in part, that ACM members have the general moral imperative to contribute to society and human well-being, to avoid harm to others, to be honest and trustworthy, to give proper credit for intellectual property, to access computing and communication resources only when authorized to do so, to respect the privacy of others, and to honor confidentiality.

Beyond that, there are professional responsibilities, such as the obligation to honor contracts, agreements, and assigned responsibilities, and to give comprehensive and thorough evaluations of computing systems and their impacts, with special emphasis on possible risks.

Several of the people involved in the killer robot case are ACM members, and there is cause to believe that they have acted in violation of our association's code of ethics. Therefore, I am asking the ACM Board to appoint a task force to investigate ACM members at Silicon Techchronics who might be in gross violation of the code.

We do not take this step lightly. This sanction has been applied only rarely, but the killer robot incident has not only cost a human life, it has done much to damage the reputation of the computing profession.

Special to the *Silicon Valley Sentinel-Observer*, Silicon Valley, USA

The Sunday Sentinel-Observer Magazine
A CONVERSATION WITH DR. HARRY YODER

by Robert Franklin

Harry Yoder is a well-known figure on the Silicon Valley University campus. The Samuel Southerland Professor of Computer Technology and Ethics, he has written numerous articles and texts on ethics and the social impact of computers. His courses are very popular, and most of his courses are closed long before the end of the registration period. Dr. Yoder received his Ph.D. in electrical engineering from the Georgia Institute of Technology in 1958. In 1976 he received a Master of Divinity degree from the Harvard Divinity School. In 1983 he received an M.S. in computer science from the University of Washington. He joined the faculty at Silicon Valley University in 1988.

I interviewed Dr. Yoder in his office on campus. My purpose was to get his reaction to the case of the killer robot and to "pick his brain" about the ethical issues involved in this case.

SENTINEL-OBSERVER: Going from electrical engineering to the study of religion seems like quite a jump.

YODER: I was an electrical engineer by profession, but all human beings have an inner life. Don't you?

SENTINEL-OBSERVER: Yes.

YODER: What is your inner life about?

SENTINEL-OBSERVER: It's about doing the right thing. It's also about achieving excellence in what I do. Is that what sent you to Harvard Divinity School? You wanted to clarify your inner life?

YODER: Virtuosity, I call it. You want to be a virtuoso performer in the miracle of life. I'm just like you.

There was a lot going on at the Divinity School, and much of it was very compelling. However, most of all I wanted to understand the difference between what was right and what was wrong.

SENTINEL-OBSERVER: What about God?

YODER: Yes, I studied my own Christian religion and most of the major world religions, and they all had interesting things to say about God. However, when I discuss ethics in my computer ethics courses, I do not place that discussion in a religious context. I think religious faith can help a person to become ethical, but on the other hand, we all know that certain notorious

56

people who have claimed to be religious have been highly unethical. Thus, when I discuss computer ethics, the starting point is not religion, but rather a common agreement between myself and my students that we want to be ethical people, that striving for ethical excellence—and more generally, for virtuosity—is a worthwhile human endeavor. At the very least, we do not want to hurt other people; we do not want to lie, cheat, steal, maim, murder, and so forth.

SENTINEL-OBSERVER: Let's see how these concepts apply to the matter at hand. Who, in your opinion, was responsible for the death of Bart Matthews, the robot operator?

YODER: Please forgive me for taking us back to the Harvard Divinity School, but I think one of my professors there had the correct answer to your question. He was an elderly man, perhaps seventy, from eastern Europe, a rabbi. This rabbi said that according to the Talmud, an ancient tradition of Jewish law, if innocent blood is shed in a town, then the *leaders* of that town must go to the edge of the town and perform an act of penance. This was in addition to any justice that would be meted out to the person or persons who committed the murder.

SENTINEL-OBSERVER: That's an interesting concept.

YODER: And a truthful one! A town, a city, a corporation—these are systems in which the part is related to the whole and the whole to the part.

SENTINEL-OBSERVER: You are implying that the leaders at Silicon Techchronics, such as Mike Waterson and Ray Johnson, should have assumed responsibility for this incident right from the start. In addition, perhaps other individuals, such as Randy Samuels and Cindy Yardley, bear special burdens of responsibility.

YODER: Yes, responsibility, not guilt. Let's view guilt versus innocence as a legal issue to be decided in the courts. I guess a person bears responsibility for the death of Bart Matthews if his or her actions helped to cause the incident—it's a matter of causality, independent of ethical and legal judgments. This issue of causality might be of interest to software engineers and managers, who might want to analyze what went wrong so as to avoid similar problems in the future.

A lot of what has emerged in the media concerning this case indicates that Silicon Techchronics was a sick organization. That sickness created the accident. Who created that sickness? Management created that sickness, but employees who did not make the right ethical decisions also contributed.

Randy Samuels and Cindy Yardley were both just out of school. They received degrees in computer science, and their first experience in the working world was at Silicon Techchronics. One has to wonder whether they received any instruction in ethics. Related to this is the question of whether either of them had much prior experience with group work. At the time that they were involved in the development of the killer robot, did they see the need to become ethical persons? Did they see that success as a professional requires ethical behavior? There is much more to being a computer scientist or a software engineer than technical knowledge and skills.

SENTINEL-OBSERVER: Who, in your opinion, contributed to the death of Bart Matthews?

YODER: Let's look at Randy Samuels. Based on what I've read in your newspaper and elsewhere, he was basically a hacker type. He loved computers and programming. He started programming in junior high school and continued right through college. The important point is that Samuels was still a hacker when he got to Silicon Techchronics, and they allowed him to remain a hacker.

I am using the term *hacker* here in a somewhat pejorative sense, but the term *hacker* does not always have a negative connotation. The point that I am trying to make is that Samuels never matured beyond his narrow focus on hacking. At Silicon Techchronics, Samuels had the same attitude toward his programming that he had in junior high school. His perception of his life and of his responsibilities did not grow. He did not mature. There is no evidence that he was trying to develop as a professional or as an *ethical person*.

SENTINEL-OBSERVER: One difficulty, insofar as teaching ethics is concerned, is that students generally do not like being told "this is right and that is wrong."

YODER: Dealing with ethical issues is a part of being a professional computer scientist or software engineer.

One thing that has fascinated me about the Silicon Techchronics situation is that it is sometimes difficult to see the boundaries between legal, technical, and ethical issues. I have come to the conclusion that this blurring of boundaries results from the fact that the software industry is still in its infancy. The ethical issues loom large in part because of the absence of legal and technical guidelines.

In particular, there are no standard practices for the development and testing of software. There are standards, but these are not true standards. A common joke among computer scientists is that the good thing about standards is that there are so many to choose from.

In the absence of universally accepted standard practices for software engineering, there are many value judgments, probably more than in other professions. For example, in the case of the killer robot, there was a controversy concerning the use of the waterfall model versus prototyping. Because there was no standard software development process, this became a controversy, and ethical issues are raised by the manner in which the controversy was resolved. You might recall that the waterfall model was chosen not because of its merits but because of the background of the project manager, George Cuzzins.

SENTINEL-OBSERVER: Did Cindy Yardley act ethically?

YODER: At first, her argument seems compelling: She lied, in effect, to save the jobs of her co-workers and, of course, her own job. But is it ever correct to lie, to create a falsehood, in a professional setting? What she did was clearly in violation of the ACM Code of Ethics.

One book I have used in my computer ethics course is *Ethical Decision Making and Information Technology* by Kallman and Grillo. This book gives some of the principles and theories behind ethical decision making. I use this and other books to help develop the students' appreciation for the nature of ethical dilemmas and ethical decision making.

Kallman and Grillo present a method for ethical decision making, and part of their method involves the use of five tests: the mom test, *Would you tell your mother what you did?*; the TV test, *Would you tell a national TV audience what you did?*; the smell test, *Does what you did have a bad smell to it?*; the other person's shoes test, *Would you like what you did to be done to you?*; and the market test, *Would your action be a good sales pitch?*

I think we can all agree that the TV test doesn't carry quite the punch that it used to because of the trashy talk shows on television. One wonders whether the whole intent of trash TV is to invalidate all ethical tests and all ethical judgments.

I think nearly everyone would agree that what Yardley did fails all of these tests. For example, imagine Silicon Techchronics running an ad campaign that goes something like this:

> *At Silicon Techchronics, the software you get from us is bug free, because even if there is a bug, we will distort the test results to hide it, and you will never know about it. Ignorance is bliss!*

Cindy Yardley's behavior shows that apparent altruism is not a sufficient indicator of ethical behavior. One might wonder what other unstated motives Ms. Yardley had. Could it be that personal ambition led her to accept Ray Johnson's explanation and his assurance that the robot was safe?

SENTINEL-OBSERVER: Are there any sources of ethical guidance for people who are confronted with an ethical dilemma?

YODER: Some companies provide ethical guidelines in the form of corporate policies, and there is such a document at Silicon Techchronics, or so I am told. I haven't seen it. When I called Silicon Techchronics and asked them whether they could send me a copy of their corporate code of ethics, I was told, "We will get back to you on that," but they never did.

Employees can also refer to ethical guidelines provided by professional societies, such as the ACM. Beyond that, they could read up on the subject to get a better feel for ethical decision making. Of course, one must always consult with one's conscience and innermost convictions.

One useful guideline is Kant's categorical imperative. This is discussed in the Kallman and Grillo text. Imagine if everyone acted in the manner in which you are proposing. Would you like to live in a culture like that? For example, would you like to live in a culture where everyone fakes test results? Would you like to live in a culture where tests for drug safety, food safety, airplane structural integrity, and so on are faked? Obviously not.

SENTINEL-OBSERVER: Did Randy Samuels act ethically?

YODER: Stealing software the way that he did was both unethical and illegal.

I think the most important issue with Randy Samuels has never been discussed in the press. I truly doubt that Samuels had the requisite knowledge that his job required. This kind of knowledge is called domain knowledge. Samuels had a knowledge of computers and programming, but not a very strong background in robotics and physics, especially classical mechanics. His lack of knowledge in the application domain was a direct cause of the horrible accident. If someone knowledgeable in robotics, mathematics, and physics had been programming the robot instead of Samuels, Bart Matthews would be alive today. I have no doubt about that. Samuels misinterpreted the physics formula because he didn't understand its meaning and import in the robot application. It may be that management is partly responsible for the situation. Samuels might have told them about his limitations, and management might have said, "What the hell!"

Samuels had difficulty with group work, peer reviews, and egoless programming. Was he trying to hide his lack of expertise in the application domain?

SENTINEL-OBSERVER: What about John Cramer's role in all of this?

YODER: He's a central character because he put the project way behind schedule due to his attempt to tie in the CX30 robot project with his own business interests. He violated the trust of his co-workers by hiding his degree of involvement in that Lucrative company. His leaping into object technology also raises ethical difficulties. He was trying to force his group into a new technology that he himself did not fully appreciate. It seems that he misled his colleagues concerning his own lack of expertise with the new technology.

Obviously, Ray Johnson should have been more alert to Cramer's psychological problems, especially his drinking following his divorce.

SENTINEL-OBSERVER: Did Ray Johnson act ethically?

YODER: Ray Johnson's behavior borders on the criminal. He ordered the faking of the software tests. Then, there's this "Ivory Snow" business! The trouble with the Ivory Snow theory is that it is just a theory. If it were more than a theory and an actual methodology for keeping the likelihood of failure within statistically determined limits, such as an actual methodology called "clean room software engineering," then there would be less culpability here.

Based upon the information that I have, the Ivory Snow theory was just a rationalization for getting flawed software out the door on time. The Ivory Snow theory is only valid, ethically and professionally, if the customer is told of known bugs. In the case of Silicon Techchronics, the Ivory Snow theory worked like this: We know it's not pure, but the customer thinks it is!

One thing we do not know is whether Ray Johnson actually thought that the robot was safe. However, his failure to discuss the real situation with Cyber-Widgets and the other clients indicates that he probably had some doubts about the safety of the robot. At the very least he believed that the clients would not consider the robot safe if they were told the truth.

SENTINEL-OBSERVER: Mike Waterson?

YODER: If Johnson is the father of the Ivory Snow theory, Waterson is the grandfather. His demand that the robot be completed by a certain date or that "heads would roll" might have caused Johnson to formulate the Ivory Snow theory. You see, it is apparent that Johnson realized that the robot could not be perfected by the scheduled delivery date.

In many regards, I feel that Waterson acted unethically and irresponsibly. He placed George Cuzzins in charge of the robot project, yet Cuzzins lacked experience with robots and modern user interfaces. Cuzzins rejected the idea of developing a prototype, which might have allowed for the development of a better user interface.

Waterson created an oppressive atmosphere for his employees, which is unethical in itself. Not only did he threaten to fire everyone in the Robotics Division if the robot was not completed on time, he eavesdropped on private electronic mail communications throughout the corporation, a controversial right that some companies do exercise.

My personal belief is that this kind of eavesdropping is unethical. The nature of e-mail is somewhat a hybrid of normal mail and a telephone conversation. Monitoring or spying on someone else's mail is considered unethical, as is tapping a telephone, except in special circumstances. Indeed, these activities are also illegal under most circumstances. So I believe it is an abuse of power to monitor employees the way that Waterson did.

SENTINEL-OBSERVER: Does the prosecutor have a case here?

YODER: Against Randy Samuels?

SENTINEL-OBSERVER: Yes.

YODER: I doubt it, unless she has information that has not been made public thus far. I know of no legal precedent for an indictment of this nature. Manslaughter, to my understanding, implies a kind of reckless and irresponsible act, causing death of another. Does this description apply to Samuels? I do not believe so.

I read last week that 89 percent of people favor acquittal. People are inclined to blame the corporation and its managers. Last night, one of the network news anchors said, "Randy Samuels is not a murderer; he's a product of his environment."

I believe the indictment of Randy Samuels to be irresponsible, even unethical and unprofessional. It probably represents an attempt on the part of Jane McMurdock and her supporter, Mike Waterson, to obscure the truth in this case.

SENTINEL-OBSERVER: Could you restate your position on the matter of ultimate responsibility in the case of the killer robot?

YODER: In my mind, the issue of individual versus corporate responsibility is very important. The corporation created an environment in which this kind of accident could occur. Yet individuals within that system acted unethically and irresponsibly and actually caused the accident. A company can create an environment that brings out the worst in its employees, but individual employees can also contribute to the worsening of the corporate environment. This is a feedback loop, a system in the classical sense. Thus, there is some corporate responsibility and some individual responsibility in the case of the killer robot.

SENTINEL-OBSERVER: Thank you, Professor Yoder.

Special Sentinel-Observer Magazine Feature

ETHICS AND COMPUTING: THE ACM CODE OF ETHICS

by Dr. Turina Babbage
President, ACM

As president of an international organization with tens of thousands of members, I must deal with many difficult issues. Nothing in recent memory compares to the situation that has been created by the killer robot incident. The intense public reaction to this tragedy is threatening the reputations of those of us who work in the computer industry. To some extent, this public scrutiny is good because it is forcing us to reexamine our values and our operating procedures.

The ACM and other international organizations in computing have codes of ethics that establish standards of professional conduct for our members. Unfortunately, these codes are voluntary, and too many people who consider themselves professionals do not adhere to any ethical code. In my opinion, codes of ethics can make professionals more effective at what they do.

I would like to review my organization's code of ethics with the readership of the *Sentinel-Observer*. I would also like to show how various employees of Silicon Techchronics have violated the provisions of the code. The lesson that I would like the readership to draw from this exercise is that if codes of ethics were adhered to in the computer industry, the risk of accidents like the killer robot would be greatly reduced.

A movement is afoot to make software development, or software engineering more specifically, a true profession with licensed practitioners. Some members of my own organization and of the IEEE Computer Society are pushing for licensing of computer professionals. Licensing could possibly involve some kind of test or, at the very least, accreditation standards such as those that exist within the traditional engineering disciplines. This is very controversial and has been so for a long time. The impact of legislation requiring licensing of computing professionals would be enormous, especially for older practitioners who have been out of school for a long time and who might have become specialized in their knowledge. One thing is clear, however: Incidents such as the killer robot tragedy make licensing much more likely.

We do not have enough space to present the entire text of the ACM Code of Ethics in this magazine, but I will quote from each and every provision. The reader can refer to the reference given at the end of this article for the complete text of the ACM code.

The code is divided into four sections:

1. General Moral Imperatives
2. More Specific Professional Responsibilities
3. Organizational Leadership Imperatives
4. Compliance with the Code

The first section, "General Moral Imperatives," has eight parts:

As an ACM member I will . . .

1.1 Contribute to society and human well-being
1.2 Avoid harm to others
1.3 Be honest and trustworthy
1.4 Be fair and take action not to discriminate
1.5 Honor property rights including copyrights and patents
1.6 Give proper credit for intellectual property
1.7 Respect the privacy of others
1.8 Honor confidentiality

CONTRIBUTE TO SOCIETY
AND HUMAN WELL-BEING

The code states, in part, "When designing or implementing systems, computing professionals must attempt to ensure that the products of their efforts will be used in socially responsible ways, will meet social needs, and will avoid harmful effects to health and welfare."

It should be obvious that a concern for the safety and well-being of users was not evident in the behavior of employees at Silicon Techchronics.

AVOID HARM TO OTHERS

Computer systems are capable of causing many different kinds of harm. The code states, in part, "Harmful actions include intentional destruction or modification of files and programs leading to serious loss of resources or unnecessary expenditure of human resources such as the time and effort required to purge systems of computer viruses."

The code is concerned with both intentional or malicious harm and unintentional harm. It would seem that the killer robot incident involved unintentional harm. On this subject the code states, "One way to avoid unintentional harm is to carefully consider potential impacts on all of those affected by decisions made during design and implementation."

I think it is clear that Silicon Techchronics did not take sufficient precautions to ensure the safety of the robot operators. Taking perhaps even extraordinary precautions to avoid harming others is part of one's professional responsibility as a computer scientist or engineer. Many decisions were made at Silicon Techchronics that had predictably dire consequences. These included managerial decisions, such as the decision made by upper-level management to proceed on schedule despite the death of John Cramer, and personal decisions, such as that of Cindy Yardley to fake software tests.

BE HONEST AND TRUSTWORTHY

The ACM Code states in part, "Honesty is an essential component of trust. Without trust an organization cannot function effectively." This provision in the code requires honesty about the system one is developing and about one's own qualifications. In the case of Silicon Techchronics, we find quite a few cases of deception. For example, Silicon Techchronics tried to deceive CyberWidgets by withholding information about problems with the robot. Ray Johnson and Cindy Yardley conspired to fake a software test and to keep that information from George Cuzzins. John Cramer hid the fact that he would profit personally if Silicon Techchronics bought the SHEOL CASE tool. Mike Waterson was dishonest in not telling his employees that he was monitoring their e-mail.

The code further states, "A computer professional has a duty to be honest about his or her own qualifications, and about any circumstances that might lead to conflicts of interest." Some people have speculated that Randy Samuels may not have been forthright concerning his qualifications when he was hired. George Cuzzins did not express reservations about taking on a leadership role in an entirely new field.

BE FAIR AND TAKE ACTION NOT TO DISCRIMINATE

Professionals must be committed to high standards of justice so that historically disadvantaged groups such as women, the disabled, and minorities are not discriminated against. Also, the ACM is concerned about the growing disparity between those who are information rich and those who are information poor. Silicon Techchronics and its employees have not violated this provision of the code.

HONOR PROPERTY RIGHTS INCLUDING COPYRIGHTS AND PATENTS

The code states further that "violation of copyrights, patents, trade secrets and the terms of license agreements is prohibited by law in most circumstances." Randy Samuels is reported to have stolen software for his flawed program, and that is a violation of this provision of the ACM code. It is also a violation of the law.

GIVE PROPER CREDIT FOR INTELLECTUAL PROPERTY

Ideas, for example, are intellectual property that are not normally covered by copyrights, patents, and trade secrets. Yet credit must be given when using someone else's ideas. There is no instance in the killer robot case where this provision was violated except to the extent that Randy Samuels was also in violation of this provision when he stole software.

RESPECT THE PRIVACY OF OTHERS

The code states, "It is the responsibility of professionals to maintain the privacy and integrity of data describing individuals." Mike Waterson, in monitoring the mail of his employees, is explicitly in violation of this section of the code, which also states, "These principles apply to electronic communications, including electronic mail, and prohibit procedures that capture or monitor electronic user data, including messages, without the permission of users or bona fide authorization related to system operation and maintenance."

There is no evidence that Silicon Techchronics informed its employees that electronic communications were being monitored.

HONOR CONFIDENTIALITY

The code requires that private information be treated with respect and that confidences not be violated. At Silicon Techchronics, some of the leaks to the press involved information that I would consider confidential in nature. For example, consider Max Worthington's whistle-blowing and the manner in which he provided confidential information to the press. Did he behave in an ethical manner?

There are eight principles under the heading "More Specific Professional Responsibilities":

As an ACM computing professional I will . . .

2.1 Strive to achieve the highest quality, effectiveness, and dignity in both the process and products of professional work
2.2 Acquire and maintain professional competence
2.3 Know and respect existing laws pertaining to professional work
2.4 Accept and provide appropriate professional review
2.5 Give comprehensive and thorough evaluations of computer systems and their impacts, including analysis of possible risks
2.6 Honor contracts, agreements, and assigned responsibilities
2.7 Improve public understanding of computing and its consequences
2.8 Access computing and communication resources only when authorized to do so

STRIVE TO ACHIEVE THE HIGHEST QUALITY, EFFECTIVENESS, AND DIGNITY IN BOTH THE PROCESS AND PRODUCTS OF PROFESSIONAL WORK

In the case of the killer robot, we have seen many examples of deficient standards for quality of work. There were deficiencies in terms of processes and in terms of products. For example, the testing process was not only deficient, but fraudulent. The product itself was deficient in terms of operator safety. The user interface was primitive and substandard by any measure.

ACQUIRE AND MAINTAIN PROFESSIONAL COMPETENCE

The ACM code states, "Excellence depends on individuals who take responsibility for acquiring and maintaining professional competence . . . Upgrading technical knowledge and competence can be achieved in several ways: doing independent study; attending seminars, conferences or courses; and being involved in professional organizations." Some have charged that Randy Samuels was not competent to write and understand code relating to robot dynamics, but this charge has not been substantiated. Software engineers are beginning to appreciate that new technologies must be introduced in a systematic way, after an appropriate cost-benefits analysis. This was not the case when John Cramer tried to force the robot project on a particular path using object-oriented analysis and design. The software development team never got up to snuff on object-oriented concepts as far as I can tell from press reports.

KNOW AND RESPECT EXISTING LAWS PERTAINING TO PROFESSIONAL WORK

ACM members are expected to obey local, provincial, national, and international laws unless there is a compelling ethical basis not to do so. My wording here is very close to the wording in the code itself. I am not a lawyer, but I think several people at Silicon Techchronics acted illegally: Randy Samuels when he stole copyrighted software and Cindy Yardley and Ray Johnson when they conspired to fake a software test. The prosecuting attorney is arguing that Randy Samuels also broke the law by causing the accidental death of Bart Matthews, but very few believe that she can prevail in a court of law.

ACCEPT AND PROVIDE APPROPRIATE PROFESSIONAL REVIEW

The ACM code recognizes acceptance of criticism as an important professional responsibility. In the language of the code: "Whenever appropriate, individual members should seek and utilize peer review as well as provide critical review of the work of others." Several individuals at Silicon Techchronics did not take well to criticism. Apparently, George Cuzzins fired Jan Anderson when she suggested that his choice of the waterfall model for the project was inappropriate. Randy Samuels exploded in anger when one of his algorithms was criticized. Silicon Techchronics, to its credit, did use peer review as a method for quality assurance, but I get the impression that they did not utilize this technique in an effective manner.

GIVE COMPREHENSIVE AND THOROUGH EVALUATIONS OF COMPUTER SYSTEMS AND THEIR IMPACTS, INCLUDING ANALYSIS OF POSSIBLE RISKS

Objectivity is an important part of evaluation, and conflicts of interest militate against objectivity. The ACM code states, "Computer professionals are in a position of special trust, and therefore have a special responsibility to provide objective, credible evaluations to employers, clients, users, and the public. When providing evaluations the professional must also identify any relevant conflicts of interest. . . ." John Cramer could not provide an objective evaluation of the SHEOL tool because he stood to gain financially from its use by Silicon Techchronics. Very little information has been given in the press concerning contacts between Silicon Techchronics and CyberWidgets. But it would seem that Silicon Techchronics was not forthright and truthful about the dangers inherent in the use of the robot in its flawed state. Ray Johnson conspired to hide the true state of affairs from CyberWidgets and the other clients.

HONOR CONTRACTS, AGREEMENTS, AND ASSIGNED RESPONSIBILITIES

This section of the ACM code stresses the responsibilities of professionals to be accountable for their work, both in terms of its quality and its ethical implications. For example, the code states, "A computing professional has a responsibility to request a change in any assignment that he or she feels cannot be completed as defined. Only after serious consideration and with full disclosure of risks and concerns to the employer or client, should one accept the assignment. The major underlying principle here is the obligation to accept personal accountability for professional work. On some occasions other ethical principles may take greater priority. . . . Performing assignments 'against one's own judgment' does not relieve the professional of responsibility for any negative consequences."

Cindy Yardley is obviously a person who did not deal well with a request from her boss to do something unethical: fake a software test. Perhaps other people at Silicon Techchronics at various points in time should have said, "No, this is not acceptable. This is placing a human life at risk."

Another aspect of this provision in the code is to ensure that one's contractual obligations are fulfilled, whether those of an employee to an employer or those of a software provider to a software customer. Silicon Techchronics tried to avoid disclosure of its inability to deliver a safe robot, an obligation that it had under its contract with CyberWidgets.

IMPROVE PUBLIC UNDERSTANDING OF COMPUTING AND ITS CONSEQUENCES

This is an interesting part of the code, and I wonder whether the ACM task force that authored the Code of Ethics could have imagined a situation such as the one that has arisen involving the killer robot. The code states, "Computing professionals have a responsibility to share technical knowledge with the public by encouraging understanding of computing, including the impacts of computer systems and their limitations. This imperative implies an obligation to counter any false views related to computing."

This is interesting because quite a few people at Silicon Techchronics have made an effort to get information out to the press. Perhaps this is good, because we have had a public debate, but I think that the magnitude of the debate has been a bit overwhelming. The public now knows much more about how software is produced and what the risks and the problems are.

ACCESS COMPUTING AND COMMUNICATION RESOURCES ONLY WHEN AUTHORIZED TO DO SO

The gist of this provision is stated as follows: "No one should enter or use another's computing system, software, or data files without permission. One must always have appropriate approval before using system resources. . . ." No one at Silicon Techchronics has been accused of illegal access to accounts or files. We have already discussed Michael Waterson's inappropriate violation of the privacy of his employees.

The third part of the ACM Code of Ethics is called "Organizational Leadership Imperatives." This relates to the responsibilities and obligations of organizational leaders (management). This section has six parts:

As an ACM member and an organizational leader, I will . . .

3.1 Articulate social responsibilities of members of an organizational unit and encourage full acceptance of those responsibilities
3.2 Manage personnel and resources to design and build information systems that enhance the quality of working life
3.3 Acknowledge and support proper and authorized uses of an organization's computing and communications resources
3.4 Ensure that users and those who will be affected by a system have their needs clearly articulated during the assessment and design of requirements. Later the system must be validated to meet requirements.
3.5 Articulate and support policies that protect the dignity of users and others affected by a computing system
3.6 Create opportunities for members of the organization to learn the principles and limitations of computer systems

ARTICULATE SOCIAL RESPONSIBILITIES OF MEMBERS OF AN ORGANIZATIONAL UNIT AND ENCOURAGE FULL ACCEPTANCE OF THOSE RESPONSIBILITIES

The motivation behind this provision of the code is to encourage organizations, such as Silicon Techchronics, to establish an organizational consciousness concerning responsibilities to the public. Based upon published reports, it does not seem that this sort of consciousness existed at Silicon Techchronics.

MANAGE PERSONNEL AND RESOURCES TO DESIGN AND BUILD INFORMATION SYSTEMS THAT ENHANCE THE QUALITY OF WORKING LIFE

The code states, "Organizational leaders are responsible for ensuring that computer systems enhance, not degrade, the quality of working life. . . . Appropriate human-computer ergonomic standards should be considered in system design and in the workplace." Dr. Horace Gritty has observed that the killer robot's operator console was poorly designed from the point of view of ergonomics. This is the sort of sloppiness in design that has real costs in terms of human suffering. Ethical leaders will work hard to ensure a healthful and safe work environment. The sad truth is that many people are suffering from work-related injuries because their work environment is not designed with human factors in mind. In addition, workers are not being given the information they need to protect themselves against repetitive strain injuries such as carpal tunnel syndrome.

ACKNOWLEDGE AND SUPPORT PROPER AND AUTHORIZED USES OF AN ORGANIZATION'S COMPUTING AND COMMUNICATIONS RESOURCES

This provision states, in part, "Because computer systems can become tools to harm as well as to benefit an organization, the leadership has the responsibility to clearly define appropriate and inappropriate uses of organizational computing resources."

For all of the faults of Silicon Techchronics, we cannot fault them for their computer security.

ENSURE THAT USERS AND THOSE WHO WILL BE AFFECTED BY A SYSTEM HAVE THEIR NEEDS CLEARLY ARTICULATED DURING THE ASSESSMENT AND DESIGN OF REQUIREMENTS. LATER THE SYSTEM MUST BE VALIDATED TO MEET REQUIREMENTS.

The code states, "Current system users, potential users, and other persons whose lives may be affected by a system must have their needs assessed and incorporated in the statement of requirements. System validation should ensure compliance with those requirements."

The agreed-upon requirements for the Robbie CX30 robot could not possibly have taken into account the needs of all of its potential users. It seems inconceivable that users such as Bart Matthews were part of the analysis process or that they could have agreed to that abysmal interface.

We know that system validation was only partial and not complete.

ARTICULATE AND SUPPORT POLICIES THAT PROTECT THE DIGNITY OF USERS AND OTHERS AFFECTED BY A COMPUTING SYSTEM

The code states, "Designing or implementing systems that deliberately demean individuals or groups is ethically unacceptable. Computer professionals who are in decision-making positions should verify that systems are designed and implemented to protect personal privacy and enhance personal dignity."

It does not appear that Silicon Techchronics has violated this provision of the code. However, designing a user interface that makes a human being feel less creative or less intelligent might be in violation of this provision, although this issue was already covered in section 3.2.

CREATE OPPORTUNITIES FOR MEMBERS OF THE ORGANIZATION TO LEARN THE PRINCIPLES AND LIMITATIONS OF COMPUTER SYSTEMS

The code states, "Opportunities must be available to all members to help them improve their knowledge and skills in computing, including courses that familiarize them with the consequences and limitations of particular types of systems."

Based on the published evidence, I would say that Silicon Techchronics did not have an organizational strategy for educating employees and for upgrading their knowledge. Education at Silicon Techchronics seems rather ad hoc. For example, the training in object-oriented technology was clearly inadequate.

The code continues, "[P]rofessionals must be made aware of the dangers of building systems around oversimplified models, the improbability of anticipating and designing for every possible operating condition, and other issues related to the complexity of this profession." At first glance this seems to favor Ray Johnson's propagandizing in favor of his Ivory Snow theory. However, his subsequent behavior—for example, his entering into a conspiracy to fake software tests—does not suggest that his motives were based on sound ethical and professional judgments.

The last part of the ACM code is brief. It is called "Compliance with the Code" and it contains two provisions:

As an ACM member I will . . .

4.1 Uphold and promote the principles of this Code.
4.2 Treat violations of this Code as inconsistent with membership in the ACM.

Under the first provision the code states, "The future of the computing profession depends upon both technical and ethical excellence. Not only is it important for ACM computing professionals to adhere to the principles expressed in this Code, each member should encourage and support adherence by other members."

I hope that I have convinced the reader that adherence to a code of ethics is essential for the computer industry. Many employees at Silicon Techchronics violated the ACM Code of Ethics. Moreover, it is clear that *if they had followed the ACM Code of Ethics, the killer robot incident would never have happened.* Many of the previously reported shortcomings of processes and decisions at Silicon Techchronics were rooted in ethical misconduct. I am referring to everything from the faked software tests to the immaturity of individuals on the project to the user interface that was apparently designed without user input or consideration of the user's safety and comfort. Even where there are technical shortcomings, truly ethical behavior can help to avert disaster.

REFERENCE

The complete text of the ACM Code of Ethics can be found in the following reference.

1. Anderson, R. E.; Johnson, D. G.; Gotterbam, D.; and Perrolle, J., "Using the New ACM Code of Ethics in Decision Making," *Communications of the ACM*, February 1993, 98–107.

At the Angry Ostrich Bar and Grill

SOFTWARE DEVELOPERS DISCUSS ETHICS AND PROFESSIONALISM

by **Sam Richardson**
Human Interest Editor

The Angry Ostrich does not appear to be the kind of place that would attract the high priests and priestesses of high technology, but it has become one of the most popular watering holes for computer industry professionals. Instead of the pack of Harley-Davidsons that one might expect at such a place, one finds an assortment of sporty foreign cars, Jeep Cherokees, and a few Acuras and BMWs. The message is plain: "The upwardly mobile replenish themselves here."

The Angry Ostrich seems out of place in Silicon Valley. It looks like an old, dilapidated barn that has had a half dozen additions slapped onto it in a rather haphazard fashion. Inside there is a lot of space, and the music soothes rather than stimulates. The Angry Ostrich is large enough that professionals with different interests in beverages, music, and food can find a room with people much like themselves.

My guests and I had a room all to ourselves, thanks to the Angry Ostrich owner, Frank Zemmel. A large-screen television hanging on the wall was showing a college baseball game, but the sound was muted. There were six of us: myself and five software developers from various companies around the Valley. Since they all desired anonymity, I have changed their names to Sue, Bob, Ted, Ann, and George. Sue, Bob, Ted, and Ann all graduated from college (Sue with a master's degree) within the past five years. George is an old-timer, having worked in the software business for nearly twenty years. He looks his forty-five years, but sometimes his laugh makes him look much younger. I gave them an assignment prior to our meeting: Read the ACM Code of Ethics and give your reaction to it. (The ACM Code is discussed in the magazine section of today's *Sentinel-Observer* in the article by Dr. Turina Babbage, president of the ACM.)

We ordered beverages, and a few of my guests ordered sandwiches. Bob in particular seemed to be very hungry, and he washed down a submarine sandwich with several beers. We eventually got down to business. I asked my guests to react to the ACM Code of Ethics from their individual perspectives in the computer industry. A transcript of our surprising conversation follows.

BOB: That code has nothing to do with what I do on a day-to-day basis. I see the ACM code being broken at work every day. There's just no awareness of ethics. It's irrelevant.

ANN: I get a gut negative reaction to rules of any kind. I cherish the freedom to do what I damn well please. I treasure my autonomy. There are no rules like this where I work. This just represents some kind of religious feeling or belief system that someone is trying to impose on all programmers, and I resent it.

SUE: This code is not a religious belief system. It's a code of professional conduct. All professions have such codes, and practitioners are held accountable to the code. We need a code of ethics in computing. Otherwise, we will gain a reputation for being unethical.

ANN: Lawyers have a code of ethics. Are they ethical?

TED: Is the ACM code actually in place? I mean, are we supposed to follow it?

SUE: No, it only applies to ACM members. If an ACM member violates the code he or she can be kicked out of the organization, but that is rare. It's a voluntary code.

GEORGE: It's not voluntary where I work. Our president has been active in ACM for many years, and this code is part of our corporate code of ethics. People have been fired for gross violations of the code. We work with sensitive data, and several people were recently fired for carelessly violating a client's confidentiality. Some poor woman who was HIV positive had her identity released to her employer. What a mess!

[I asked George whether having a code of ethics in place where he worked made any difference to him.]

GEORGE: It makes a great deal of difference. I have worked for three different companies, and I have a basis for drawing comparisons. I started out at the company where Bob currently works, and there were no ethical standards in place at that company, at least back then. I found working in an environment like that depressing.

BOB: I'm happy this is going to be confidential, because I can state right out that I hate my job. I hate it! It's not the work so much as the atmosphere. I wish we had better guidelines about how to do things. Apparently, things haven't changed much since when you were there, George. It doesn't help that management doesn't seem to be bound by any ethical principles at their level.

GEORGE: That's what I'm trying to say. It's better to work with a company that has clear ethics policies and that considers ethics important. If I were advising young people, I would tell them to carefully consider the environment where they work. Is software development treated with respect, and does management adhere to ethical guidelines similar to the ACM code? Twenty years ago I was where Bob is now. I hated it. I hated the lying to customers. I hated the unprofessional work that was done, the undocumented and sloppily tested software. I hated the cynical attitude of management, which was very similar to what we see in this killer robot case. Sometimes I say, "Thank God the killer robot brought all of this out in the open!" but then I catch myself. After all, an innocent man was killed.

BOB: I'd like to find another job. I can't stand it where I'm working now. We delivered a million-dollar system last month, and we knew it would not work, and then my boss sent me to the east coast to hold our customer's hand. You can't debug fatally flawed software by holding the customer's hand. The user interface is totally incomprehensible. I can't see how we can expect a human being to sit in front of that interface all day and remain sane. And this bothers me. This is not consistent with who I am! Do you understand what I'm trying to say? This job is not letting me be who I am!

ANN: I just can't relate to all of this whining. Business is business. Buyer beware. All of this touchy-feely stuff is based on religion. And that's what I have a problem with. Why don't we just accept the world view of Darwin and admit that it's tooth and nail, fang and claw out there? The next thing, someone will be bringing up our obligations to the homeless! It's in the air. I can smell it.

BOB: I don't think that's what you're smelling.

SUE: I think it's useful to have Ann in this discussion because I know people like Ann at work. So I would like someone to tell me how a person like myself, who cares about other people and ethical principles, how a person like myself can function in a world where there are people who think the way Ann does.

GEORGE: That's what I'm trying to contribute to this discussion, although I guess I'm not doing a very good job. Look, I'm speaking from many years of experience, but the fundamental deficiency of people without experience is that they cannot imagine what experience is.

BOB: Some of us younger folks know a lot of new technologies that most of you older folks haven't even heard of yet.

GEORGE: I wasn't trying to be confrontational. I'm talking about the kind of experience one has when one gets older and realizes, in a flash, "So this is what life is about!" Take my word for it. You do not want to reach age forty-five thinking that your life has been wasted or that you sold your soul to a company whose values you fundamentally oppose.

BOB: So, what's your advice, o learned one who is wise to the ways of the world?

GEORGE: Try to find an environment where there is a feeling for ethics and a concern for human dignity. Find a good working environment where you can grow professionally and as a human being.

SUE: I think George is trying to make an important point. Ethics and professionalism go hand in hand. You cannot have professionalism without ethics. You cannot have ethics without professionalism. I was impressed with those parts of the ACM code that dealt with management responsibilities. Management must ensure that requirements are clarified and that the interests of the client are carefully considered. This is the ethical bottom line, as far as I am concerned.

So, I think what George is saying is really profound—if I'm understanding him correctly. People coming out of college and people like ourselves who might want to change jobs should consider the professionalism and the ethics of the companies that we're considering for possible employment. For example, if I go to work with a company like the one where George works, I would grow professionally. I would feel better about myself. I wouldn't feel a clash of values between myself and my employer.

TED: In other words, don't accept just any old job. Be selective, if the job market allows that.

SUE: Or at least make professionalism and ethical standards two of the bases for deciding whether you will accept a particular job, if offered.

TED: I read that some companies are looking for applicants who have good business ethics.

GEORGE: Yes, but you had better walk your talk. You'd better not foul up.

TED: My present employer is currently like Bob's. Issues of professionalism and ethics are never discussed. And I have this vague feeling of stagnating, of being stuck. The software that we work with has lots of bugs, and the code has no documentation. There are no design documents. No formal analysis process is engaged in. When I think back on the software engineering course that I took in college, I think, "Now, that was a joke!" We don't do any of that stuff at our company. Is there anything I can do to improve the climate where I work?

ANN: Why not get yourself a soapbox and quote chapter and verse to the sinning masses?

GEORGE: I tried that at my second company, and it didn't work. My second company was just like the first. You see, I fooled myself into believing that I was unhappy because of technical issues. My first company was working on some old DEC operating system, and I wanted to get into the new UNIX operating system—this was almost twenty years ago. I had a whole list of technical reasons for leaving. What I didn't realize is that it was the lack of ethics and professionalism at work that was killing me. It's stressful to lie all the time.

BOB: You're speaking figuratively, I hope. Your job wasn't *literally* killing you, was it?

GEORGE: I think the stress *was* killing me. I had all sorts of aches and pains. The thing was I couldn't stand the constant lying: the lying to customers, management lying to us, our lying to management, our lying to one another, and our lying to ourselves. One morning I got up and looked into the mirror and I said, "Who in hell are you?"

SUE: If you can't trust and don't like the people you work with five or six days a week, that is hell.

BOB: I lost track of where George is. Are you at your first or your second job?

GEORGE: I'm at both jobs. The environment was hell at both companies, but I thought by changing jobs I would become happier, but that didn't happen. The second job was just as lousy as the first, except with a different operating system. Correct me if I am wrong, but lying about systems running on VAX is much the same as lying about systems running on UNIX. Am I right or am I wrong?

SUE: No argument.

GEORGE: The point is that the atmosphere at work is critical. I did some reading—this is back around 1980—about professional issues, but there wasn't as much to read back then. There was an old ACM Code of Professional Conduct and some early books on software engineering. In any event, I started to talk about ethics and software engineering as much as possible, and at first people seemed interested. Then all of a sudden, as if the word had come down from on high, people started treating me like a pariah, and I was eventually laid off.

TED: Were you fired because you were trying to change things?

GEORGE: I think so. But you also need to bear in mind that my personality was different back then. I might have been too aggressive. Fortunately, I got a much better job at the company where I am today. I think you can make a difference at a small company, but you have to be very diplomatic. You have to test the waters. People aren't always happy to hear the constructive criticisms you might have to offer.

[Turning toward Ann] Just on the basis of what you've said here today, I feel that if I were working with you in a professional setting I would find it difficult to trust you.

ANN: You can see how much that upsets me.

[I then asked my guests which part of the ACM Code of Ethics they liked the most.]

BOB: The part about management responsibilities and the mixing of professionalism and ethics.

GEORGE: Same here. Also the stuff about the importance of honesty and trust.

ANN: I liked the very last part because it meant that I had reached the end.

SUE: I liked the whole emphasis on the potential for harm and the necessity to avoid doing harm, whether personal or social, whether local or global, whether intentional or accidental.

TED: I also liked the emphasis on honesty and trust. At my job I'm beginning to see the importance of trust. Everything breaks down without trust. Also, I liked anything that related to important social issues, like the acknowledgment that there is a huge gap between the rich and the poor.

[I asked Ann why she was so antagonistic toward the subject of ethics.]

ANN: Frankly, I was trained as a computer *scientist,* and as a scientist I do not have to worry about ethics. I'm like a physicist or a chemist. It's not my job to worry about what people do with the discoveries that I make.

SUE: So you are a scientist, in the pure sense?

ANN: I would say so. I'm writing software for an advanced, top-secret autonomous land vehicle, that is, a robotlike tank. So, I think I'm like a scientist. I'm developing algorithms for distinguishing between enemy tanks and friendly tanks when all of the tanks are moving at high speed over a rough terrain. It's an incredibly difficult problem. Also, we're hoping we can program our autonomous land vehicle to avoid civilian targets.

SUE: That's not pure science! That's applied science, and it's important to consider the social implications of what you are doing. You're creating a computer application.

TED: It's not science. It's perversity!

ANN: It's science and I am a scientist. I create new knowledge, new technologies.

GEORGE: Still, don't you find the ACM code relevant to what you do, your responsibilities to your clients—the military, for example?

ANN: No, I don't.

TED: Actually, I think the ACM code failed to address this whole issue of using technology to create more and more gruesome weapons of mass destruction. Is it ethical for someone to work on a cruise missile guidance system when that cruise missile is going to kill hundreds of civilians? What if Ann's robot tank kills innocent civilians? Wouldn't that put Ann in the same category as Randy Samuels?

BOB: One can argue that the intelligence in the missile makes it less harmful to civilians. You can't expect the ACM code to reflect your own pacifist beliefs.

[No one wanted to pursue this issue further, so I asked my guests whether there was anything that they did not like about the Code of Ethics, beyond what Ted had just said concerning military applications of computers.]

GEORGE, BOB, SUE: No.

TED: Well, I thought that the code could have been more concerned with social issues. There is some concern, but it is minimal and qualified.

ANN: I do not like professional societies attempting to speak for me, an autonomous person.

[I had asked my guests, as part of their preparation for our meeting, to come prepared to state one new proposition that they would like to add to the ACM code.]

GEORGE: I wanted a statement about the obligations of management to workers in terms of job security, health insurance, and so forth. I think management has important obligations that do not have to do with computing per se but that do have to do with the larger business environment.

ANN: I couldn't come up with anything.

TED: I wanted a stronger statement about the military uses of computers.

BOB: I think there should have been a special section for educators. The code discusses the obligations of practitioners and managers and organizations. But what about the educational institutions and educators who are preparing people for work in the computer industry? Don't they have ethical obligations to their students?

SUE: That's just what I wrote down for my "missing principle"!

GEORGE: It seems to me that ethical obligations of educators should not be part of the ACM code. Computer science educators should have their own code.

TED: I agree with George, but I still think that it would be worthwhile for us to discuss the ethical obligations of educators. It seems to me that the content of the curriculum should follow from those ethical obligations.

[I then told my guests that Peter Denning, a well-known computer scientist, had written an article that expressed the related idea that a curriculum should follow from the obligations of educators to their students. I asked my guests to express themselves concerning the education that they received in undergraduate and (for Sue) graduate school.]

BOB: I wish computer science had been taught as a profession rather than as a science. The nature of professional knowledge and scientific knowledge are distinct to some extent. Professional knowledge includes the ethical dimension and the dimension of working with others.

ANN: I really have no complaints about instruction in my major. Overall, I thought college was good because it helped me to become an autonomous person. Fortunately, I had no exposure to ethics in college, and if I had, I would have made my professor's life very unpleasant.

SUE: I thought the emphasis in my undergraduate courses was okay. I learned the basic principles of computer science, the formal foundations, and that has been very useful in my career. Analysis of algorithms is very important in my work, which involves graphics. However, in graduate school, I was disappointed that there was not more of a professional emphasis.

TED: I think I know what Bob meant by his comment. Some of the professors were trying to teach computer science like a science, but it seems different from a normal science. For example, a lot of the problems posed during my student years were solved by me alone. But, in the workplace, problems are solved in teams, and one has to interact with lots of people. The thing is that communicating in this way is not trivial. The most difficult part is dealing with different types of people.

BOB: I wonder whether the usual academic model fits our field. What does it mean when a student gets an A in operating systems? It's not clear to me that grades and courses have any kind of uniform meaning.

GEORGE: If a student gets an A that means that the student was one of the best in his or her class.

BOB: But what does it mean in practical terms? The grade does not tell us what the student can do. Can the student build an operating system emulation? Can the student do UNIX script programming? Can the student solve theoretical problems in operating systems? Does the student have any practical competency with respect to operating systems?

SUE: I see what you mean. There is not a close fit between competencies that employers might need and grades on a transcript.

TED: Yes, it would have been helpful for me if my undergraduate career helped me to develop and identify specific competencies that I could then show to my prospective employers—like a portfolio. I had a few programs to show them, but it was not organized in an impressive way.

GEORGE: Well, I majored in mathematics, and I learned about business the hard way. However, I think the business environment today is more brutal, and it's good to have some idea about the business world before you leave college.

SUE: My internship at college helped me in that regard.

BOB: I felt that my education was too narrow. I think it is unfair for a college or university to educate its students in some narrow, technical way and then expect them to meet life fully, with all of its challenges and with all of its grandeur.

GEORGE: Good point! But what can any of us do about it?

BOB: Somewhere along the line students need to be taught more about the professional world that they are going to have to deal with. I think a good student should be able to graduate from an undergraduate program thinking, "I am ready to make a contribution, and I have the knowledge and skills I need to engage in life-long learning. I have the ethical, social, and communications skills that I need in order to succeed in today's working environment. Beyond that, I see the challenge of life and its beauty, and I am ready to deal with whatever might come my way." If the graduates of a program cannot graduate with that kind of confidence and spiritual depth, then something is wrong.

GEORGE: Thank you for donating your time so that our readers can get a deeper insight into the ethical issues of computing.

BOB: Thanks for lunch!

A *Sentinel-Observer* Human Interest Story

LONG-AWAITED SUITS FILED IN KILLER ROBOT CASE

Widow of Robot Operator Sues Samuels and Silicon Techchronics for Negligence

CyberWidgets Sues Silicon Techchronics on Grounds of Strict Liability

by Pam Pulitzer

Experts have been predicting a blizzard of lawsuits in the killer robot incident, and that blizzard began today in the Silicon Valley Courthouse. Sally Matthews, widow of Bart Matthews, the slain robot operator, sued Randy Samuels and Silicon Techchronics for negligence. In a courtroom down the hall, papers were filed in a strict liability suit that is now formally called *CyberWidgets, Inc., v. Silicon Techchronics, Inc.*

When a person kills another person with a gun, the case can be fairly straightforward, especially when there is good forensic evidence. However, readers who have been following the killer robot case are well aware of the case's complexities. Who is ultimately responsible for the death of Bart Matthews? Can anyone be held criminally responsible? For example, can the charge of manslaughter made against Randy Samuels stick? Can parties be held responsible to the extent that they are held liable to pay compensatory damages?

As software becomes more pervasive and touches on more and more aspects of our lives, these issues are gaining attention among those responsible for producing software: computer scientists and software engineers.

Randolph Yerges, attorney for Sally Matthews, spoke to reporters on the steps of the Silicon Valley Courthouse: "Mrs. Matthews is suing Randy Samuels and Silicon Techchronics for negligence. This means that we are accusing both Mr. Samuels and his employer of not conducting themselves with sufficient care for the lives and safety of those who would be using their robot, now known as 'the killer robot.' Our suit is based on our firm conviction that neither Mr. Samuels nor Silicon Techchronics more generally conducted themselves in accordance with the professional standards of computing and of software engineering."

When pressed for more information, Mr. Yerges indicated that, if necessary, he would place witnesses on the stand who would state clearly and unequivocally that Randy Samuels did not conduct himself in a professional manner. Mr. Yerges went on to say, "Managers at Silicon Techchronics, especially Ray Johnson, did not behave in a responsible manner and with sufficient care for the safety of my client's husband."

Mr. Yerges indicated that he was prepared to file depositions from software engineering experts who had studied software development procedures at Silicon Techchronics. According to Mr. Yerges, these experts were prepared to testify under oath that Silicon Techchronics operates at the very lowest level of what they call "process maturity." Process maturity is a measure of how well-organized software development is at a given company.

Joseph Green, attorney for Silicon Techchronics, charged Mr. Yerges with creating a media circus. "I am speaking to you under the glare of those television lights only reluctantly," Mr. Green said. "Our defense [of Silicon Techchronics] is based on the fact that there are no standard practices in software engineering. Consequently, how can you say that the defendant in this case [Silicon Techchronics] is not living up to its 'duty of care'? Silicon Techchronics is not a hospital, where the standards are more clearly established."

Alex Allendale, attorney for Randy Samuels, made a similar argument on a local television talk show last night. "I don't think you can charge Randy with negligence. He's not a doctor. There are no standards in software development. My client is not even a professional in the true sense, bound to a code of ethics or bound to a set of accepted practices. There are no professional standards that can be cited as establishing a standard of care. So, I do not think that this charge of negligence has any merit. How does software development, when you get right down to it, differ from magic or sorcery?"

Trisha Wembley, professor of law at Silicon Valley University, disagreed with these assessments from the defense attorneys. "I think courts will be more and more willing to impose a 'duty of care' for software developers who are involved in developing embedded software systems, like robots. Consequently, negligence suits against computing professionals are a distinct possibility at some point in the future. However, in today's legal environment, it will be difficult, but not impossible, for Mrs. Matthews to win these negligence cases."

Professor Wembley pointed out that one factor acting in favor of the defendants [Randy Samuels and Silicon Techchronics] in these negligence cases is that they will find it easy to find industry experts who will claim that there are no standard practices in software development. "I think the credibility of the witnesses will play a key role in the way the courts decide these cases. For every witness for the plaintiff who will claim that a duty of care was neglected, there will be another witness for the defense who will say, 'What duty of care? According to which licensing procedure? Which professional society? According to whom?'"

Professor Wembley added that different kinds of software products are held to different standards under the law. "Producers of embedded software, software that is machinelike, will be held to stricter standards for cases of liability than producers of information-providing software, such as an on-line dictionary or encyclopedia. This favors the plaintiff in the liability suit that CyberWidgets filed against Silicon Techchronics. Developers of embedded software are definitely vulnerable to product liability suits."

According to Professor Wembley, the situation is evolving, and she expects stricter forms of accountability to be applied to more and more forms of software. "This will occur," she told the *Sentinel-Observer*, "if software developers continue to move toward more formal processes, toward more rigorous software engineering, toward standards that are more like those used in the manufacturing sector."

In suing Silicon Techchronics on the grounds of strict liability, Cyber-Widgets in effect is trying to circumvent the implications of its own contract with Silicon Techchronics. That contract assigned CyberWidgets certain responsibilities that were not carried out very well. For example, CyberWidgets was responsible for ensuring that robot operators received sufficient training. With this lawsuit CyberWidgets is trying to say, "You sold us a faulty and dangerous robot, and we want to be compensated for that. We don't care how this situation came about, we just want compensation for the damages done."

Professor Wembley commented on the notion of strict liability and the implications of the CyberWidgets suit: "This form of liability is called 'strict liability in tort,' that is, independent of the contractual agreements existing between the parties. Some computer scientists are arguing in favor of this sort of liability for faulty software products. The emphasis would be on establishing the extent of the damages as opposed to tracking down responsibility. A suit based on strict liability will (almost always) progress without any effort to blame any particular employee. A more extensive kind of investigation would be necessary in a case involving negligence."

Silicon Techchronics attorney Joseph Green appeared on the steps of the Silicon Valley Courthouse with CyberWidgets attorneys George Annapolis and Sally Winfield. Mr. Green issued a terse statement: "Silicon Techchronics feels that this suit filed by CyberWidgets is reasonable and we do not contest the idea behind it. We hope to settle this suit without going to trial. We produced a faulty robot. At issue then is the amount to be paid to Cyber-Widgets by my client. We reiterate that there is a major difference between a strict liability suit and a negligence suit. The latter is a direct attack on the good name of Silicon Techchronics and its employees. Naturally, we will fight the negligence suit filed by Sally Matthews with all of the resources at our disposal."

George Annapolis read a statement on behalf of CyberWidgets: "In accepting the reasonableness of my client's strict liability suit, Silicon Techchronics is once again demonstrating that it can be a good partner in the business community. CyberWidgets, in avoiding a more costly court battle, is demonstrating its interest in helping to establish responsible means of resolving disputes of this nature."

Sally Matthews was clearly upset when we asked her about Joseph Green's comments regarding her negligence suit. "It just makes me so mad!

Don't you see what's going on here? Big business and the courts are deciding that no single individual can be held responsible for deaths caused by
computer programs. They are shutting out any possibility of personal
accountability for harm done by computer systems. Their only concern is to
make sure that the wheels of industry are running smoothly. Meanwhile,
someone like myself is *widowed—widowed*—by an irresponsible programmer
like Randy Samuels. I have three fatherless children to take care of! Do you
see what I am trying to say? They are just trying to protect themselves and
the programmers. They don't want the programmers to be treated like true
professionals, held to a code of ethics and to a set of professional practices.
The big companies can absorb the cost of strict liability suits. Do you get my
point? They can do some calculations, and they can decide that they can
absorb a certain number of dead robot operators and that will be cheaper
than actually building a safe robot. Their ability to absorb these costs will
only encourage them to act irresponsibly."

Joseph Green, reached by telephone late last night at an attorney's conference in Las Vegas, responded to Sally Matthews's remarks: "My client
will gladly compensate Sally Matthews for her loss. However, not on the
grounds of negligence, for that implies substandard practices, and Silicon
Techchronics is not substandard or negligent in the manner in which it conducts business."

Despite the new lawsuits, the central legal issue in the case of the killer
robot is whether Randy Samuels can be convicted for manslaughter in a
court of law before a jury of his peers. Opinion polls show that the public
feels by an overwhelming majority (91 percent) that the criminal charges
against Randy Samuels should be dropped. Manslaughter involves causing
the death of another, but without premeditation or intent. If a programmer
writes code that is directly responsible for the death of another human
being, is that manslaughter?

Law Professor Wembley has been a vocal opponent of the prosecution
of this case: "Samuels guilty of manslaughter? That is a stretch! I see it as
politics. It's no secret that Jane McMurdock would like a seat in Congress
and that she isn't going to get to go to Washington without the financial
backing of one Michael Waterson, chief executive officer of Silicon Techchronics. The killer robot affair is her attempt to make a name for herself and
to serve the interests of Mr. Waterson. Beyond that, I think she really
believes what she says about setting a precedent that would force software
developers to accept responsibility for their actions.

"Certainly, her desire to set this precedent stems from her sense of justice. Just think about the complexity of software and the 'many hands' that
are laid on a piece of software, literally hundreds. If you think about those
facts, you will conclude that a manslaughter conviction against Samuels
would be a true injustice. My computer science colleagues tell me that the
killer robot software, which includes sophisticated AI components for vision
and decision making, cannot be completely understood by a single human
being. *No one person fully understands it!*"

Sally Matthews has made it clear in all of her public statements that she wants to see Randy Samuels behind bars. "It's easy for this Professor Wembley—is that what you said her name was?—it's easy for her to talk up there in that ivory tower of hers. Injustice? What about me and my children? Don't we deserve any justice? Randy Samuels wrote the code that caused the death of my husband. If Randy Samuels were sitting inside the robot and flailing the robot arms and if he killed my husband accidentally, then he would be charged with manslaughter. Well, *in my opinion, the programmer is in the robot, flailing those arms!* The code that a programmer writes is just an extension of that person and should be considered as such. Who else can be held responsible for the robot's behavior? The robot doesn't make up its own mind! The manslaughter charge is justified, and I am going to be in that courtroom, and I am going to see to it that Randy Samuels gets what he deserves."

Special to the *Silicon Valley Sentinel-Observer*, Silicon Valley, USA

HACKER EXPOSES "PROCESS MATURITY" CONTROVERSY AT SILICON TECHCHRONICS

Samuels Bitter Opponent of Rigorous Software Process

Sentinel-Observer Decides to Report Story after Tabloid Reveals Hacker Files

by Pam Pulitzer

Miasma, a figure previously known only in the underground world of hackers and cyberpunks, emerged this week as a new figure in the case of the "killer robot." Two weeks ago Miasma, who is rumored to live somewhere in central Europe, mailed this reporter a package containing sensitive documents relating to software development at Silicon Techchronics. These documents also raised new questions about Randy Samuels and his relationship to his employer.

Miasma came upon this material illegally by entering a computer system at Silicon Techchronics. In his boastful cover letter, Miasma stated that he has been the de facto system administrator for all Silicon Techchronics computers for many years "even though I was obviously not on their payroll."

Soon after the receipt of the "Miasma papers," a meeting was held involving the publisher of the *Sentinel-Observer* and various editors and reporters. At issue was whether we should publish the story that Miasma uncovered. Finally, our publisher, Ben Bentley, said, "We can't go with this. It's a [expletive deleted] good story, but this Miasma character got this stuff illegally."

Last Monday the notorious tabloid, the *National Squealer*, published its version of the "Miasma Papers" in a front-page story that was read in supermarket check-out lines throughout the United States. At that point the *Sentinel-Observer* decided that we had to publish the Miasma story so as to set the record straight.

None of the papers that the *Sentinel-Observer* received from Miasma indicated in any way, manner, or form that Ray Johnson was having a torrid affair with Cindy Yardley, as was reported by the *National Squealer* in its front-page story. We question the ethics of our sister newspapers who reported this rumor for the sole purpose of refuting it.

The Miasma papers in our possession consist of computer files and electronic mail messages that were exchanged over a private and secret computer system established by Silicon Techchronics CEO Michael Waterson.

We asked Max Worthington, former security chief at Silicon Techchronics, to explain the existence of this secret computer system. Mr. Worthington described the system as follows:

"Waterson wanted to create a computer system that would be accessible only to his most trusted managers and employees, people who he knew would never betray him, such as myself. Consequently, we had two computer systems, one for routine communications and administrative computing, and another for secret, highly sensitive communications between Waterson and those in the 'inner circle.' The inner circle consisted of myself and all of the vice-presidents. Of course, there were lots of other computers at Silicon Techchronics, but these two systems provided the communications backbone."

This reporter then asked Mr. Worthington to comment on the apparently lax security on the "secret" computer system.

"Unfortunately, it was an old bare-bones UNIX system with plenty of holes, and Waterson insisted on putting it onto the Internet. I warned him against this, given its purpose, which was one of maintaining the highest security. Waterson can be real stubborn. This computer system was an easy target for hackers. No one was ever made system administrator for the secret computer system. It just ran on its own once it was set up with only occasional maintenance."

Professor John McElroy is a leading expert on hackers, hacking, and the ethical implications of hacking. Interviewed by phone from his office at Silicon Valley University, he had this to say about the Miasma developments:

"Everyone knows how I feel about hacking—hacking in the sense of gaining access to computer systems without permission of the owners of that system. Hackers do a tremendous amount of damage to the computing community. In the simplest analysis, and in the most benign instance, hacking is stealing. Computer time and resources are being consumed without permission. It's also a form of intrusion into a person's personal space. Sometimes private data is stolen, and if we cannot call stealing stealing, then our culture has truly descended to a new low. Hackers often do at least some damage to system administration files, including programs, so their intrusion into a system may not be harmless even when they claim it is. Also, we must acknowledge that some hackers are malicious and do great damage to files, even if they do so only to prevent getting tracked down. In other words, a hacking incident can cause the malicious destruction of programs and data that represent many, many hours of work."

Professor McElroy then mentioned the famous hacking incident reported by Clifford Stoll in his book *The Cuckoo's Egg*. "Stoll points out that this hacker, although his intention was just to get information, did indeed damage systems administration files. Furthermore, the hacker obtained access to a computer that was being used to treat a hospital patient. In gaining access to a computer of that nature, the hacker might have caused the death of the patient."

Professor McElroy apologized for giving a lecture over the telephone, but he explained that hacking is an emotional subject for him. "I would like to see the cyberspace that we are creating, that is so exciting, embody certain fundamental values, and these include the right to privacy and safety from attack and unwanted intrusions. Ironically, in order to have a truly open cyberspace, we must respect the right to private space in cyberspace.

"If the framework of trust breaks down within that cyberspace, then it will be rendered useless. If you cannot trust that the message you received is really from the person who apparently sent it, if you cannot trust that your communications over the global network are private and secure, then you will abandon that network."

Professor McElroy suggested that Miasma might have been engaging in industrial espionage when he gained access to the Silicon Techchronics computer. "I think he was after information about Silicon Techchronics that he could sell to his clients, newly developing computer companies in Europe. Perhaps he was looking for business plans or trade secrets. Waterson's secret computer system was a big gaping hole in computer security at Silicon Techchronics."

The Miasma papers have created a sensation because of what they contain, in addition to the controversial manner in which the information was gathered. The Miasma papers show that at the very time that the Robbie CX30 robot project was getting under way with the late John Cramer at the helm, managers at the vice-presidential level at Silicon Techchronics were proposing that Silicon Techchronics devote itself to something called "process improvement."

"Process improvement" is a movement afoot in the software industry that involves improving the manner in which software is developed. Its ultimate goal is to create a software process that is predictable and continuously improving. Predictability is important so that corporations, such as Silicon Techchronics, can better predict project costs in terms of time and money.

There are several models for process improvement. The most popular model comes from the Software Engineering Institute (SEI) of Carnegie Mellon University in Pittsburgh. Their model is called CMM, the capability maturity model. However, the International Standards Organization (ISO) is developing a new international standard for process improvement that will probably differ, at least in the details, from CMM. SEI spokespeople say that CMM will probably evolve in response to the ISO effort.

CMM, the process improvement model that was being considered at Silicon Techchronics, involves assessment and improvement. A company that wants to improve its software development processes would need to undergo an assessment. The company would be assessed as being at either level 1 (initial), level 2 (repeatable), level 3 (defined), level 4 (managed), or level 5 (optimizing). The higher the level, the more mature the process, that is, the better the process from the point of view of producing high-quality software that is on target in terms of both cost and time.

Level 1 is the most immature level. An organization at this level of maturity does not really have a standardized process for developing and maintaining software. The success of a project will depend upon the individuals, their skills, and their personalities. If the good people leave such a company, the good methodology leaves with them. Eighty percent of companies that have been assessed were found to be at level 1.

A company gets to level 2 from level 1 by introducing more discipline into the software development process. Discipline includes better project tracking and more stable behavior from one software project to the next. Project standards for various stages in the life cycle are more rigorously defined than for an organization at level 1.

At level 3, a standard and consistent process for software engineering and management is introduced and documented. The standards are comprehensive throughout the life cycle and include standards for work quality and for quality assurance.

Level 4 introduces the idea of numerical control, that is, gathering data that can be used to help predict project behaviors and to control projects so that they do not get off track. A lot of the effort for achieving this level goes into developing metrics that can measure where a project is and how it is doing. A database must be set up to keep track of project data. There is much emphasis on measuring how good a product is according to various criteria.

Level 5 involves utilizing the data organized at level 4 in order to introduce a continuously improving process. An important goal of level 5 is to prevent defects and to eliminate waste. A systematic mechanism for evaluating and adopting new technologies is introduced.

According to an expert that we spoke to at SEI, a company should expect to invest ten years in a process maturity program in order to reach the highest level of maturity.

An organization that is willing to participate in process improvement will be subject to two different kinds of evaluations. The first is formally called *assessment*, a self-assessment process that is performed internally within an organization with the help of professionals who are expert at the CMM process maturity model. This self-assessment allows an organization to determine its maturity level so that it can map out a strategy for reaching the next maturity level. *Evaluation,* in contrast, is an external review of an organization's level of maturity. This is done so that the organization can compete for a contract that requires a certain level of maturity. For example, if company X wants to bid on a contract that requires a maturity level of 3, then company X would need to submit to a formal evaluation and it would need to establish itself as a level 3 organization before it would be considered as a possible software provider under the contract.

The Miasma papers reveal that Michael Waterson met with his "inner circle" for the purpose of considering SEI's model for process improvement. Some of the Miasma papers are transcripts of these meetings.

At one meeting Waterson expressed concern that Silicon Techchronics might prove to be at level 1, the lowest level of maturity. What follows is a portion of the transcript for that meeting. We are reproducing the transcript here despite the fact that Miasma obtained this information illegally on the grounds that this transcript has already appeared in full in the *National Squealer*. Harris, Wilson, and Toomey are vice-presidents at Silicon Techchronics. Wilson is the immediate superior of Ray Johnson, Robotics Division chief.

WATERSON: But what if we assess ourselves and it turns out that we are at level one?

HARRIS: Michael, we *are* at level one. We—are—at—level one!

WATERSON: How could that be? You're just speculating.

WILSON: Michael, we are at level one. We know. We've studied the assessment criteria. It doesn't take a genius.

WATERSON (shouting): You mean that Silicon Techchronics, *my company,* is an immature company!!!

(PAUSE)

Maybe I should just fire the bunch of you and hire better people!

HARRIS: It's very difficult to get to the higher levels of maturity, but I think if we don't act now, we're in a situation of an accident waiting to happen. What if a robot kills somebody, for Pete's sake? [sic]

WATERSON: What if we go through a formal assessment and we are at level one—what will happen to our customer base?

TOOMEY: That's what I've been trying to tell you folks! I'm opposed to getting involved with process improvement for this very reason. If we submit to assessment and if our customers learn that we are at the lowest maturity level, they'll . . . We'll lose our [expletive deleted] customer base!

WILSON: You want to talk about losing our customer base? Listen to this: Some defense department agencies are now requiring level three! Do you understand what this could mean for us? Imagine the impact if SiliTech is at level one and [the Department of] Defense moves more uniformly in the direction of demanding level three as a condition for even considering a bid on a contract!

HARRIS: It would be fatal!

TOOMEY: Okay. I get the picture.

WILSON: Look, the truth is that a lot of big companies are at level one. The important thing is that Silicon Techchronics be viewed as a company going forward. Also, we need to anticipate that Defense, in particular, and other clients might become more interested in process improvement.

WATERSON: The argument that major clients might begin insisting on maturity levels three or higher has convinced me that we must go for process improvement. Does everyone agree?

HARRIS, TOOMEY, WILSON: Yes.

WILSON: Mike, I would also like to add that if we do not go this route, then we could face lawsuits five or ten years down the line. I mean, if our practices become substandard as compared to our competition, we could be sued for negligence. If de facto standards are established, then they can be applied in courts of law. We have no choice but to keep up with the rest of the industry.

WATERSON: I see the writing on the wall. Okay, let's have a meeting within each division announcing our intention to implement process improvement, and let's see how people react to that idea.

WILSON: Does this mean that the decision is final?

WATERSON: No. Let's see how it goes over with the troops.

TOOMEY: They're not going to like it, I can tell you that.

WILSON: Does this apply to ongoing projects?

WATERSON: No.

WILSON: Good! I'd hate to throw a monkey wrench into the Robbie CX30 project.

WATERSON: What do you mean, a monkey wrench?

WILSON: I mean that this represents a revolutionary change, and I would hate to throw it at people in the middle of a project. It's stressful enough that

[John] Cramer has them learning object-oriented technology! He swears by this SHEOL tool that they're using.

WATERSON: But make it clear to those people down there that if there is a CX40 robot, it will be developed under the new regime, under the new banner of process improvement. Otherwise—

WILSON: You're going to cut robotics? Is that what that motion across your throat meant?

WATERSON: Look, it's the law of the corporate jungle. If you're in the red, you're as good as dead.

Two weeks later meetings were held in each division of Silicon Techchronics, including the Robotics Division. These meetings were mandatory. At the Robotics Division meeting, Vice-President for Autonomous Technologies Jim Wilson explained process improvement and what it would mean. The Miasma papers include a transcript of that meeting, obtained from Michael Waterson's secret computer system.

The transcript shows that Randy Samuels became increasingly agitated as Jim Wilson explained what process improvement would mean for programmers. Here is the transcript of the critical portion of that meeting. Ray Johnson is the Robotics Division chief.

WILSON: Who is that man in the rear who is shouting obscenities at me?

JOHNSON: That's Randy Samuels. He's got some kind of mouth. He's working on Robbie CX30.

WILSON: Come up here, Mr. Samuels, and speak into the microphone so that we can all hear what you have to say.

SAMUELS: This is the biggest [expletive deleted] I've ever heard in my whole life. I was hired to *program,* not to do all this [expletive deleted] [expletive deleted].

JOHNSON: Randy, why don't you just go back to your seat and cool down!

WILSON: Cool it, Ray! I asked him to come forward. He'll cool down once he understands the benefits.

SAMUELS: I swear, if Silicon Techchronics expects me to do documentation of the kind Jim Wilson is suggesting, if they expect me to do all of that paperwork and specification stuff, then I don't know what I'm going to do!

WILSON: We need to do this so that we can eventually avoid errors and produce a safer and better product.

SAMUELS: Well, you see, I belong to a religion that you probably can't understand, because you've never written a line of code. . . .

WILSON: And what religion is that?

SAMUELS: It's called "Freedom for Programmers." It stands for freedom for people like me who love to program and don't want some kind of totalitarian regime shoved down our throats. Mr. Wilson, I'm warning you! Don't destroy my freedom! Don't destroy the work I love to do. Programming is not engineering as you would have us believe. It's an art and I'm an artist!

WILSON: Well, Mr. Samuels, I am happy you've regained your composure. I beg to disagree with you, however. Programming is an art, but all good art needs discipline. We can't have flawed and dangerous robots, for instance, going out the door, now can we? You know, Mr. Samuels, I see myself as a young man in young men like you. I used to be a programmer at a big aeronautics company. And you know, I am impressed with your passion—I really like that! It reminds me of the way I was when I was younger.

SAMUELS: You're not listening to what I am saying! "Freedom for Programmers" is a religion! If you try to kill my religion, I will have to fight back.

WILSON: That's good, Randy! I love that passion and I'll be looking out for you, *because I think you'll be one of the big names here at Silicon Techchronics before too long.*

Various sources have told the *Sentinel-Observer* that programmers often resent process improvement when it is first introduced. Ruth Hallman of RuHa Software Group in Silicon Valley has introduced the CMM process improvement model at her thriving software company. Ms. Hallman told the *Sentinel-Observer* that programmers resist process improvement because it means doing less coding and spending more time with documenting designs and code. Ms. Hallman had this to say in a telephone conversation with this reporter: "Randy's attitude is not acceptable, especially when the software being developed is safety-critical or finance-critical. We are getting into an era, I think, where software developers will be held more accountable for what they do. There are applications where the artistic element is important, but building a robot is not one of them."

The Miasma papers have opened up a new dimension in the case of the killer robot: Is it possible that Randy Samuels deliberately sabotaged the Robbie CX30 robot as an act of revenge against his employer? As a responsible newspaper, we must refute the rumors to the effect that the prosecuting attorney has concrete evidence that Samuels intentionally sabotaged the robot.

Attorney Alex Allendale, representing Randy Samuels, issued a statement on behalf of his client yesterday evening on the KSVT eleven o'clock news: "This kind of speculation is shameless, scurrilous, and obscene. To say anything further would be to dignify something that is beneath contempt. My client is not the sort of person who would deliberately create a killer robot. I will not discuss the wild speculations that have been aired on several television talk shows any further."

Special to the *Silicon Valley Sentinel-Observer*, Silicon Valley, USA

Silicon Techchronics:
THE UNHEALTHY WORKPLACE

by Pam Pulitzer

For several months the *Sentinel-Observer* has been investigating rumors that Silicon Techchronics has been conducting research on the physical and psychological effects of various working environments on its employees. We can now report the essential truthfulness of these rumors. In so doing, we are raising new questions about the awareness that some employers apparently have of unhealthy working conditions at their offices, plants, and factories.

The *Sentinel-Observer* is in possession of numerous documents that show that upper-level management at Silicon Techchronics—including its CEO, Michael Waterson—ordered a deliberate study of the effects of poor working conditions on their employees. The study took the form of a closely monitored experiment in which the corporation's Chip Creek plant was set up as a model environment, specifically designed to prevent repetitive strain injuries. In contrast, the Silicon Valley plant was set up as a control, and the corporation made deliberate efforts to prevent workers from obtaining a healthier work environment at the Silicon Valley plant.

Repetitive strain injuries (RSIs) are of great concern among workers who spend many hours working at a computer. These injuries are often painful, and in the worst case they can be debilitating.

Within two years after the initial concept was developed among Waterson's "inner circle," the two plants, Chip Creek and Silicon Valley, had diverged markedly in terms of the quality of the working environment.

The systematic improvements introduced at Chip Creek came to be called the "new regime." The new regime called for new workstations and special training to help workers keep their workstations well designed for safe operation. One Chip Creek worker told the *Sentinel-Observer* that a world-class expert on repetitive strain injuries was hired to set up the workstations and to organize classes on posture, typing techniques, resting, stretching and strengthening exercises for the upper body, and strain-relieving exercises for the eyes. This worker said that she felt an immediate improvement in her health because of the measures that were taken. "I stopped taking the anti-inflammatory medication that had become a part of my daily routine. People do not realize how much damage can be done by the apparently unathletic activity of hitting a keyboard," she said. "The classes that we received at Chip Creek allowed us to greatly reduce the routine aches and pains that had become a part of our lives."

"My entire office work area was redesigned when that RSI expert came in," a Chip Creek computer programmer told this reporter. "First of all, we were all given more space to work in, which reduced stress. In addition, they improved the lighting and reduced the noise level by putting in noise-absorbing ceilings. They installed an improved air circulation system over a period of several years. Finally, they gave us new workstations that allowed us to work with the proper posture and with the proper positioning of our hands. Our workstations had ergonomic keyboards and low-radiation, low-glare computer monitors."

This Chip Creek computer programmer described the new working environment in detail. "They instituted a musical chime system every half hour to remind people to break up their work so that they wouldn't spend hour after hour at that computer keyboard, which can potentially cause great damage to muscles, nerves, and tendons. Of course, you didn't have to take a break when the chimes sounded, but I got into the habit of taking a break at least once an hour with the help of the chime system. A new exercise facility was set up, and everyone was encouraged to work with the exercise equipment that was specifically designed to prevent the sort of injuries computer workers are prone to. A new staff of nurses and physical therapists was put in place to provide classes on RSI and to provide massage and physical therapy for those who had already been injured."

Unfortunately, documents in the possession of the *Sentinel-Observer* also show that Silicon Techchronics was determined to keep the Silicon Valley plant in a primitive state in terms of the quality of the work environment. The rationale behind this strange corporate behavior is found in a secret memo that is in our possession. This memo bears the signature of Max Worthington, who was chief security officer at Silicon Techchronics before his resignation several months ago. Max Worthington would often sign a controversial memo with the understanding (within the "inner circle") that the memo bore the seal of approval of Michael Waterson. Here is an excerpt from the Worthington memo:

> The purpose of Project Shooting Pain is to do a cost-benefit analysis on the efficacy of introducing a healthier work environment for our computer workers. This can only be done if at least one of our plants is not allowed to improve in terms of worker comfort and safety. Because of his commitment to justice and fairness, Michael feels very strongly that the plant that must bear the burden of this sacrifice must be our own facility here in Silicon Valley. This will give us a basis for comparison with the plant that has been designated as our "model plant." The model plant will embody the most advanced concepts in ergonomically designed work environments. We have chosen the Chip Creek plant to serve as our model plant.

> By keeping careful data on worker compensation claims, health insurance costs, and lost worker productivity due to injuries at these two plants, we can determine whether it is economically feasible for Silicon Techchronics to maintain a state-of-the-art work environment for all of our employees at our twenty-two sites here in the States.

In other words, if the added expense of providing a healthful environment is less than the savings in medical costs that derive from such an environment, then it will be economically feasible for Silicon Techchronics to provide an ideal work environment for all of its stateside employees. We must not hurt our ability to compete with our competitors both here and overseas. If we cannot afford to provide a healthful environment, then we have no choice but to force our workers to absorb the financial and emotional costs of their disabilities and their career-ending handicaps. Let's hope that this will not be the case.

Many computer workers at the Silicon Valley plant, including several who have become media personalities because of the killer robot incident, describe the working environment at the Silicon Valley plant as hellish. One computer programmer, however, declined to characterize the plant environment in this way. His exact words were, "I haven't been to hell as yet, so I have no basis for a comparison."

Max Worthington played an important role in preventing workplace improvements at the Silicon Valley plant. He defended his role by stating, "Without my efforts to prevent improvements, the study could not show the efficacy of the improvements taking place at Chip Creek. My goal was to make sure the 'new regime' would eventually be implemented throughout the corporation. In other words, I was trying to guarantee the needed improvements by preventing them from occurring. Am I making myself clear?"

One programmer at the Silicon Valley plant described Worthington's activities as follows: "All of a sudden we were all told that some new computer software would be monitoring our keystrokes as a measure of our productivity. This not only increased stress, it made many of us angry and resentful toward management. You cannot measure programming productivity in terms of keystrokes."

Another feature of Worthington's efforts to keep Silicon Valley as "unhealthy" as possible was a new emphasis on overtime and weekend work. One programmer who is permanently disabled from a severe repetitive strain injury told this reporter that she used to work until ten o'clock at night four nights a week. "I would also work all day Saturday and at least part of the day on Sunday. It felt good that I was being such a good employee, and I received the highest praise from my boss. I received a plaque at a farewell banquet they gave me when I was forced to retire because of carpal tunnel syndrome. What an irony! My husband had to accept the plaque for me because I cannot hold things with my hands any longer. He had to feed me in front of all of my co-workers, because I was unable to hold a fork or knife in my hands. How humiliating, and *for what*? My boss made a phony speech about how dedicated I was and how he always saw me pecking away, pecking away, at my computer. He got himself a nice round of applause when he turned to me and said, 'I wish I had a dozen more just like you!' I didn't hang up the plaque in my house. I guess you know where I'd like to put it, but you wouldn't print that in your newspaper."

The Silicon Valley plant became the exact opposite of the Chip Creek plant. Working spaces, which were not generous, were made less so. Workers who brought in new devices to help improve the ergonomic quality of their workstations were criticized. One worker said that Max Worthington came to his cubicle and criticized the way he had set up his keyboard on a stand so that he could adjust its height, based upon advice from a doctor. Worthington told him, "We're a team, and we've got to look like a team. If everyone is typing *up here* and you're the only one typing *down here*, it doesn't look good, now does it? What if everyone on the 49ers wore the same uniform except for one Sad Sack?"

Exercise classes and classes about repetitive strain injuries were discouraged at the Silicon Valley plant while the experiment was being conducted.

It is not clear whether Silicon Techchronics was able to determine the cost-effectiveness of a healthful environment for its workers. However, we do know that the toll in terms of RSI injuries at the Silicon Valley plant has been enormous. One of those seriously injured is Randy Samuels, the programmer who has been indicted for manslaughter in the case of the killer robot.

Apparently, Samuels's injuries are quite severe, and he is bitter about Silicon Techchronics and their shoddy treatment of workers. He spoke to this reporter on condition that we not ask him about the killer robot case. Samuels said that he had surgery performed for carpal tunnel syndrome only months after he was forced to take a leave of absence from Silicon Techchronics because of his indictment. He described carpal tunnel syndrome as incredibly painful. "People know that I love to program, and several years ago, before the robot incident, I was deathly afraid of losing my job and my livelihood due to this pain that is just indescribable. This news that Silicon Techchronics conducted a deliberate experiment at my expense just enrages me."

Samuels explained that not all doctors are equipped to understand and deal with RSIs. "I went to this doctor here in town and he said, 'Take two aspirin and see me in the morning.' It was a long time before I found a doctor who could really appreciate the damage to the body that can come about from working at a computer day in and day out."

The *Sentinel-Observer* contacted Dr. Fatima Jones, professor of medicine at the Silicon Valley University Medical School. She agreed with Samuels's observation that many doctors do not know how to deal with RSIs. She explained that carpal tunnel syndrome is just one of many repetitive stress injuries. Generally, these injuries involve damage to the muscles, tendons, and nerves in the shoulders, arms, and hands that are involved in computer keyboard use. Dr. Jones offered the following suggestions for preventing RSIs:

- Get medical help from someone who is knowledgeable about RSIs.
- Exercise, stretch, and otherwise keep the muscles of the upper body healthy; maintain good health habits with a good diet; avoid overweight, smoking, and excessive drinking; avoid a sedentary lifestyle.

- Pay attention to posture and typing technique.
- Learn healthy posture and technique from qualified professionals.
- Take frequent breaks; stretch and do eye exercises to prevent eye strain; prevent long, uninterrupted stretches at the keyboard.
- Learn how to reduce and manage stress at work.
- Prepare yourself psychologically for a long recovery period once damage has been done.

Dr. Jones indicated that there are many symptoms of RSI. These include pain and tremors in the hands, forearms, and shoulders; weakness in the hands and forearms; heaviness in the hands and arms; clumsiness and dropping things; and difficulty using the hands for carrying, opening, and so on.

The *Sentinel-Observer* has been able to obtain, through legal public channels, information concerning claims for workmen's compensation at Chip Creek and Silicon Valley. In the last year there were only two claims for computer-related injuries at Chip Creek as compared with thirty-one at Silicon Valley.

Workmen's compensation prevents the thirty-one claimants at the Silicon Valley plant from suing Silicon Techchronics for damages. Workmen's compensation is a state-run program. However, some of the injured workers at Silicon Valley are suing the FastTrack keyboard company, which manufactures all of the keyboards used at the Silicon Valley plant, under product liability laws.

The Silicon Techchronics "experiment" raises some ethical questions. Corporations probably have the right to study the cost effectiveness of various procedures, in effect, to perform experiments on humans. It is clear that the kind of study described here would be considered unethical under normal guidelines for academic and scientific research, because the human subjects were not informed of the purpose and nature of the experiment. Thus, the workers at the Silicon Valley plant were involuntary guinea pigs in an experiment that took a high toll in terms of their health and well-being.

No one in the "inner circle" at Silicon Techchronics was willing to speak to this reporter on the record. Max Worthington, who was once a powerful figure in the "inner circle" but who has since left Silicon Techchronics, did speak to us. He defended the experiment in this way: "All we did was keep the Silicon Valley plant at a normal level as compared to the rest of the industry. So if the Silicon Valley plant was just run as it would be normally, where is the ethical problem that you see? Chip Creek was run at an extraordinary level that few companies achieve. Chip Creek is not the norm. It was an experiment about the effectiveness of new equipment and new work spaces that had to get done. We did not know in advance that the new regime at Chip Creek would diminish repetitive strain injuries to the extent that it did. I think that the study was a resounding success. It proved that the new regime would almost eliminate repetitive strain injuries from a computer-based work force. Furthermore, as a company, we were under no obligation to provide a working environment that was much better than that provided by our competitors."

I asked Mr. Worthington about his efforts at the Silicon Valley plant to discourage people from improving their workstations, not to mention the monitoring of keystrokes and the emphasis on overtime work.

"There was an ethical lapse there," Worthington admitted. "There were a few flaws in the way that we implemented our study. However, my intention was to ensure the success of the study because, in the long term, that would result in better working conditions for everybody. Perhaps some of our employees were overly zealous in the way that we handled things."

We asked Mr. Worthington whether he had been overly zealous, in retrospect.

"I was. Whatever song the boss played, I goose-stepped to his tune. That's the kind of mentality I had. Being a good soldier in the corporate world gave me a sense of doing good regardless of what I was doing. I was Waterson's loyal foot soldier, and he manipulated me knowing that I thought of myself in that way. Thinking of myself as loyal made me feel righteous. Now I have come to realize that my allegiance to Michael Waterson was foolish, to say the least. I feel like a complete fool."

Special to the *Silicon Valley Sentinel-Observer*, Investigative Report

---

Chip Creek versus Silicon Valley:

A TALE OF TWO CITIES

by Pam Pulitzer

Over five years ago, Silicon Techchronics initiated an attempt to create two very different work environments: one worker-friendly and the other worker-unfriendly. The Chip Creek facility was chosen to be a representative worker-friendly environment. The Silicon Valley plant, birthplace of the infamous killer robot, was chosen to be a representative worker-unfriendly environment. This was accomplished by forcing the Silicon Valley plant to remain at the same rather primitive level of worker friendliness while the Chip Creek plant entered what was called the "new regime." The new regime involved new guidelines for worker participation in management decisions, participation in creating a healthier working environment, and opportunities for exercise and intellectual enrichment.

The *Sentinel-Observer* has conducted an investigation into these environments from the points of view of worker satisfaction, stress, and health. Our study focused on software developers and did not include other kinds of workers at the two plants. Not surprisingly, we found the Chip Creek software developers to be happier, less stressed, and healthier than their counterparts here in Silicon Valley.

We did not subject the data we collected to statistical analysis. For the most part, we collected anecdotal information. We believe that this information demonstrates that software developers at Chip Creek have a totally different attitude toward their jobs than the software developers at Silicon Creek. In this article we will present a summary of the information we collected, including comments by the employees themselves. We shall also present some suggestions that employees might follow in order to reduce stress and increase the happiness in their lives.

We interviewed software developers at Chip Creek and Silicon Valley about their work. We gathered their responses to the following questions:

1. To what extent do you feel that you are in control of what goes on at work?
2. To what extent do you feel that you know what you need to know in order to do your job well?
3. To what extent do you find that your co-workers and managers give you the kind of social support that you need to do your job?
4. To what extent do you feel yourself in a values conflict with your co-workers, your bosses, and your company?
5. To what extent would you characterize your work load as optimal, as opposed to too great or too small?
6. To what extent do you feel that you are in a good situation to advance in your career?
7. To what extent do you feel that the physical environment at work is conducive to your own physical and mental health?

These questions are derived from a list of criteria for analyzing the stressfulness of a job given in *The Relaxation and Stress Reduction Workbook* by Martha Davis et al., New Harbinger Press.

Here are typical responses that we received from the software developers that we interviewed at the two plants. These responses are grouped by question and by facility (Chip Creek versus Silicon Valley).

BEING IN CONTROL

Chip Creek

"There are good lines of communication between the programmers and project leaders. We're never given anything to do unless we know what we're doing and why we're doing it."

"Evaluations are a two-way street. My boss is interested in my own growth, and I want to contribute as much as possible to the team effort."

"Everyone feels like a member of a team instead of a cog in a machine."

Silicon Valley

"Management at the higher levels has no interest in what the programmers are feeling. I feel that I am totally at my boss's mercy."

"Sometimes I am asked to do things that I am not qualified to do."

"On my particular project, there is so much paperwork that needs to get done that I rarely get to the interesting part of my job."

"I read about an experiment about helplessness where dogs were given electric shocks, and they had no way to control the administration of the shocks. After a while the poor dogs became lethargic. They would just lie down passively on the electric grid. They stopped making any kind of effort to avoid the shocks. Well, that's how I feel."

"We don't get feedback. A lot of times I feel like I am adrift."

"My own sense of how I am performing almost never corresponds to how I get evaluated by my boss. I never know in advance what the evaluation criteria are going to be."

KNOWING WHAT NEEDS TO BE KNOWN

Chip Creek

"When I get my marching orders, I know exactly where I'm going and who the enemy is and how many steps it's going to take to get there. I know everything I need to know in order to understand the project I'm working on. I feel like I'm participating in the whole effort. Management deserves a lot of the credit for this."

"We have excellent training at Chip Creek. It's almost like being back at school, which I like."

Silicon Valley

"I've had assignments where I didn't have the slightest idea as to what I was supposed to do. It finally dawned on me that my boss didn't know either. That's when I began to drink and smoke a lot more than I used to."

"My boss refuses to give me the constructive criticism that I need. He's afraid I might get mad at him. Well, I am mad at him."

"On this robot project that's been in the papers, you know which one, well I swear I knew less than one percent of what I wanted to know about the entire project. Each person dealt with a tiny fragment and never got any perspective on the entire system."

"My boss never gives me any feedback, and he never tells me when he is filing a performance review. It's all so secretive. I have to go to the personnel office to see what he's been saying about me behind my back."

SOCIAL SUPPORT

Chip Creek

"We have excellent conflict management and resolution procedures in our division. That keeps the infighting low and the morale high."

"We have excellent, open, professional relationships on our team. We genuinely like and appreciate one another."

"I went through a personal tragedy, and the people on my team went out of their way to show their concern and support. I'm lucky to work with people like this."

Silicon Valley

"If you ask me right now who I like on my team, I can't come up with anyone."

"I hate the constant bickering and arguing. It's hell just to come to work. I've gained forty-five pounds since I took this job. The first thing I do when I get home is raid the refrigerator."

"It's like we're always working at cross-purposes."

"When I looked at my co-workers and management and asked 'who around here gives a damn about me,' I came up empty-handed."

"There are two people at work who I dislike with such a passion that it's driving me crazy."

"Can you imagine being on a starship in another galaxy somewhere, and you're put on a team of nine beings from nine different planets? That's what it's like working on my team here at work."

VALUES CONFLICT

Chip Creek

"I have never been asked to do anything that I considered to be in conflict with my own values, and I think that my values are pretty damn high."

Silicon Valley

"I have thought about quitting on several occasions when they asked me to do things that I considered to be fundamentally in opposition to my own personal values."

"You're only interviewing the ones who are still here. Why don't you find some of the people who left in disgust?"

"I try to keep my nose clean, but I see things going on around here that are just plain wrong."

WORK LOAD

Chip Creek

"My work is challenging and satisfying."

"I've never been bored ever since the 'new regime' went into effect."

Silicon Valley

"It's flood or drought, feast or famine. Sometimes I work over sixty hours per week. Other times I'm reading World Weekly News *at my desk.*

"I usually feel like I'm on the edge of total burnout. Sometimes I work such long hours that I have to guzzle coffee just to stay awake. Sometimes I am so bored that I have to guzzle coffee just to stay awake."

"I was one of those people they hired onto the 'killer robot' project when it fell behind schedule. That's when I learned the meaning of boredom. I became an expert on the poetry of Emily Dickinson. Would you like me to recite some of it for you?"

"If you see my wife and kids, say hello to them for me."

"To me the saddest part is that I don't have time for the things that I used to love to do, because of this crushing work load. In my mind I was a tennis star once. I coulda been a contendah. But no more. My husband used to call me 'sugar plum.' Now, I'm his 'honeydew melon.'"

CAREER ADVANCEMENT

Chip Creek

"I know where I stand and how I can advance my career along one of several alternative career paths."

Silicon Valley

"At this point I only work for a paycheck and for some good hard booze at the end of the week. Sad, but true. I have no idea as to where I go from here. When I brought up the subject of advancement in the company, my boss started to call me 'Young Turk.' He still calls me that. I don't even know what it means, but I think it has something to do with taking over—like I want his job!"

"My boss takes every opportunity to criticize my work. This makes me anxious about my prospects in the company. Given what's been in the news, maybe it's time to abandon ship."

ENVIRONMENT

Chip Creek

"There's been a remarkable improvement since the 'new regime' came in. I don't rub in as much Ben Gay as I used to."

"The best part of the 'new regime' is the encouragement to exercise. I know I would have had some kind of repetitive strain injury if it weren't for the upper-body exercises that I do."

Silicon Valley

"When the air blower turns on, some kind of noxious fumes come out of that vent. That can't be healthy, can it?"

"I work in an office with no air circulation whatsoever. How can you think clearly if it feels like you are suffocating?"

"I work in a tiny cubicle that I share with a female colleague. If my wife knew how close we were, she wouldn't let me come to work."

"I get up and stretch and walk around every hour and my boss gives me the strangest look. I decided that that was his problem. My health comes first!"

Our informal survey shows just how much more "worker-friendly" the Chip Creek facility has become as compared with Silicon Valley. Experts agree that the conditions that the Silicon Valley workers were describing correlate with high stress, low job satisfaction, and stress-related illness. In particular, the following perceptions and feelings are indicative of a stressful workplace (these correspond to the questions that we asked the software developers):

1. A perception of not being in control
2. A perception of not having the information that one needs in order to do one's job effectively
3. A feeling of alienation from one's co-workers and a perception that social support is lacking
4. A perception that one's values are not consistent with the values being practiced by one's co-workers and/or the organization
5. A perception that one's work is too demanding or that one's work is not demanding enough
6. A sense that one is not advancing in one's career
7. A perception that the environment is physically stressful and unhealthy

Research has shown that a stressful work environment correlates with high blood pressure, high serum cholesterol levels, and symptoms of cardiac disease. We took blood pressure readings over five days for each of the workers that we interviewed. No worker turned down being interviewed when they found out that we wanted to take these blood pressure readings. Thus, the fact that we took blood pressure readings did not bias our results. Our informal study, which is not a formal scientific study, found that workers at Chip Creek had lower blood pressure than those at Silicon Valley. The average systolic blood pressure for Chip Creek workers was 132. The average systolic blood pressure reading for Silicon Valley was 161. Several workers at Silicon Valley had dangerously high blood pressure, and we convinced them to see their physicians.

The poor health of workers who work in a stressful environment is partly caused by poor health habits that result from the pressures of that environment. Note that quite a few Silicon Valley workers mentioned increased drinking, smoking, and eating. One mentioned that she no longer had time for tennis, and another mentioned, somewhat tongue in cheek, that he no longer got to see his wife and kids because of his work load. So here we have a prescription for poor health: reduced exercise, obesity, more drinking, smoking, and caffeine. This amounts to a pathway from a poorly designed job to an early health crisis.

Professor Hiram Milton of Silicon Valley University is an expert on the nature of the work that programmers do. He described stress in these terms: *"Stress is physiological reaction to the desire to be in a situation other than the one that one is actually in.* The unpleasant working conditions at the Silicon Valley plant are stressful because the programmers would rather not be in those situations. In many cases, the programmer is wise to desire change. It is wise to desire more reasonable work loads and a healthier physical environment. In other words, there is wisdom in stress. It is a message from our bodies that we either need to change the environment or that we need to change ourselves."

Professor Milton continued: "It is not wise to avoid stress altogether. For example, any new situation contains an element of stress. Things are happening physiologically and mentally just because it is a new situation, but it may be just the kind of new situation that our own personal growth demands."

Professor Milton emphasized that the goal was not to eliminate stress but to bring it to a level where one's health and performance were optimized. Professor Milton offered the following list of suggestions for managing stress and bringing it to a more healthful level:

1. *Analyze your thinking.* See to what extent your thoughts are contributing to stress. Change your thoughts. Sometimes emotional thoughts are not based on objective reality. You may dislike someone when, with a little effort, you could get to like that person.

2. *Negotiate reasonable goals.* This requires more assertiveness than some people have. Those people should consider assertiveness training. Good communications skills are also needed. Defend yourself against unreasonable expectations without selling yourself short. Evaluate and change, if necessary, the way in which you manage your time.

3. *Be humble.* Not act humble, but be humble. Have the attitude of a student who is always willing to learn. Check your sense of self-importance at the door.

4. *Be wary of perfectionist tendencies.* Perfectionism creates stress in many ways. For example, in analyzing our thoughts, we may find perfectionist thoughts that prevent us from accepting anything less than a perfect performance from ourselves. In addition, we exaggerate the negative reaction others might have to our shortcomings. Perfectionism can also contribute to stress when we expect too much out of others. Being wary of perfectionism in this sense has nothing to do with the technical perfection that we need to strive for in terms of the reliability and effectiveness of software systems.

5. *Find effective techniques for controlling anger and hostility.* Have you ever raged at another person? What were you raging at? Were you angry about an objective injustice, or were you raging about something very subjective and personal within yourself?

6. *Avoid activities that create more stress than you care to handle.* Don't create a situation for yourself that, after you create it, will be overly stressful. On the other hand, don't avoid situations that, although novel and stressful, will contribute to your personal growth. Avoid impulsive and especially angry acts, for example, that e-mail message to your boss that puts you in the doghouse, that idiotic remark that you wish you could take back. Don't volunteer for a new responsibility when you already have more responsibilities than you can handle.

7. *Maintain a healthy lifestyle.* A good diet, adequate exercise, and rest are essential.

8. *Investigate the value of meditation and prayer.* Meditation and prayer can give a person deeper insights into his or her personal weaknesses and strengths. Some forms of meditation and prayer can improve a person's imaginative powers so that he or she can discover creative solutions to difficult problems.

9. *Nurture close and supportive relationships.*

10. *Reserve time for pleasurable activities.*

Professor Milton stressed the need to research the issue of stress and the workplace environment carefully. "A simple list like mine is just an indication that stress in the workplace is not an unalterable reality."

Professor Milton added that too many of his students believe that the purpose of life is to make a lot of money. "Sometimes I think my students do not realize that human life is as great as the mystery of existence itself. Life is about attaining true happiness. Before you can have true happiness, you need wisdom so that you can make the right choices. The ten rules I gave contain some wisdom about circumstances at work. I see them as echoing the wisdom of a Zen saying: What we do to ourselves and what happens to us are not that very different. We should not blame others for our difficulties. We need to understand how we participate in the creation of our own difficulties. We create a lot of our own difficult circumstances because we are not relating to life in the right way. If a person cannot find happiness in his or her work, then I doubt that that person will find happiness in his or her life as a whole. Work is an important part of one's life. That's why I tell my students to carefully consider the work that they will be doing and the impact that their work will have on their lives and on the lives of others. Life is not a sitcom. Life is not a corporation. Life is a beautiful thing."

Special to the *Silicon Valley Sentinel-Observer*, Investigative Report

WEB OF DECEPTION

by Frank Kafka
Science and Technology Reporter

htpp://www/silitech.com

Shortly before Randy Samuels was indicted for manslaughter, he established a storefront for himself on the World Wide Web. Silicon Techchronics at the time was encouraging its employees to explore the Web as a possible source of valuable information. In addition, management hoped that the good name of Silicon Techchronics could be spread by means of the corporate home page and the employee home pages that people could access from it.

For those with access to the Web from around the world, visiting Silicon Techchronics was easy. Using special programs that provide a user-friendly interface to the Web, such as Mosaic or Netscape, they could access the Silicon Techchronics home page at the URL (Web "address") http://www/silitech.com. From there, they could follow links to obtain information about Silicon Techchronics and its products, or they could follow links to the home pages of important clients, such as CyberWidgets, Inc. Finally, there were links to the employee home pages, including the one created by Randy Samuels. The employee home pages contained links to new documents and pictures, some of a fairly personal nature.

As Michael Waterson, CEO of Silicon Techchronics, put it in a memo to his employees: "We want you to create your home page to communicate what you know and to reflect upon the good name of Silicon Techchronics." This memo was written before the killer robot incident.

Management personnel at Silicon Techchronics were not aware of the fact that Randy Samuels was fast becoming a cult figure among a small cadre of disgruntled programmers around the world. Samuels used his home page to post revolutionary manifestos about a new "religion" that he was founding. The central tenet of this new religion was its hostility to software engineering and to all efforts to rein in the freedom of programmers. Its mantra, if you will, was "Freedom for Programmers."

Bob Henderson of Vienna, Virginia, was one of Randy's most fervent "followers." Henderson viewed Randy's home page as a brilliant piece of black humor. Henderson had this to say in a telephone interview with this reporter: "Randy's home page was extremely funny. It was a wonderful diversion for the guys, and gals, at work. Whenever Randy posted anything new, I alerted my colleagues via e-mail. I don't see how anyone could read 'In Praise of Obscurity' and think anything but that it was an outrageous satire."

Sean Culligan of Dublin, Ireland, was another programmer who enjoyed Randy's home page. Sean sent this message to us via e-mail as part of an interview using that medium: "Well, you know that we in Ireland are making great strides in high technology. I'm the manager of a software company that does contract work for some major U.S. corporations. I thought the Samuels stuff was hilarious. I don't see how anyone could interpret his 'new religion' as anything but a satirical comment on the way in which software is developed. I know that some of the men and women who work here were reading Samuels's essays and everyone knew it was a big put-on. It's satire, that's all."

Rifkah Agnon of Eilat, Israel, checked out the Samuels home page at least once a week to see if there were any new postings. This reporter spoke to her via telephone. She made the following observation: "When you live in Eilat, you want to feel like you're connected to things, so I was always using the Web. I was a big Samuels fan. I loved his essay on software reuse. It was enormously funny, and no one could possibly take it as serious professional advice."

Kevin Chen of Taipei started a Samuels fan club at the software company where he works. Mr. Chen said that as soon as Randy posted a new essay, word would spread by e-mail throughout his company, one of Taiwan's most prestigious financial institutions. In a telephone interview, he told this reporter that no one that he knew took the essays seriously. "My favorite essay was 'On Reducing Stress.' It was very dry humor. Anyone who actually followed his advice would be dead within a week. On the other hand, once you understand how Mr. Samuels writes, then you can learn from his essays because they are always the opposite of the truth. I wonder if he ever considered going into politics."

The global character of the Web is striking. One lone programmer in Silicon Valley had become a minor celebrity at sites as far-flung as Virginia, Ireland, Israel, and Taiwan. All of the software developers that we interviewed viewed the material as being satirical in nature. No one believed that Randy Samuels took his "religion" espousing freedom for programmers seriously. Yet Randy Samuels himself took it seriously enough to rail against process improvement at a meeting reported several months ago in the *Sentinel-Observer*. On that occasion, he bitterly opposed all process improvement efforts as constituting an attack upon his "religion" of freedom for programmers.

Samuels's home page has been on the Web for several years. Silicon Techchronics failed to remove it from the Web when Samuels was forced to take a leave of absence following his indictment for manslaughter in the killer robot incident. Since his indictment, Samuels has had access to his home page and has been able to add new links to new documents. One wonders whether the newer documents, posted after his indictment, were as innocent as the earlier documents? Did Samuels's intent become more subversive and sinister after his indictment?

The *Sentinel-Observer* knows of two instances in which people used Randy's material without realizing its humorous intent. This raises questions concerning the quality of information available over the World Wide Web. In the rest of this article, we will meet these two victims of Randy's home page. We will also discuss the social and ethical implications of the Web with Professor John Clark of Silicon Valley University.

html FILES

Randy's essays were contained in what are called *html files*. The acronym *html* stands for *hypertext markup language*. This language is used to describe hypertext documents with links to other hypertext documents. Hypertext documents are thus nonlinear documents that can include pictures and sounds. The html language is extraordinary because implicit in the language is the whole power of the Web and its high degree of connectivity.

Samuels's home page was implemented as an html file that included links to other html files. It was trivial for someone with access to the Web to access Samuels's home page. All a Web user needed to know was the URL (address) of the corporate home page, which was http://www/silitech.com. Once the home page appears on the computer screen, it has sensitive areas that allow the user to follow links to other resources by the click of a mouse button. One of those links gave access to Randy's home page.

At the height of its glory, the Randy Samuels home page contained dozens of statements and essays that all had to do with his rather sarcastic view of the computing profession. The centerpiece was a manic manifesto concerning the rights of programmers to work in freedom and without constraints. Other parts of his home page did not seem to make much sense, at least from the point of view that they did not contribute to his agenda, be it humorous or political, in any obvious way. He included a picture of his boss, George Cuzzins, without comment and a picture of a colleague, Fred Worthington, also without comment. His home page included a picture of his girlfriend clad in a skimpy bikini. One html file gave a listing of his favorite movies, which included *M, War Games, Westworld,* and *Tron.* Another listed his favorite junk foods and fast-food restaurants. He also included an essay on the controversial rap star, Nano Sex, whom he apparently idolized, at least until the tough and belligerent rapper was shot by police in a blazing gun battle after a drug deal gone sour. Randy identified Nano Sex as "my favorite female vocalist of any genre."

But most of Samuels's home page was devoted to his missives about programming and software engineering. This was the Samuels canon about programmer freedom and resisting management calls for process improvement, software engineering, and software reuse. This is the material that has won a worldwide following, and this is the material that was taken seriously by two independent parties: a freshman engineering student in Apu, India, and an overworked home page author in Hoboken, New Jersey.

MOSAIC MASALA

The village of Apu is on the eastern coast of India, south of Bombay. It is an ancient village surrounded by hot, sandy farms, with the steamy sea to the west. The farmers still use animals to plow their fields and to haul their harvest to the village market. When I arrived, it was the middle of the dry season and the air was hot and dusty.

A middle-aged woman in a colorful sari welcomed me into the house. A group of women, young and old, all colorfully dressed, were frying some pastries in a vat of oil. The women instinctively hid their faces when I entered. I tried to smile politely, but I found their modesty both appealing and unsettling.

The house was ancient by American standards. I was told that this house was built when Columbus was still a baby. The room where the women were cooking has been used for the same purpose for hundreds of years. Still, the house had all of the modern conveniences, including a few portable air conditioners. The woman who greeted me at the door led me into a room that apparently served as a home office for my host. This room had two computers and dozens of computer manuals and books.

My host was Satyajit Murthi. He and his son were waiting for me when I entered the office. A short man with a moonlike face and engaging eyes, Satyajit was dressed elegantly in the Indian style, with a white shirt that hung straight down over his hips. He also wore white trousers and sandals but no socks. He greeted me warmly, as did his son, Ananda Murthi, who stood beside him. Ananda was of college age. He was lanky and quite a bit taller than his father. He had a thin mustache that did not hide his youth. Unlike his father, he wore a colorful, western-style shirt.

"My son was thrown out of school because of your Randy Samuels," Satyajit Murthi said when we finally got down to business. He turned to his son: "Show Mr. Kafka your test."

Ananda Murthi showed me a software engineering test that was marked with a great red zero. The grader added insult to injury by writing "PURE RUBBISH!" in bright red letters across the face of the exam.

I opened the exam book and the first question was, "Choose the single most important concept in software engineering and write an essay of 2–3 pages on it." Ananda's answer appeared beneath the question in his own writing. It began as follows:

> Just as animals have evolved to ensure their survival by means of camouflage and other such devices, so software has one preeminent self-protection mechanism, to wit, obscurity.

Further down the page our aspiring young software engineer wrote, "Obscurity is a mark of true genius." This was followed by nine additional points in praise of obscurity.

I knew enough about software engineering to understand that obscurity was not a desirable trait, but I was not totally sure why Ananda had received a zero. Not knowing how to break the embarrassed silence I said, "Your son writes very well."

"That's just the point! It's not his writing!" Satyajit Murthi shouted, hitting the top of his son's head with the palm of his hand, almost affectionately rather than in anger. "It's plagiarized. It comes from your Randy Samuels."

Politely, I told Satyajit Murthi that Randy Samuels did not belong to me and was not mine in any conceivable sense.

"How did Ananda get this material?" I asked.

Satyajit Murthi walked over to one of the computers, and as he pecked and clicked he told me a bit of his story. "I myself am a software engineer, and I expected Ananda to follow in my footsteps. I graduated in the first rank at the Indian Institute of Technology, the M.I.T. of India, and then I completed a master's degree at M.I.T. itself, the Cal Tech of Massachusetts. Then, I returned to India and started a successful software development company."

As Satyajit Murthi typed at the keyboard, my eyes wandered over the computer screen and then to the window just behind the computer. The window looked out over an agricultural scene that could have been stolen from five hundred years ago. A farmer was plowing his field behind a water buffalo. Behind him and his plow, a cloud of dust billowed into the air beneath a sultry yellow sky. As the farmer plowed his field, my host surfed the net.

A distinguished looking woman, Satyajit's wife and a medical doctor as it turned out, came in with a platter of fried potato pastries. "Please take one, Mr. Kafka," she said gently. "Take some mint chutney, too."

"It's delicious," I said. "What is this?"

"Samosas. Please take another one!" She left the samosas on a table and quietly left the room. At that point Satyajit Murthi exclaimed, "I found it!"

It was Randy Samuels's home page in all of its glory. The URL was http://www/hobo.infosearch/resources/prog.advice.

"This Hoboken InfoSearch company is in Hoboken, New Jersey. Do you know where that is?"

"Why, yes. It's near New York. I think you can *see* Hoboken from New York," I replied, remembering a time as a youngster when my father pointed out Hoboken across the Hudson River as our ancient '49 Ford sped down the West Side Highway. That was before my father was relocated to California. From that point in time when I was six, I knew Hoboken only as a place that you could see across the river from New York from the West Side Highway. Yet in the forty intervening years I had never found any use for that particular piece of information until this very moment. I wondered what that information had been doing in my brain all that time.

ıis company has posted several of Samuels's essays. Look, they have
___ ____ on 'obscurity' that Ananda plagiarized and the one called 'Reuse Is
the Enemy.' I'm bringing up his html file that contains the essay on obscurity."

A document appeared on the screen. The document began like this:

In Praise of Obscurity: The goal of every piece of code that I write is
survival—its survival and mine. Software engineering is just a trick to
make all programmers as interchangeable as cogs in a machine. Well,
I'm not a cog. Thus, I am writing these guidelines so that other programmers will be able to write code that cannot be maintained. Thus,
once installed, it will become irreplaceable and indispensable. If the
software is irreplaceable, then its author, yours truly, will also be irreplaceable.

Just as animals have evolved to ensure their survival by means of camouflage and other such devices, so software has one preeminent self-
protection mechanism, to wit, obscurity. Almost all of the laws stated
below have to do with obscurity and obfuscation.

"My son plagiarized this material off the Web, and he has been punished for that. But he did not have enough knowledge of programming
and software engineering to realize that this information was of poor
quality. He was only a freshman, and perhaps he was a little over his
head at I.I.T. To his naive mind, obscurity might be a good trait for software.

"The question I want to leave you with, Mr. Kafka," Satyajit Murthi said
as he offered me another samosa, "is how can we distinguish between high-
quality information and trash on this World Wide Web of yours? My son
was only a student writing an exam question, but is it possible that people
are using other bogus information available over the Web without realizing
it?"

I assured Satyajit Murthi that I would let him know the results of my
investigation.

At that very moment, the woman who was indeed Satyajit's wife
entered the room and insisted that I eat some sweets that she had prepared.
These were golden cheese balls in a honey sauce. She insisted that I eat several servings, although I had already consumed four samosas. The sweets
were delicious. I asked Mrs. Murthi what they were called, and she said,
"Gulab jaman." I soon realized, because of the looks on their faces, that if I
did not eat my quota, my host and hostess would both feel insulted. I
dug in.

Mrs. Murthi forced me to take a bag of sweets back to my hotel
room. These sweets were different from the sweets I had enjoyed earlier.

They looked like tiny cheesecakes. I called my host from my hotel room that evening in order to thank him and his wife for the delicious sweets, which I finished off despite the fact that I had enjoyed a generous dinner in the hotel restaurant. "What is this confection called?" I asked innocently.

"Barfi," he replied.

INFORMATION McNUGGETS

This was my first trip to Hoboken, and it came as no surprise to me that you could see New York from the Hoboken side of the river.

I was visiting the international headquarters of Hoboken InfoSearch, a rising new star on the information superhighway. I was seated in the spacious offices of the president of Hoboken InfoSearch, Marge Allen. She was an energetic woman with blonde hair and a pretty face. The two of us were seated on comfortable chairs arranged around a glass coffee table.

Behind Ms. Allen was a wonderful panorama that included not only the New York skyline but also what was left of northern New Jersey's original wildlife heritage. It was a dirty and nervous-looking English sparrow that was perched on the ledge outside Ms. Allen's window.

Almost immediately, Ms. Allen started to force some extremely rich milk-chocolate candies upon me, despite my protests. They were arranged on an ornate glass serving plate with gold-leaf trim. "You've got to eat these," she insisted. "They have our corporate logo on them."

We spent quite some time sipping cappuccino and eating chocolates. Finally, she asked, "Exactly what is it that you want to know, Mr. Kafka?"

"What does your company do?" I asked, wiping cappuccino foam from my upper lip.

"We collect information on a tremendous scale such as has never before been possible in all of human history. Our essential service is to find the information that our clients need using the resources of the Net and the Web. In addition, we will create home pages for clients who want to get their storefront established on the Web. For example, we just established a home page for one of the biggest fast-food chains. Their home page gives people menus, prices, locations of stores, nutritional breakdown of menu items, and so forth." Ms. Allen was obviously proud of the service that her company provides.

"Do you recognize this?" I showed her a slip of paper that had "http://www/hobo.infosearch/resources" written on it.

"Of course. That's the URL for our corporate home page," she replied, returning the slip of paper to me.

"What's the purpose of your home page?" I asked.

"Well, we need a storefront on the information superhighway as much as anyone. Look, I don't know the details, I'm only the head honcho, but the general idea is to provide an ever-changing sampling of the kind of information that we can track down for our clients. It's organized by industry. For example, we have a link to a health care provider home page that gives a sampling of the kind of information that we can provide for health care providers. When they see the sample, they will want to buy the real thing by subscribing to our service."

I noticed that Ms. Allen had become agitated and nervous. She turned toward the window in an apparent attempt to interrupt the flow of our conversation. "Isn't that a cute bird? I've never seen one like that before."

"It's an English sparrow," I said, with just enough bite to communicate that I hadn't come to Hoboken to play games. "Ms. Allen, do you know anything about the programming advice that people can access from your home page?"

Ms. Allen's muscles tightened, and she twisted in her chair. She stood up and went over to her huge mahogany desk. She pressed a button on her desk phone and said, "Please get McPhearson up here, quick!"

Still standing behind her desk, she said, "You'd better talk to McPhearson. He's the one who set that up. I don't know the least bit about programming. I took a FORTRAN course at Stevens Tech, but that was years ago."

Fred McPhearson entered with a cheerful smile. When Marge Allen mentioned the programming advice home page, the smile disappeared. He looked more puzzled than worried. "Tell Mr. Kafka here about the programming advice page that you put on the Web."

Ms. Allen sat down at the coffee table while McPhearson, standing and shuffling from one foot to the other, gave his report. He described the home page in considerable detail, except that he failed to mention the essays by Samuels. The motivation for the home page sounded reasonable in theory. McPhearson explained it in this way: "The idea is to show prospective clients that we have a unique ability to track down technical information about software development from anywhere around the world. The home page gives them a sampling of that material so that they can appreciate our global reach. We try to use material that is cutting edge and difficult to come by in books or printed media." Ms. Allen smiled appreciatively at her employee.

"Okay, but what about the essay on obscurity? What is that doing there?" I asked.

Ms. Allen's smile turned into a puzzled look and then a frown. McPhearson became defensive. "Look, I am not an expert on programming and computer science. My job is to find information and not to evaluate it. I just surf the net looking for stuff. One day, in a software engineering news group, I found a posting that said, 'For the BEST programming advice you've ever seen check out the Randy Samuels home page at Silicon Techchronics. It's AWE-SOME.' I looked it up. It seemed deep, but maybe a little tongue in cheek. I couldn't tell. I'm not a software developer. However, in the weeks that followed, I found dozens of references to Randy Samuels's programming advice in various news groups and bulletin boards. These references all said that this was the best programming advice around, so how could I possibly not use it? I linked our programming advice home page to Randy Samuels's obscurity html and to his software reuse html."

Ms. Allen turned toward me. "Are you trying to say that the programming advice Fred posted was phony?"

"As phony as a three-dollar bill," I answered.

I could feel the ax being raised over McPhearson's head. I decided to speak up. "Before you fire Mr. McPhearson, perhaps you should consider your own ethics in allowing information to be posted without the appropriate professional filters. Shouldn't people who are creating a resource for software professionals be competent in issues of software development and engineering?"

I then informed Ms. Allen of the incident in Apu. "Ananda Murthi got burnt because of the poor information that you posted on the Web. It was through your programming advice page, which presented itself as containing high-quality programming advice, that this student accessed Samuels's essay, 'In Praise of Obscurity.' Ananda thought that he had the right to copy this material for his take-home exam because Randy Samuels explicitly stated that the material could be copied freely as long as it was not used to commercial advantage. Of course, this kind of plagiarism is not acceptable in academia regardless of any copyrights or copylefts or whatever they are called. Any competent computer scientist would recognize Randy's material as being satirical in nature. However, even Mr. McPhearson was fooled by the dry satirical writing style that Samuels employed."

Ms. Allen was clearly grateful that I had brought this issue to her attention. She gave me a large gift box of the custom-made chocolates with the company logo. As she bid me farewell, I could see a workman in janitor's overalls wielding a broom and crawling out on the ledge outside Ms. Allen's window.

Ms. Allen looked embarrassed. "Look, I'm all for the environment, but we can't have these birds messing up our beautiful, marble building face, now can we?"

LAZY FARE

There is a growing awareness around the world that the information superhighway is a significant phenomenon that contains many dangers and pitfalls for humanity. One of the leading proponents of this view is Professor John Clark, professor of communications at Silicon Valley University. He is developing a course that will explore the technical, ethical, social, and policy issues relating to the Web and the Internet.

Professor Clark invited me to join him for lunch at the Silicon Valley faculty club. It was crowded, and Professor Clark stopped to chat with at least five colleagues before we finally got to our table.

I couldn't help but notice the angry professor seated alone at the table next to ours. As Clark and I were reading our menus, this professor suddenly shouted, "Waiter! Waiter! I've been waiting here for you to take my order for thirty minutes, and those people who arrived after me are getting their food already." The waiter's reply was memorable: "Professor Wilcox.

Don't you remember me? I was in your organic chemistry class last year. You know, the one that you said would separate the men from the boys. Well, I'm one of the boys."

I asked Professor Clark if he had read Clifford Stoll's new book on the information superhighway. "I haven't gotten my hands on a copy yet, but I did read an opinion piece he wrote for the "Week in Review" section of the *New York Times*. It appears that he and I and many others are starting to take a long, hard look at this information superhighway phenomenon. The information superhighway may not have been well thought out. It contains a lot of dangerous curves, intersections, and potholes."

After our food arrived, Professor Clark spoke almost nonstop, and the extensive comments reported here are transcribed from a tape recording of our conversation. Here is an extended excerpt from what he had to say:

"We have this new and amazing information highway, but it seems to have come upon us with great speed and without the careful planning that went into the development, say, of the interstate highway system. I think we need to look at several issues with respect to the information highway and the way that it is being used.

"One issue is the quality of information. I am concerned that students, in particular, may not appreciate the difference between high-quality information and low-quality information. This is the issue that you are raising with respect to the Randy Samuels home page and what happened to that student in India.

"Clearly, this is a relatively minor mishap compared to what could potentially happen. A colleague of mine who teaches computer science assigned a paper in a research seminar. The students started to come to him with literally dozens of technical reports and papers that they had gotten off the Web. The students did not seem to appreciate that only a tiny minority of these papers were refereed papers. In other words, these were papers posted on the Web by their authors without any form of peer review. This is an unacceptable situation from the perspective of scholarly and professional standards.

"Traditionally, a paper gains acceptance by a process of peer review that involves a careful reading of that paper by three or more colleagues. If accepted for publication, the paper might appear in a journal, in conference proceedings, or as a book. In each case, the paper has gone through a rigorous process of writing, review, revision, and editing. Most of the papers that these students had gotten off the Web had not been reviewed and revised in this way.

"The peer review process is essential to maintain standards of scientific truth in academia and in the professions. Imagine if any medical researcher could post a paper over the Web about the efficacy of some treatment for a serious disease without subjecting his or her methodology to the careful review of peers.

"Thus, my first concern about the Web is that the information flowing over the information superhighway is not as reliable as the information one needs for scientific and professional decision making. A special effort must be made to teach students the distinction between a paper appearing in a peer-reviewed journal and a paper posted without review on the Web. . . .

"Another problem I see is that we are creating a culture in which the desire for information is being overly stimulated. I believe, as Clifford Stoll wrote in his *New York Times* article, that this artificial stimulation will abate when people realize its limitations. I do not believe that information, beyond a certain point, contributes to human happiness, which should be the central issue in evaluating any new technology. I believe that an artificially stimulated demand for information is contrary to human happiness.

"Another issue is the ethics of speech as it relates to the information highway. Three technologies have arisen since the first half of the nineteenth century that augment ordinary conversation: the telegraph, the telephone, and now the Net. These technologies are freely accessible, unlike radio and television. Anyone can send a telegram, make a phone call, or send messages over the Net. You and I do not have access to radio and television in exactly this same way. Thus, I do not view radio and television as media for ordinary conversation, despite the phenomenon of the talk show. The Net dramatically 'pumps up the volume' as far as ordinary conversation between ordinary people is concerned. A message that two hundred years ago would be heard by one or two or maybe thirty people can now be 'heard' by millions, if that message is posted on the Net.

"This augmented form of human conversation greatly magnifies the damage that is done by hurtful and malicious speech. Gossip in the village barbershop becomes gossip on a worldwide scale. Lying and racist language are similarly magnified. Anyone with a grudge against a person, a race, or an organization can defame that person, race, or organization over the Net. At this point in time it is not clear what the legal status of that kind of libelous speech is going to be. So, the danger is that we have greatly augmented our ability to communicate and to disseminate information, but we have not changed our values or our ethical convictions. In fact, several years ago one of the major weekly news magazines featured an article on the fact that lying was epidemic in America. People did not view lying as an ethical or moral problem on the same scale as murder or stealing, but lying is stealing the truth from another.

"We may feel that we have the choice to lie or not, but the consequences of our choices do not belong to us. Lying is not a minor offense. A murderer or a thief needs to have a willingness to lie before he or she can embark upon a criminal career. A person who was committed to truthfulness could not become a criminal or a tyrant.

"When there is a change in the fundamental manner in which information is disseminated in a culture, that culture must change in a fundamental way. Although futurists told us this would be coming, I know that I did not truly appreciate how revolutionary the new global network would be. The fact that people today are not more ethical than people of thirty or fifty years ago, combined with the fact that people now have a much more powerful means of communication, amounts to a dangerous situation in my opinion. We need to educate people about the ethical use of language and communications. People need to understand the implications of gossip, backbiting, slander, lies, and deception more than ever.

"Another great danger is the fragmentation of the American community and, beyond that, of the world community. The Net bypasses the public square that has evolved here in America. That public square includes newspapers, magazines, publishing houses, and the broadcast media. That public square was already disintegrating with the rise of cable television and the decline of the daily newspaper. The public square had a fairly standard language of discourse and a fairly standard set of assumptions about government, the Constitution, and human rights. The Net bypasses the public square, and each group can establish its own private square with its own language and its own truths. The result is fragmentation, the inability of one group to communicate with another.

"The citizens of a democracy need a public square that all of the citizens can share in a civil way. You cannot have a free republic without an open and civil public square. When the entertainment industry tries to dominate a public square that was created for the purpose of engaging in serious discussions of public policy issues, then the result is going to be disastrous. Add to that the fragmentation brought on by computer-mediated communications, and you have a great challenge to our free society.

"I blame some of the fragmentation that is taking place on the politicians and talk show hosts that have invaded the public square and have turned it into such an inhospitable place. Many of them are doing this for their own political and pecuniary gain. That is, the lack of civility in the public square and the existence of the Net promote the existence of groups that splintered off from the public square. By implication, these splinter groups have abandoned our democratic institutions as well. The citizens in a democracy need to be tied in to some freely accessible, independent, responsible, and professional source of information. We need to be tied in to the publishers of responsible newspapers, magazines, and books—institutions that respect truth and the dignity of all citizens. If we allow the Web with its fractious communities to replace the public square, we will no longer have a viable republic.

"Another great danger of the current situation is the deterioration of language. Until this point scholars, the publishers of books, magazines, and newspapers, as well as the broadcast media to a lesser extent, have helped to establish the nature of the English language. This overlaps with my previous point in that the language that we speak and the meanings that we share *are* the public square that I just spoke about. The public square is really an agreement about language and meanings. One effect of the Net could be a loosening of these standards and the creation of specialized languages and communities.

"We need to take a look at the Net from the point of view of public policy and education. It may be that there is no way to control the fragmentation that is occurring without violating the Constitution. Freedom of speech has been essential for the vitality and creativity of our country. Thus, I would recommend extensive efforts to educate people about values and ethics, especially about the value of honesty, about the damage that is done by hurtful and unethical speech, and about caring for one's neighbor. We need to educate people about the ethical and responsible use of this powerful new technology."

I was shocked at the bleak picture that Professor Clark painted. His blackened tuna sat cold and untouched on his plate. On his plate was also a baked potato, wrapped in aluminum foil. He had a side dish of steamed broccoli. I was a bit embarrassed that I had finished my pasta salad down to the last piece of macaroni. "Professor, isn't there something cheerful you can say about this situation?"

"Yes. It may be that the power of the World Wide Web will force people to reconsider the ethics of communications and the ways in which they use information. It's like a man whose health is suffering because his diet is too rich. He is going to have to reevaluate his relationship to food. I think the Net will cause people to reevaluate their relationship to information."

At this point we were joined by Professor Malcolm Denton, also of the Department of Communications. He was a large man, tall and noticeably overweight. He sat down at our table. He was holding a box of doughnuts. He offered me one, but I refused. He didn't offer Professor Clark a doughnut. I got the impression that the two gentlemen did not like each other very much.

An entire doughnut disappeared into Professor Denton's mouth. He then licked the sugar off his fingers. "Has my colleague here been bending your ear about the 'dangers' of the Internet?"

I replied, "Yes."

Denton laughed as he reached for another doughnut. Every time he ate another doughnut his otherwise handsome face puffed up like a blowfish. "Clark thinks that people are artificially stimulated to desire more and more information, but my opinion is that you can never get too much information."

Denton literally punched a hole in his next doughnut with his index finger and, holding the doughnut only with this one finger, he maneuvered the doughnut into his mouth, finally extracting his finger, which was covered with grape jelly. Finally, his face filled with delight as he sucked the grape jelly off his finger. "Information is knowledge and you cannot get too much knowledge."

"Information is not knowledge!" Professor Clark snapped back, evidently unaware of the fact that he was bending his fork in his hands. "Knowledge is the result of the processing of information. Knowledge is actually diminished if there is too much information to process. Knowledge comes about when you have processed and digested the information that you have received. Information is a lot like food, and knowledge is like the tissues and structures that the body builds using the nutrition contained in food. There is nutritious information and there is 'junk' information. Too much information, even if it is of high quality, leads to excess fat. This excess fat manifests as incoherent ideas and confusion. This excess fat prevents the functioning of genuine knowledge."

The next doughnut that Denton attacked was a honey-dipped cruller. "It's just not possible to get too much information," Denton reiterated, cruller crumbs flying from between his honey-frosted lips.

Professor Clark was clearly annoyed. He had just noticed what he had done to his fork. "Look, information is just like anything else that a human being consumes. It is possible to get too much. Now, if we cannot utilize all of the information that we take in, what happens to the excess? That excess information must have an impact on the brain. It is possible to have too little information, and it is also possible to have too much information."

Denton attacked a chocolate cruller, all the while staring at Professor Clark with a look that bordered on contempt.

Professor Clark continued, "Another issue is the quality of the information. There is a big difference between eating a balanced lunch and eating a box of doughnuts. In other words, I see one danger of the Internet as being that people will be eating excessive amounts of junk food. Too much low-quality information."

Denton stuffed the last doughnut, a sugar-frosted, lemon-filled beauty, into his mouth. Clark asked, "Did it ever occur to you that you eat too much?"

Denton looked surprised. "How can you even *think* that? I enjoy every bite."

Denton stood up and excused himself. He left behind his empty doughnut box.

Clark pushed aside his plate of cold, blackened tuna. "There's another thing that is troubling me about the Internet, and that is the issue of cultural imperialism. I think it is very valuable for my students to study other cultures so that they can see the American culture against a broader global landscape. When a foreign country plugs into the Internet, they are plugging into the American culture and into American values. American culture is gaining everywhere, and this is good insofar as this promotes constitutional government, freedom, and human rights, but it is bad, in my opinion, when it means that a country is exposed to aspects of American culture that are not consistent with that country's traditional values."

At this point the student waiter that confronted Professor Wilcox at the beginning of our lunch reappeared carrying a platter of steaming hot food. "Has anyone seen Professor Wilcox?" he asked.

"He left," I said.

Seeing the untouched blackened tuna on our table, the waiter asked Professor Clark if he would enjoy Professor Wilcox's poached salmon. Professor Clark nodded in the affirmative, and that seemed like a good time for me to stop recording.

When he finished eating his salmon, I asked Professor Clark if he could tell me about the new course he was developing.

"Everything you want to know about my new course is on the Web," he said. He wrote down the URL on a piece of paper.

obscurity.html

The sidebar shows the beginning of the file *obscurity.html* that Randy Samuels linked into his home page and put onto the Web. This file is his satirical hymn in praise of obscurity.

IN PRAISE OF OBSCURITY

The goal of every piece of code that I write is survival—its survival and mine. Software engineering is just a trick to make all programmers as interchangeable as cogs in a machine. Well, I'm not a cog. Thus, I am writing these guidelines so that other programmers will be able to write code that cannot be maintained. Thus, once installed, it will be irreplaceable and indispensable. If the software is irreplaceable, then its author, yours truly, will also be irreplaceable.

Just as animals have evolved to ensure their survival by means of camouflage and other such devices, so software has one preeminent self-protection mechanism, to wit, obscurity. Almost all of the laws stated below have do to with obscurity and obfuscation.

1. Obscurity is a mark of true genius. If the man on the street could understand general relativity, Einstein would not be considered a genius.
2. Obscurity is universal, in that it can be achieved in any programming language, except perhaps for Logo. Some languages support obscurity better than others.
3. Definition: A language that has strong support for obscurity is said to be *strongly obscure.*
4. If a language is popular among practitioners, then it must be strongly obscure. C is popular among practitioners. Therefore, C is strongly obscure. The "++" in C++ means that C++ is even more strongly obscure than C.
5. Languages that attempt to do away with obscurity never get much further than the front door of the Pentagon.
6. Obscure code is never clearly correct, but the beautiful part is that it is never clearly incorrect either. In fact, by definition, obscure code is never clearly anything.
7. Documenting your code makes it less obscure. Documenting your code is like writing out instructions for your own funeral. Remember: Anyone who can understand what you did can do what you do and for less money.

---

8. If your company requires documentation, then use it as part of your arsenal of obscurity tools. Explaining an algorithm by referring to scribbled lecture notes from a class taught by a professor who was forced to retire is my favorite.
9. If subjected to the indignity of a code review, put on your "if you don't understand what I did, then you must really be dumb" face.
10. Use a notational convention that looks like Hungarian notation but really isn't. This should confuse the kejabbers out of people who are trying to understand your code. One of my favorite naming conventions for C and C++ identifiers is to capitalize every other letter, iFyOuGeTmYdRiFt.

Human Interest Feature

The Sunday Sentinel-Observer Magazine
VISITING A SOFTWARE VISUALIZATION LABORATORY

by **Frank Kafka**
Science and Technology Reporter

A MAN WITH A UNIQUE GIFT

The Computer Process Visualization Laboratory at Silicon Valley University has won several awards for its startling design. Each corner turned in this impressive building reveals new vistas of sparkling crystal and luminous steel. Wavy strands of glowing neon lead visitors in every direction.

"Dr. Cleareye? Just follow the green neon strands," the helpful young lady at the reception desk intoned.

She was embarrassed when I informed her that I was color-blind. "This building seems to attract more color-blind people every day," she said testily. "Follow me. I'll take you there."

Things had gone too far, and I did not have the courage to tell the young lady that I was not really color-blind. I was just trying to make a point about the user interface implicit in the building design.

The door to Dr. Cleareye's laboratory read "Computer Process Visualization Lab, Dr. John Cleareye, Project Director." The laboratory was filled with state-of-the-art computer equipment, including an extremely expensive parallel processing machine. Three graduate assistants were hacking away at computer terminals as I entered. Professor Cleareye greeted me with great warmth. His handshake was firm and sincere.

I asked Professor Cleareye how he managed to get himself involved in killer robot maintenance.

"Silicon Techchronics had a major maintenance problem on its hands as soon as Bart Matthews was killed. The Robbie CX30 robot had been ordered by several companies, and each company ordered an average of about ten robots apiece. Each robot had its own unique section of code, but ninety percent of the code was common to all of the robots. It was economically unfeasible to take the robots off-line permanently or even for a long period. The immediate task, then, was to fix Randy Samuels's violent swing_arm function, which was common to all of the robots."

Professor Cleareye had amazingly clear eyes. They sparkled with vitality and the love of life. They seemed to plead, "Please find this as interesting as I find it!"

I asked Professor Cleareye how that initial software patch was accomplished.

"Simple. We replaced the swing_arm function with a function stub that printed out a warning message and turned off the robot. After this patch was made, there were about a half dozen incidents where robots shut down at various sites when the swing_arm function was called. No one was hurt in any of these incidents. Operators were given intensive training in using the operator console, but all of the shutdowns were automatic. No operator had to take emergency measures to shut down the robot." Professor Cleareye presented the facts casually and in a friendly manner.

"Fortunately, the swing_arm function is not called very often, only in a very specialized circumstance.

"I guess you know my story," Cleareye said unexpectedly.

I told him that I knew that his field of expertise was computer program visualization, that is, creating visual representations of and animations for computer programs. I told him that I was curious how this ties in with program maintenance.

"It has to do with my power to see things," Cleareye replied, catching my eyes with his own. His stare made me increasingly nervous. "My father and his father and his father before him were holy men for our tribe. They were men who could see, that's what a holy man is really, and they passed on that power to me. Much against their wishes, I left our village and studied mathematics, and I had enormous success as a topologist. My grandfather died shortly after I left for the university. My father taught me to see on our sacred mountain when I was twelve, so I guess it was not surprising that I discovered that I had the ability to see four, five, six, and eventually seven dimensions as clearly as you see this laboratory before you. I was able to prove specific theorems about shapes and surfaces in seven-dimensional space because I had the ability to see them as concrete objects."

I admitted having heard about his famous theorem about intersecting knots in seven-dimensional space.

"They almost used my result in a 'Star Trek' episode," he boasted. After a thoughtful pause, he added: "Only one man ever saw the eighth dimension, a Frenchman who left mathematics to become a Buddhist monk.

"At the age of forty, I suddenly lost my ability to see the seventh dimension, and with that, the source of my theorems dried up, so I became a computer scientist," Cleareye explained, perhaps with a hint of regret. "I love what I do, don't get me wrong," he added.

Cleareye went on to connect his earlier work in mathematics with his current work in computer science. "My work has to do with visualizing computer systems. A famous software engineer, Fred Brooks, asserted that software systems were not visualizable, and that this property was an essential feature of software systems. A 'silver bullet,' as he called it, for software development would have to allow for the visualization of the software. But Brooks was skeptical that an effective system for visualizing software in a single coherent vision could ever be developed.

"Over the years I have developed literally dozens of graphical schemes that represent aspects of systems, but no scheme really captures the entire system, and I am beginning to agree with Brooks that no such scheme is possible. What we do get, however, are plentiful and complementary perspectives that allow one to understand different aspects of software, both its static and dynamic properties."

Cleareye drew my attention to a specialized graphics computer. He clicked his way through several menus and soon I was viewing a split video image showing the Robbie CX30 robot on one side and the operator console on the other. "Here you see the Robbie CX30 robot operating at the widget bath, and the operator is entering some new information. A green error message appears with a beep. Now, one of our first tasks was to change the color of the error message to red to conform to the other error messages in the system. My friend Horace Gritty pointed out these user interface problems in his widely read robot journal article. Now I am going to show you what happened when our maintenance programmer changed the color of the error message."

Cleareye clicked on some menus, and a new video screen image appeared. The robot operator keyed in some values, and the error message appeared in red, as required. But now the robot dropped the widget bath, almost burning the robot operator with acid. Then the robot began a repetitive, back-and-forth rocking motion.

"Do you see these gray hairs here?" Professor Cleareye asked. "I didn't have these before Silicon Techchronics gave me this grant. The grant is about using visual tools in support of the maintenance effort. I am not doing any maintenance myself, but I do work closely with the maintenance programmers who are at another site."

"At Silicon Techchronics here in the valley?" I volunteered, to fill in the details.

"No, they are in Bombay, India," he said without blinking an eye. "Can we get back to my video demonstration? The point that I want you to see is that by changing the color of the error window in the user interface, there were some strange side effects on the behavior of the robot. This means that the routine controlling the error message window color is somehow coupled with the routine or routines controlling the robot motion. There's some kind of undocumented interaction there. This is very bad programming. Do you know how long it took us to track that down?"

I stood there not quite knowing how to respond.

Cleareye seemed to relish my indecision. "Whatever you're thinking it was longer than that, because we still haven't figured it out. We resorted to a software patch that is not totally satisfactory. We made all error messages green, and that seemed to work better than making all error messages red. The robot still turns around a few times, but it puts down the acid bath first, and no harm is done."

Cleareye stared into my face as if trying to see if I had absorbed what he had said to that point. "Now come over here, Mr. Reporter, and I'll show you some visualization techniques that my students and I have come up with to investigate the coupling between routines in a program. We are not talking object-oriented here. I'll show you the object-oriented visualizations later."

COUPLING

Cleareye went over to a computer where a graduate student was working. She deferentially moved away. "Her final defense is coming soon," he said nonchalantly. Cleareye clicked on some menus and called up a screen that showed a large array of small boxes. A special box in the upper right had buttons with the words "data," "stamp," "control," and "common." He gestured toward that box and said, "These are some of the forms of coupling that occur between routines. Coupling has to do with the ways in which routines communicate and interact with one another. Common coupling is bad; data coupling is good. Control coupling and stamp coupling are acceptable."

Cleareye explained that data coupling is the usual passing of parameters between routines. Only the required data is passed. In stamp coupling structures might be passed containing more data than is absolutely necessary. Control coupling involves the passing of control flags between routines. A control flag from a called routine might communicate the result of some process to the calling routine, which would then use that result to determine what actions to take. Common coupling involves the use of global variables. Common coupling is very bad from the perspectives of software maintenance and reuse.

"A variable is global to a routine if it is used there but is not defined there. This creates a dangerous form of coupling between routines. Now this box shows all of the global variables in the system. You need to use the scroll bar to see all of them. If you click on one of the global variables, you will see which routines in the program use that global variable. Each box in the grid is a function in the killer robot program. All of the boxes that become colorized when you click on a global variable represent functions that are bound together by common coupling. Use these scroll bars to see the functions that won't fit on this screen."

I clicked on the error_color variable icon and about ten percent of the boxes representing functions changed from a neutral color to a bright yellow.

"The yellow boxes represent the routines that use the global variable error_color. These routines are tightly coupled to one another. Making a change in one of the routines, a change that affects error_color, can have an effect on all of the other routines. Incredibly, error_color has at least three different meanings that we could find. It has one meaning for the user interface and another meaning for robot actions and one incredibly obscure meaning that I cannot remember right now. This third meaning is so obscure that Rachel, that's the young woman that you just met, devoted an entire chapter of her dissertation to it. It's so obscure that it would be ingenious if it weren't so damn dangerous.

"Now click on the data-coupling icon and then click on any function box," he instructed.

I did as he said, and the result was that a few boxes turned blue after I clicked on the get_wgdata function. Also, blue lines appeared connecting the get_wgdata box to the other function boxes.

"These are the functions that get_wgdata is connected to by means of parameter passing and the function call relationship. If this is the only form of coupling permitted in a system, it is easier to track down where the effects of change will be. Stamp and control coupling are also acceptable, and the visual representation for these is similar to what you see before you."

Professor Cleareye waited until I looked up at him from my position at the computer. "The killer robot code is atrocious. It's not documented in any systematic way, there are no coding standards that are obviously being adhered to, and the design stinks. Please forgive me, but I have to be blunt!"

SOFTWARE MAINTENANCE

Professor Cleareye then went on to explain the kinds of maintenance that he was performing on the killer robot.

The maintenance process, according to Professor Cleareye, is the most time-consuming phase of a software project. It involves all of the basic project activities, including requirements analysis, design, implementation, and testing. Changing environmental conditions—for example, the need to process widgets more quickly than previously—could cause a change in the requirements, and this could necessitate a change in the design and in the implementation. All of this has to be documented as well.

"One thing I found with the documentation that Silicon Techchronics provided," Cleareye said, "is that the various life cycle stages seemed discontinuous. There was no traceability back from the implementation through the design back to the analysis. For example, the delivered system places widgets on a moving conveyor belt, but nowhere in the original analysis was there any mention of the need for that capability. Yet clearly, this was an essential capability that was actually required by the application. So, where did this new functionality come from, and why is it never mentioned in the analysis documents? One would like to see the delivered system flowing, as it were, from the original requirements, and one would like to see the original requirements done to completeness."

Cleareye continued, "Each life cycle stage should be well documented to facilitate this traceability concept, but the documentation from Silicon Techchronics was woefully inadequate. I don't know how many times I came across a page that had a title and then just a little note saying, 'fill this in later.'"

According to Cleareye there are four fundamental kinds of maintenance: corrective, adaptive, perfective, and preventive. Corrective maintenance involves fixing errors as they arise during daily operations. For example, an operator notices that the robot is removing widgets from the drying chamber before they are dry. The operator makes note of this and passes this information on to the maintenance people.

"We have received over one hundred complaints about Robbie CX30 problems from the various industrial sites where the robot is still in operation," Cleareye said.

Adaptive maintenance involves fixing problems caused by other fixes. "An example of adaptive maintenance is when we fixed the color of the error message window and then found that the robot behaved in a new, bizarre manner. This forces us to fix the new problem," Cleareye said.

Perfective maintenance has to do with improving the performance of the system, or tuning the system the way one would tune a piano. Cleareye gave this example: "Suppose the algorithm to compute the next fixed point for a robot arm motion is slow, and this limits the number of widgets that can be processed per hour. Finding a better algorithm to improve the robot's performance would be perfective maintenance."

Finally, there is preventive maintenance. This is maintenance that is aimed at preventing crashes or errors before they occur. So preventive maintenance is a special form of perfective maintenance. Cleareye gave this example: "Suppose we know that under certain circumstances the robot might toss a widget toward the operator console. Preventive maintenance would try to forestall that."

Cleareye explained that typically most maintenance is perfective. He gave a figure of fifty percent of the maintenance effort being perfective, twenty-five percent adaptive, twenty-one percent corrective, and four percent preventive. "The killer robot is in a category by itself," Cleareye explained, and he gave the following percentages:

MAINTENANCE EFFORT	NORMAL	KILLER ROBOT
Adaptive	25	82
Corrective	21	12
Preventive	4	6
Perfective	50	0

"In other words, we spend most of our time trying to fix bugs caused by our fixes. This is mostly because of the tight coupling between our functions and also the fact that the functions are not cohesive. In addition, the designers and implementors did not practice information hiding."

COHESION

In order to explain the concept of cohesion, Professor Cleareye replaced me at the computer and brought up a new visual image. "This is a visualization of the cohesion concept that Rachel and I have been working on. Each rectangle in the array of rectangles that you see on the screen represents a function, and these functions are only in the C code, not the visual processing code that is done in an object-oriented manner. You need to scroll to the right and down to see the full array of hundreds of functions."

Cleareye now looked intently at the screen. "Now, if I click on this button, then I am asking the computer to show me how many discrete tasks are implemented in each function. That is part of the procedure for measuring the cohesiveness of the function. It's not really a procedure, because some subjective judgment is involved. In this visualization, each rectangle will be partitioned into smaller rectangles with different colors. Okay, here goes."

The screen became alive with a multiplicity of colors. Initially, the screen was a uniform gray with black lines and letters. Now some boxes had five or six distinct colors in them. "The more colors you see in a function," Cleareye explained, "the more likely it is that the function is not cohesive. But the real test has to do with how the tasks are related to one another. We're not at the cohesion concept yet."

Cleareye now pointed the cursor at another button. "When I click on this button, each function will be illuminated with a color that indicates the level of cohesion achieved by that function. The level of cohesion is determined by looking at the tasks identified in the previous step and then asking questions about the conceptual 'glue' that is holding them together. In other words, we ask how the tasks are related. The weaker the relationships between the tasks, the weaker the cohesion; the stronger the relationships, the stronger the cohesion. Strong cohesion is good. Weak cohesion is bad.

Some authors have identified seven levels of cohesion, and that's the model that Rachel used for her program."

Cleareye clicked on the button and the boxes returned to solid colors: white, green, blue, yellow, orange, red, and black. Cleareye then explained the meanings behind the colors. "White means functional cohesion, the best form of cohesion. All tasks in the function are related to a single purpose, and that purpose is achieved completely. Green represents sequential cohesion, the second-best level. All tasks in the function are related in that the output from one task is the input into the next task. Blue means communicational cohesion, also good. All tasks performed by a function are related in that they work with the same data or data store. Yellow represents procedural cohesion. All tasks are related in that they are to be executed one after the other, but without the data flow effect of sequential cohesion. Orange represents temporal cohesion. This is getting into the less acceptable forms of cohesion. The tasks are related in that they should all occur at about the same time—for example, at the beginning or end of the execution of the program—but they have no stronger connection between them. Red represents logical cohesion, which is very poor. Basically, you have logical cohesion if there is some concept linking the tasks, but nothing better. Black represents coincidental cohesion, in which tasks have no conceptual glue relating one to the other. Now, tell me, Mr. Reporter, what do you see?"

There were relatively few white or blue boxes on the screen, representing functional and communicational cohesion. There were as many black as white boxes, but there were many orange and red boxes, representing temporal and logical cohesion, and an equal number of green and yellow boxes, representing sequential and procedural cohesion.

"When a function lacks cohesion, it makes maintenance quite difficult. It has an even more profound negative impact on reuse. For example, this coincidentally cohesive function that I am pointing to with the mouse cursor is code that is being reused from the Robbie CX20 robot. It performs five unrelated tasks. They ported it to the Robbie CX30 for the purpose of performing just one of those five tasks. So, they use parameters to tell the function which task needs to be performed, and this function is called with four useless, dummy arguments. This is not a good way to make a function reusable. Lack of cohesion makes maintenance difficult because natural functional components are broken up. For example, suppose a natural task is t1, t2, t3, t4, t5. Of right, these tasks should be in one function, but lack of cohesion means that they will be spread out among several functions."

I told Cleareye that I was really impressed with the work that his graduate student Rachel had done. "But, you know," I said, "a color-blind person would not be able to follow this demonstration. This assumes that the person using the software has normal vision."

Cleareye's jaw dropped, and he suddenly became quite pale. He then turned toward the graduate students huddled in a far corner and shouted, "Rachel! I would like to speak to you later. Mr. Reporter here just made an interesting observation about your system."

INFORMATION HIDING

"The next demonstration is also part of Rachel's dissertation," Cleareye explained. He picked his way through a new set of menus, and a new graphic appeared. "This shows you what information hiding is about. Here again you have a grid showing the functions in the C part of the killer robot code. Each function is shown as a rectangle. If you click on a function, all functions that know things that they shouldn't know about that function will be illuminated in a bright color. Try it."

I clicked on a function, and a large number of rectangles turned bright blue.

Cleareye explained this latest graphic: "The illuminated functions are all implemented using information about the function you clicked on. That information might be the detailed representation of a variable or knowledge about what particular algorithm is being used. Ideally, knowledge like this should be hidden away within the function. The ideal situation is called information hiding. Other functions should not know about the implementation details. Shared knowledge is really a form of coupling."

Cleareye explained how Rachel's program visualizations were produced. "I should mention that in order to produce this visualization, as well as the previous one, Rachel had to manually make the determinations concerning levels of cohesion and the use of information that should be hidden. We are far from the point where one program can analyze another in these terms. For example, we do not have a program that can take another program as input and assign levels of cohesiveness to the various routines of the input program. Until we can create such automatic analysis tools, the usefulness of these visualization techniques will remain somewhat limited. It is very expensive to produce visualizations such as these."

OBJECT-ORIENTED VISUALIZATIONS

"Chris over there is working on his dissertation," Cleareye said, pointing to one of the graduate students working in the corner. "He's inventing new graphical representations for object-oriented systems, and he has several job offers already from companies that are building CASE tools."

Cleareye explained that object-oriented systems are not easy to maintain and that maintaining object-oriented systems may require sophisticated visual tools. "I am calling up one of the programs that Chris developed to portray properties and behaviors of object-oriented systems. This graphic shows the class hierarchy in the visual part of the killer robot system. It is quite complicated, because of the use of multiple inheritance, and some of the inheritance patterns are not good ones.

"Now, if you click on a class with the right mouse button (not the left), the class will expand into a fairly standard notation invented by Grady Booch, a class or module diagram, which shows the interface of the class on the border of the rectangle representing that class. Now if I click on one of the functions in the interface, all classes that contain at least one function that calls the original function will turn bright blue."

Cleareye performed the indicated action with an example method, and many classes turned blue.

"This is a form of coupling in object-oriented systems. Changing the function I clicked on could have an impact on all of the classes that turned blue, because the function I modified provides a service that those classes use. Notice the numbers that appeared in each box. They give the number of functions in each class that call the function I originally clicked on. So, the function that I clicked on is called by six functions in this class and seven in this class over here! Thus, if I change the function I clicked on, hundreds of functions should be retested!"

Cleareye clicked away and brought up a new screen. "Chris generated this analysis of the Smalltalk system. Now, I do not mean a program developed in Smalltalk, I mean the Smalltalk system itself. It consists of all of these classes. Now watch what happens when I click on this function in the True class."

The entire screen turned blue.

"Just about every class uses the function I clicked on, which implements the if-else control structure. If you are dumb enough to change that method, the entire system will not work correctly. In my opinion, Smalltalk is tightly coupled in a strangely perverse way. Please understand, I love Smalltalk, but this property of the system always fascinated me.

"The usual dogma is that object-oriented systems give you good cohesion at the class level. All functions in a class use the same variables, so that gives the functions as a group communicational cohesion. This is a modified notion of cohesion from the first one I gave you, because now I am discussing the cohesion of a class as opposed to the cohesion of a function. Now, this next graphic is going to show that object-oriented systems may not be all that wonderful in terms of cohesion. This is wonderful work that Chris did. He took the idea of a programming plan from Elliot Soloway, and he showed how simple programming plans are implemented in a large C++ program. Here is the class hierarchy for the program, and here is a menu of program plans. I'll choose this one. A program plan is a common programming strategy, and in my mind, this has something to do with the idea of cohesion. A plan is trying to achieve a cohesive idea: read in a file, find the average of a sequence of numbers. If I click on this plan, the graphic will show all classes that contain at least one function needed to realize the plan. Okay, see all of that blue that just appeared? Lots of classes are needed to realize this plan. If I click on one of those classes using the right mouse button, I get one of those Booch symbols again, and now the functions that were called in this class are shown in blue. Three functions from this class were called in realizing the program plan I originally clicked on. So, one plan is implemented across many functions of many classes. This makes maintenance very difficult. I have hardly begun to work with the visual processing part of the killer robot. I think we have a daunting task ahead of us."

I thanked Professor Cleareye for the tour of his lab. He escorted me into the corridor and then cautioned me against taking the elevator back to the lobby floor. "If the building air conditioning unit is on and you press 'L' for lobby, then the lights in the elevator will go out. No one has been able to figure it out, but it is clearly a bug in the design of the building's integrated, computer-controlled, hermetically sealed environment."

Human Interest Feature

Latest Silicon Techchronics Bombshell:

AI RESEARCHER QUITS TO PROTEST SYSTEM HE HELPED TO CREATE

"Visual Profiling" Was Goal of Multimillion-Dollar Project

Waterson Intended to Eliminate Robotics Division, AI Expert Claims

by **Pam Pulitzer**

Dr. John Erstwhile is not well known outside of a small circle of researchers in vision processing. But within that circle, he is considered one of the leading experts on artificial intelligence systems that can "see."

Artificial intelligence, or AI, is the branch of computer science that studies intelligence from a computational point of view. For example, an AI program might simulate human intelligence, or it might exhibit intelligent behavior without regard to how human intelligence actually operates. Vision processing systems either duplicate or imitate human visual capacities, such as identifying objects. Vision problems in computing are far from trivial, and some people believe that success can only come from computer systems that process information much as the human brain does.

Yesterday, Dr. Erstwhile quit his position at Silicon Techchronics as chief research engineer in the Vision Products Division. He made his announcement at the kind of crowded news conference that has become the norm here in Silicon Valley in recent months. "I am resigning my position because I have come to believe that the system that I was working on is highly immoral. I could not in good conscience continue to work on such a system. In addition, I accuse my former employer of unethical and probably illegal business practices, and I have documentation to back up these charges."

Dr. Erstwhile added the following remarks concerning his resignation. "Recent revelations in the media concerning Silicon Techchronics also influenced this decision. I am especially troubled by the lack of professionalism that led to the killer robot incident," he stated, reading from a prepared text.

Most of the news conference dealt with the computer system that Dr. Erstwhile himself was working on. In fact, no one at Silicon Techchronics had more technical knowledge of this system than Dr. Erstwhile himself. Erstwhile revealed that Silicon Techchronics had embarked upon an ambitious research project with significant social implications. This project involved "visual profiling," a new technology apparently developed at Silicon Techchronics that would allow surveillance cameras to look for people with specific characteristics.

"Mr. Waterson was banking the future of Silicon Techchronics on this new technology," Dr. Erstwhile claimed.

Erstwhile described "visual profiling" as follows: "The idea of visual profiling comes from the area of data surveillance, or dataveillance, as it is sometimes called. Dataveillance takes many forms, but one form is to have some kind of model, perhaps statistical, of the kind of people you are looking for in a database. For example, the IRS might develop a model that would allow them to predict who is a tax cheat. A person who has the characteristics x, y, and z might have a seventy-five percent chance, according to the model, of being a tax cheat. On that basis, they might call that person in for an audit. Profiling might be used to determine who is likely to be a drug dealer, for example, and on this basis such people might be placed under police surveillance. This same concept is being used in many domains."

A reporter for National Public Radio shouted out, "But doesn't that violate the Fourth Amendment to the Constitution? Isn't there supposed to be some evidence or cause for suspicion, other than a statistical model, that would justify the police placing someone under surveillance?"

"I'm not a lawyer, Nina," Erstwhile responded. "I'm just trying to explain what visual profiling is. Visual profiling involves picking people out of a crowd based upon visual properties or characteristics. For example, one of our big clients is a consortium of five of the largest banks in America. They are partners with Silicon Techchronics for the purpose of developing and marketing a new bank surveillance system. This surveillance system will alert bank security when a suspicious-looking person walks into a bank. Using widely available crime data, we have created a model of what a bank robber looks like in terms of height, weight, skin color, gender, facial features, and clothing."

The National Public Radio reporter expressed shock and anger. "What you're really saying is that if a person with certain racial, ethnic, and sexual characteristics walks into the bank, then security will be alerted."

"Nina, I quit my job because I agree with you! I do want to be careful, however, not to give away any of my former employer's trade secrets. I could get into legal difficulty."

"Trade secrets?" the NPR reporter snapped back. "Since when is prejudice a trade secret?"

"Automated prejudice is an accurate way of describing the system that I was developing. The system is called ARCHIE. Officially, ARCHIE stands for 'Automatic Recognition of Criminals and Hostile Individuals in the Environment.'" Unofficially, we all know that it was named after Archie Bunker, the bigoted television character," replied Erstwhile.

A famous reporter from the *New York Times,* who used to cover foreign affairs but who was recently promoted to cover the killer robot case, asked the next question. "Are you trying to tell us that you were trying to create a computerized bigot? A system that would distinguish between black and white, Anglo and Hispanic, male and female?"

"I was only trying to replicate human intelligence, Tom," Erstwhile replied. "My goal was to create a computer system that could scan a crowd and identify people with specific characteristics in that crowd. Security guards do this all the time."

"But are you replicating intelligence or stupidity?" the *Times* reporter asked.

"Well, that's what I started to ask myself. Is this artificial intelligence, or is this artificial stupidity? I guess I came to realize that a lot of the thinking that people do is just stupidity. Sometimes those who appear to be the most intelligent do the most evil. I came to understand that true intelligence and evil have nothing to do with one another. I realized that all human evil from slavery to Auschwitz arose from a thought process that had become divorced from love and from truth, a computerlike thought process. I started to ask myself, in all earnestness, *Why am I devoting my life to this [expletive deleted]?* Please pardon my French, ladies and gentlemen, but I wanted to be perfectly blunt with you. The realization that evil is the result of a computerlike thought process that is divorced from love came as a great shock to me. This realization came in a flash!"

Dr. Erstwhile paused for a while. Tears welled up in his eyes. He referred to some index cards that he had brought along to the news conference. He looked up and added, "You know, my whole adult life has been dedicated to artificial intelligence."

Dr. Erstwhile cleared his throat and then continued with his remarks. "I apologize for that outburst, but I became deeply disillusioned with the research that I was doing at Silicon Techchronics. Our research was really about creating new security systems that would recognize suspicious people based upon their visual characteristics. Now, I suppose this is how some people operate. This is how Archie Bunker operates, but I became increasingly confused about whether I was creating artificial intelligence or artificial stupidity. I realized that some forms of stupidity are really quite sophisticated and they are disguised as intelligence."

A reporter from CNN asked the next question. "But is it really stupidity? You were using actual crime data. Archie Bunker is a bigot because his prejudices had no foundation in fact. Your system uses factual data in order to determine who might be a bank robber or a terrorist or whatever."

Dr. Erstwhile was obviously prepared to answer this question. "Imagine the social consequences of installing surveillance systems that look out for people with particular racial and ethnic characteristics. Suppose that group X is targeted, and you are an innocent member of group X. How are you going to feel knowing that whenever you go to the bank or the store, a computer system is focusing on you as a potential robber or thief? Is that an acceptable burden to place on innocent people?"

The CNN reporter followed up. "But isn't that what security people are doing anyway? How does this computer system make things any worse?"

"For one thing, the new security systems will be everywhere," Erstwhile replied. "Every bank, store, business establishment, and apartment building will want to have one. They will be at airports and at railroad and bus stations. 'Big Brother' will be a reality."

Professor Harry Yoder, computer ethics consultant for the *Sentinel-Observer*, was shocked by these new allegations. We reached him at a computer ethics conference being held in Hawaii. "This confirms my worst fears, my worst fears about where computer technology is heading."

Pressed to elaborate, he said, "What we're doing is building systems that behave like us. We are bigoted, so our machines will be bigoted. We are violent, so our machines will be violent. We behave stupidly, so our machines will be created in our own image."

The next item on John Erstwhile's agenda was to share his insight into how Silicon Techchronics conducts business. He revealed some questionable business practices that, according to Erstwhile, " just add to the sordid picture we already have of Silicon Techchronics and its business practices."

Here are Erstwhile's remarks on this subject: "Visual profiling was becoming a major activity at Silicon Techchronics, and I was a major player in all of this. Silicon Techchronics was part of a consortium to produce the bank surveillance system. That consortium was set up to sell the surveillance system to banks outside the consortium at great price. Silicon Techchronics was also involved in research with the Department of Defense for the same purpose. That research involved the autonomous land vehicle that we are working on. The idea is to use visual profiling to help the autonomous land vehicle distinguish between friendly civilians and those who might be hostile—based upon racial, ethnic, and other visible characteristics. Now, I knew that this project with the Department of Defense was not doable in the time frame of our contract. It clearly was not doable, but no one at Silicon Techchronics ever expressed any doubt about the autonomous land vehicle to the Department of Defense."

He continued, "There was also a major project funded by the Department of Transportation to do surveillance at airports, to alert airport security to the presence of people with certain visual characteristics, people who might be potential terrorists. We had that Middle Eastern look down pat. Another project was funded by the Justice Department, specifically the FBI. They wanted a surveillance system that could be used to protect federal facilities against domestic and foreign terrorists. They wanted the ability to recognize specific terrorists whose visual characteristics were known and they were also interested in 'visual profiling.' Against my better professional judgment, I signed off on that grant as project director, although I knew damn well we weren't going to get to the point where we could recognize a specific terrorist.

"Finally, there is a project that we have been doing for a consortium of high-tech industries, including CyberWidgets, to work toward a Robbie CX40 robot that would be able to avoid human beings on the shop floor and a Robbie CX50 robot that would be a slave of a particular human operator, almost like a pet. These robots are merely ideas on paper. The Robbie CX50 was viewed as a project that would not come to fruition before the year 2005."

John Erstwhile went on to describe in more detail the questionable business activities at Silicon Techchronics. "About eighteen months before Bart Matthews was killed, John Cramer died. Now, I was good friends with Max Worthington, security chief at Silicon Techchronics and part of the 'inner circle,' as it is called. Soon after Cramer's death, Worthington told me in the strictest confidence that Waterson had decided to eliminate the Robotics Division as soon as the Robbie CX30 robot was finished. The idea was to get Robbie CX30 out the door and then to immediately ax the Robotics Division and all of its employees, except for a few cronies like Ray Johnson.

"In addition, Waterson insisted that the Robbie CX30 be delivered on time, warts and all. He told Ray Johnson to develop a slogan that would capture this idea, a slogan that the robot developers could live by. That's how the 'Ivory Snow theory' came to be.

"One of the implications of this is that we were getting a lot of money from the industrial consortium that included CyberWidgets to conduct research necessary for the Robbie CX40 and Robbie CX50 projects, but Silicon Techchronics already knew that these robots would never go into production. I knew all of this, but I didn't say a word. I know that you will want to ask me about this, but all I can say is that you don't understand the love I have for my work. I guess I put my work above everything else. And I didn't feel selfish about it because I felt that I was serving humanity by building these *intelligent* systems."

Erstwhile paused to catch his breath. "Silicon Techchronics took three hundred thousand dollars from that consortium and put it into visual profiling research. They had no intention of ever building the CX40 or the CX50. They did, however, have a few people working on trying to relate our visual profiling work to robotics just so the consortium wouldn't get suspicious."

Erstwhile continued, "The consortium of banks, the Departments of Defense and Transportation, and the Justice Department were all being cheated because of the overlap among their contracts. The banks, the Department of Defense, the Department of Transportation, and the Justice Department were each getting nearly identical systems, yet they were not aware that most of the required research applied to all four systems. For example, at one point I was aware that I was developing a program for four different projects, but my pay was coming from the bank consortium contract only. Worthington himself told me that the Defense Department contract by itself could have paid for the bank consortium system, the Department of Transportation system, and the FBI system."

A spokesperson for Silicon Techchronics called Erstwhile's charges "ludicrous and reprehensible." Max Worthington declined to comment on the charge that he knew that the Robotics Division would be axed.

A spokesperson for the Department of Defense stated that John Erstwhile had been ill-advised to tell the press about secret DoD research. The spokesperson also stated that the Department of Defense would not tolerate overcharges on contracts and that an investigation into the matter would soon be under way.

Apparently, Silicon Techchronics CEO Michael Waterson's plan to eliminate the Robotics Division was thwarted due to the publicity surrounding the killer robot. Waterson is rumored to be waiting for a more opportune time to dispose of the Robotics Division, according to a source close to his "inner circle."

Special to the *Silicon Valley Sentinel-Observer*, Silicon Valley, USA

The Sunday Sentinel-Observer Magazine

VISION QUEST: THE FUTURE OF COMPUTING

A True Adventure of the American West

by Frank Kafka
Science and Technology Reporter

When my editor asked me to do a story on the future of computing, I naturally turned to Professor John Cleareye, whose Computer Process Visualization Laboratory was featured in a *Sentinel-Observer* article last month. I wondered whether Professor Cleareye's ability to "see" included the ability to see the future, in particular the future of computing.

His response over the telephone was crisp and cheerful: "Certainly. Does the future interest you?"

I explained that my editor had asked me to investigate the future of computing. Before I could explain further, he shouted, "Excellent! Come down to my laboratory immediately."

When I arrived at the laboratory I was surprised to see Rachel and Chris, the two doctoral students I had met during my last visit, and a pile of baggage of various sorts, including duffel bags and backpacks. Professor Cleareye stood in front of the bags, and Chris and Rachel stood behind them.

"Where are you going?" I asked nervously.

"You wanted to see the future of computing, so we are going to take you there. This will take at least five days. I hope you have no pressing obligations." Cleareye seemed to be on the verge of laughter, as if the joke would soon be revealed.

As it turned out, Cleareye was dead serious. The next thing I knew I was in the back seat of his Jeep Cherokee, which was crammed with luggage and four passengers. We headed east out of the valley and into the mountains, and we traveled a scenic interstate for most of the afternoon.

We camped out the first night, and I must say it was exhilarating to see the natural beauty around us in a lakeside forest. The crescent moon set behind a granite peak that stood black against a star-filled sky. I was not used to the sounds of wildlife that lent poignancy to the darkness.

Cleareye asked Chris to start a campfire, and we sat around it quietly in the chilled air. Cleareye finally spoke. "It is important for a person who is going to work with technology to see. That is why I took Chris and Rachel and other students of mine on this same adventure, to teach them how to see."

"Why, Cleareye?" I asked.

The light of the campfire danced in his mystical eyes. "Creating something new, some new technology, requires seeing it, and seeing it includes understanding all of its implications. Whom will it help? Whom will it hurt? Will it hurt that majestic owl looking down upon us from that tree?"

The owl flew off into the darkness, as if on cue. The beating of its wings reminded me of the beating of my own heart.

"You can create something either out of anger or out of love or, worst of all, out of cold indifference. Creating out of anger or out of indifference is destructive. It will hurt that owl and all living things." Cleareye's comments were followed by a silence that was somehow filled with energy.

Cleareye turned away from the others and faced me directly, looking into my eyes. "Seeing allows the creative process to function, but that creative process is always a double-edged sword. The same creative process that creates a new technology or a new piece of music or literature is behind madness and insanity. Are you sure you want to learn how to see and thus to bear the awesome responsibility that the creative spirit bears?"

"But, Cleareye, I am not creating any new technologies!" I replied.

"Seeing is fundamental to all creative professions. You are a reporter, and that involves creativity. And you are an author. I have seen some of your stories in the literary supplement. So, I ask you, will you use your powers responsibly?" His voice took on a tone of great urgency.

"I will," I replied.

"Seeing and creativity are the essence of everything that has happened in technology," Cleareye said, stirring the campfire with a stick.

Sparks drifted skyward as he stirred the embers. "Tomorrow we will reach the town where I grew up. Our holy man, George Eaglefeather, will then tell me whether you are a proper candidate for initiation. If you are, I myself will take you to Elk Mountain, and there the Great Spirit will open your heart to the nature of seeing and to the creative powers that you bear within. Any questions, Mr. Reporter?"

Cleareye stood up and stretched before I could pose the question that I was trying to formulate in my mind. He indicated that it was time to go to sleep.

The next day was hot and dry during the entire drive, which started out on an interstate but ended up on a dirt road through a seemingly endless desert. Just before two o'clock that afternoon, we reached Cleareye's home town, the hub of which was a five-square-block collection of brick and adobe houses and small commercial buildings. We immediately went to the home of George Eaglefeather.

Eaglefeather was younger than I expected, younger than Cleareye. He certainly did not look anything like a holy man. He looked quite ordinary. He was wearing worn trousers and a t-shirt. Later I learned that he was an electrician who loved to repair things. I liked him immediately, but his first words were harsh.

"Is this the one?" Eaglefeather asked, inspecting me from head to toe. Most of all, he looked into my eyes. His eyes were clear and dark like Cleareye's, and they contained the same vibrant fire, only more so.

"He's the one!" Cleareye replied. I felt my muscles tensing, and I thought I would storm out of the house if either one laughed or insulted me in any way.

"Newspaper reporter?" George asked.

"Yup," Cleareye said.

"Not a good profession," George said.

"He's a good man. I know his work. He will use the ability to see in a positive way. Not all reporters are the same."

"I'm happy I brought myself a lawyer," I muttered to myself in a sarcastic undertone.

"Can't go like that," Eaglefeather said, shaking his head and frowning as if he had heard my remark.

"I brought clothes for him," Cleareye replied.

"Can't wear those WalMart shoes," Eaglefeather said. "Elk Mountain is holy ground."

"I brought ceremonial shoes for him to wear," Cleareye replied.

"Okay," Eaglefeather said. Eaglefeather and Cleareye hugged each other, and I realized there was great affection between these two men. Eaglefeather put his arms around Cleareye's shoulders, and the two of them walked toward the dining room, leaving me in the living room, so that I could not hear what they were saying. They broke into raucous laughter, and they turned their faces toward me. When Eaglefeather laughed, his face looked entirely different, almost childlike. Soon the two men turned around and walked toward me. Eaglefeather's face became serious.

Turning to Cleareye once again, Eaglefeather said, "Watch yourself on the mountain. You are like an older brother to me."

In an almost military fashion, Cleareye turned around and started barking instructions to Chris and Rachel. He then turned to me and said, "You are going to have to change into the ceremonial clothes that I give you. We will leave four hours before sunset, so we will get to our destination around sunset. It's a tough trail, so I hope you are in shape!"

Cleareye's admonition about being in shape kept on echoing through my mind as we climbed the seemingly impossible wall face of Elk Mountain. I felt like a tiny ant against the enormity of the mountain. And the mountain was just a tiny speck in the vastness of the surrounding wilderness, and I. . .

"Keep your mind on the task at hand!" Cleareye shouted back to me. "One false step and you'll end up down there!" He pointed to a dry river bed several thousand feet below, which I was trying not to acknowledge.

We were not going to the top of the mountain, but to a small plateau with a magnificent view of distant mountains and a desert valley. Cleareye had given me an entirely new wardrobe from head to toe. The ceremonial clothes were colorful, a mixture of Mexican and Native American. Cleareye handed me a beautiful wool blanket. "Wrap this around yourself!" he barked. More and more I felt like the butt of a bad joke, and occasionally that suspicion would melt into a vague fear.

We reached the holy ground, and Cleareye began chanting a prayer as he motioned to Chris and Rachel. They apparently knew exactly what he wanted. They used brightly colored pebbles to create a circle on the ground, and they motioned me to sit in the middle of the circle. As I entered the circle, Cleareye gave me a ceremonial mask. He smiled as he handed it to me. The face on the mask seemed familiar. Suddenly, a chill ran down my spine as I realized that it looked a lot like me. I again wondered whether this was some kind of elaborate joke, the nature of which would soon be revealed with much laughing and backslapping all around. I had this suspicion right up until the point when I actually traveled into the void.

"Am I really going to visit the future?" I asked, sounding like a little boy who can't believe that his parents are actually taking him to Disneyland.

Cleareye asked for silence and told me to be quiet and to stare out into the vast spaces that lay before us. Cleareye, Rachel, and Chris were all standing behind me, and I would not be permitted to see them again until I had experienced the initiation into seeing. Cleareye, Rachel, and Chris were attired much as I was, but before they moved behind me, I saw Cleareye donning his own ceremonial mask, which looked like an angry bird, probably an eagle or a hawk. The bird had enormous eyes and a grotesque beak. I saw that Cleareye had assembled various ceremonial objects around him, including an eagle's feather and a ram's horn, which he blew once with soul-piercing ferocity.

My respect for Cleareye and knowledge of his integrity gave me renewed strength whenever I found my confidence ebbing. He told me to look ahead at the beauty before me and to thank God, the Great Spirit, for the creation.

The sun had just disappeared behind the horizon, and the sky was filled with a wonderful orange light. Clouds above the horizon were dark black tinged with crimson red. The moon was more full than it had been the night before, its coppery gold sliver of a face partly obscured by the clouds. The valley before us was illuminated with the golden, orange light, and the rock formations and mountains all around us were bathed in golden tranquillity. I felt an intense sense of gratitude that merged with the indescribable beauty that was all around.

Cleareye began to chant. Occasionally, Rachel would translate some of the prayers quietly, so as not to disturb Cleareye. "He is thanking the Great Spirit for creating Man and for bestowing Man with vision," she explained softly.

Suddenly an eagle, huge and terrifying, swept by our ledge. I screamed, but no one else reacted in the least. Cleareye reacted to my scream by asking me what I had seen. I told him an eagle. He said, "That is the best possible sign. I am now going to ask the Great Spirit to grant you the gift of vision, the ability to see. You must stand up and stare straight ahead into the great space in front of you. Concentrate on your goal, which is to see the future of computing."

Cleareye began a chant that was much more animated than any of the previous ones. I felt his ceremonial eagle feather touching the ridge above my eyes, and then he started to chant a resonant word in his native language. Rachel translated in a soft undertone: "See! See! See!"

Suddenly, the space in front of me started to melt into a vision of light, and a tremendous roaring sound bombarded not so much my ears as my very sense of hearing. Then I entered a void, a space of great peace. The next thing I knew, I felt someone shaking my hand, and I heard the voice of Cleareye.

"Welcome to my Experimental Landscapes Laboratory," Cleareye said, as his face emerged from the whiteness. "It's 2011, and I knew you were coming. I warned my graduate students that this would be the day that you would visit us. If 2011 seems remote, the typical college students of the 1990s will be in their thirties and forties by now. So what I am showing you today is really quite relevant to their careers."

I looked around the laboratory. It was in the same building as the laboratory I had visited when I first met Cleareye. Cleareye laughed heartily as he informed me that the elevator still had not been fixed. The computer equipment, however, was new and unfamiliar. Some students—I assume they were students—were standing in glass booths wearing what looked like motorcycle helmets. The booths were labeled "virtual reality enclosures," or VREs. The computer screens in the laboratory were very large and had very high resolution, almost like reality itself. Most of the screens had a slight wrap-around effect. Two computer screens were shaped like light-filled cubes, and Cleareye explained that these were experimental holographic screens from Silicon Graphics. Cleareye brought me over to see one of the cubes. "Each cube costs about one million of our dollars, which is about nine hundred thousand of your dollars. The Federal Reserve's GREENSPAN has kept a lid on inflation."

"Greenspan? You mean, Alan Greenspan?" I asked.

"No, I mean GREENSPAN, the Fed's inflation-fighting computer program. As soon as it detects any sign of true robust health in the economy, it recommends a boost in interest rates. The Fed always goes along with what GREENSPAN recommends, because GREENSPAN knows more about monetary policy than any single human being."

Cleareye then escorted me to a classroom with a gigantic television screen. "Because time is short, I have prepared a lecture for you about computing in 2011. After the lecture, I can give you a hands-on experience with some of the technology, if time permits. However, whatever you do must be limited in its impact to our laboratory, because we are very concerned about a time-travel accident where you create an irreconcilable time-space paradox over the global network. I don't have time to explain to you what that is, but it is not good. You'll know you created one if you start to see two of everything."

I didn't have time to absorb what Cleareye was telling me about the dangers of time travel. He changed the topic and started to tell me about the lecture that he had prepared. "The lecturer is a computer-generated image of a famous television personality of your time, since we thought that would make you feel more comfortable. The image, the voice, are all computer generated, but the lecture is mine. What you are going to see is not unlike an actual lecture that I give to my students, except for the specific references to your time—the 1990s. So sit back, absorb, but remember: When the wind, which is the voice of the Spirit, comes for you, you will have to return."

We sat next to each other in the darkened lecture hall, and the video began. I realized that Cleareye really was trying to steer me away from any actual use of the new computer systems. Maybe there was some kind of danger involved in time travel that I did not understand.

LECTURE 1: THE GLOBAL LANDSCAPE

Hello, I am Dan Rather, Virtual, of CBS News, and welcome to this presentation of Technology 2011. Time is brief, so I will give you the basic concepts, although we will also use actual computer demonstrations to illustrate those concepts. Computing in 2011 is highly visual. Ideas generated during the 1990s have had a tremendous impact, but some things have evolved in unexpected ways.

The changes in hardware have been dramatic. We have new memory devices based upon light-wave physics that are enormously fast and also high capacity. We have very high bandwidth communications channels. Holographic memories are used for huge databases with high security needs. The holography implies that if a part of the database is destroyed, then the entire database can be reconstructed from any fragment. This is an age of massive parallelism of processors and massive distribution of processes. There are new screen technologies that allow for lifelike images, and there are now experimental holographic screens for truly three-dimensional images. There is much more reliance on natural language processing. Many computer users today wear headsets with microphones so as not to disturb their co-workers. The headsets allow for a natural language dialogue between the user and the computer. Mice, track balls, and related pointing devices are still used. Keyboards are ergonomically designed. They are so comfortable that it's hard to pull people away from them. The technology has advanced so far that some people just like to rest their hands on the new keyboards as a means of attaining a peaceful, meditative state. The user interface contains many modalities and technologies, including very high definition television—what we call VTV or veritable television—film, music, natural language, and so forth.

The most exciting development, in our opinion, is the Global Landscape Initiative, or GLI. The GLI is an attempt to create a true infosphere, paralleling the biosphere. The infosphere is a shell of densely connected processors all over the globe that mediate the flow of information in many spheres of human activity. This infosphere is also called the Global Landscape, or GL. The ideas for the GL arose during the 1990s but owe a special debt to the work of Wiederhold, Wegner, and Ceri, who described the megaprogramming concept.

The Global Landscape was developed in part as a reaction to the poor quality of information on the World Wide Web in the 1990s and the poor security over the Internet. Government, business, and cultural leaders wanted a more sophisticated network that would be based upon readily available, high-quality information.

Now, I want to define terms, and as I do so, visual images will appear on the screen as illustrations of those terms. These images will include animations and actual videos of computer systems that are currently in use.

Global Landscape. This is the infosphere I mentioned earlier. It is the complete electronic image of all government, business, technical, entertainment, artistic, and educational activities that need to be reflected in the infosphere. The Global Landscape is planned, deliberate, and self-governing. It stores all relevant information about the status of enterprises that are engaged in business, scientific, educational, and cultural activities.

Realm. This refers to a specific realm of human activity that needs to be reflected in the infosphere. The realms include the business realm, the educational realm, the artistic realm. The most important function of a realm is to organize the domains that constitute that realm and to promote communications between those domains.

Domain. A domain is a specific kind of activity within a realm. For example, the business realm includes the banking, manufacturing, and health care domains.

Enterprise. An enterprise is an actual entity in a given domain. For example, enterprises in the banking domain include First National Bank of Silicon Valley and World Chase Bank of Singapore.

Cooperatives. Cooperatives are international governing boards that regulate hardware and software standards in the Global Landscape, in the various realms, and in the domains. The most important cooperatives are the Global Landscape Cooperative, which formulates policies and standards for the entire landscape, and the domain cooperatives, which formulate policies and standards for each individual domain. The main purpose of the realm cooperatives is to facilitate cooperation among domain cooperatives.

Let me now explain how the various cooperatives function to provide standards and to govern activities in the Global Landscape.

Global Landscape Cooperative. The Global Landscape Cooperative (GLC) creates the most general policies for the Global Landscape. These include specification language standards, data representation standards, data communications standards, and ethics policies. It establishes judicial bodies that might be needed to resolve disputes between realms and/or domains.

The members of the GLC Executive Council are among the most influential men and women in the world. They have the power, for example, to expel a nation from the Global Landscape if that nation violates basic human rights or if that nation does not provide equal opportunities to all of its citizens. While this policy is not perfectly enforced, we are proud to tell you people of the 1990s that there are no dictatorships anywhere in the world today, in part because of the power of the GLC.

Domain cooperatives. The domain cooperatives have enormous power and are at the heart of the Global Landscape, how it works, and how it relates to earlier ideas in computing. Each domain cooperative has one fundamental purpose: to create the megamodule for its domain. A megamodule has two aspects: an inner aspect and an outer aspect. The outer aspect is a collection of services provided by the megamodule. This is the public interface of the megamodule. The services provided in this interface can be viewed as constituting a domain-specific programming language. Each domain has its own megamodule with its own domain-specific programming language. We call the domain-specific programming language a common domain language, or CDL. The inner aspect of a megamodule has to do with the formal semantics of the CDL. The semantics is described in terms of a domain-specific specification language. Specification languages are called metamegalanguages or MMLs.

A megamodule is formulated by the domain cooperative. It must then be approved by the community that the cooperative serves. This is the megamodule standardization process. A megamodule standard is a formal description of the services provided by a megamodule as well as a set of formal specifications for those services. The formal specifications give the semantics for those services.

The megamodule standards are developed iteratively. The domain cooperative publishes a report; the member enterprises and other interested parties provide feedback. Eventually, the domain cooperative publishes a formal specification of the megamodule for its domain. This is the official megamodule standard for a given domain, and it corresponds to the language standards of your time. Once a standard has been agreed upon, all software manufacturers that have the requisite level of maturity are invited to become vendors of the new megamodule standard. Each megamodule implementation must pass a rigorous set of tests specified by the domain cooperative before it can be certified as being in compliance with the standard.

For example, at present there are twelve vendors of banking megamodules, and banks can be sure that all of these megamodule implementations are compliant with the standard established for the banking domain. This means that the software is certified to function correctly for important banking processes, such as creating accounts or transferring funds.

As time goes on, the domain cooperative monitors the existing megamodule standard in order to ensure that it is up to date. We anticipate that every ten years or so a new standard will have to be developed using the same iterative process that was used to develop the original standard. That would involve getting feedback from member enterprises and interested parties, agreeing on a new standard, and then allowing vendors to implement megamodules based upon the new standard.

The megamodule provides a set of tools, or services, for application development within a given domain. For example, in the banking domain these tools are reliable and efficient realizations of banking processes. An application is essentially a creative combination of these standard processes.

It's time for some new and expanded definitions:

Common Domain Language (CDL). This refers to the set of services provided by a megamodule, or more specifically, the public part of a megamodule that constitutes a language of service calls. Applications are created by threading together the service calls provided by the CDL. The CDL code describes what needs to get done, but it makes no commitment to how it will get done nor to the detailed manner in which the service call will manifest at the user interface.

Megalanguages. The lower-level languages, including object-oriented languages, that are used to implement megamodules. Thus, CDL service calls are ultimately implemented using megalanguage code. Among the concepts that we have discussed or shall discuss in this lecture, megalanguages most closely resemble the programming languages of the 1990s.

Metamegalanguages (MMLs). The languages that are used to specify megamodules and megaprograms. We shall discuss megaprograms briefly. An MML is a formal specification language. Today, these languages are based upon the formal specification language MML-I that was developed at the Software Engineering Institute at Bill Gates University in Pittsburgh.

The Software Engineering Institute has guided the effort to adopt MML-I so that it can be used in specific domains. MML-I is not domain-specific but is extensible to a domain-specific language that incorporates facts and knowledge relating to a specific domain. For example, the banking megamodule is specified using BANK/MML version 1.0, which is a banking domain-specific extension to MML-I. In fact, a given banking domain megamodule service can be specified either in MML-I or in BANK/MML. However, the MML-I specification is extremely difficult to understand, while the BANK/MML specification can be understood even by bankers. This is important because it allows bankers to provide feedback during the megamodule standardization process. One can view a BANK/MML specification as a human-oriented version of an underlying MML-I specification.

Megaprogram. What a megamodule is for a domain, a megaprogram is for a set of domains. Megaprograms are sponsored by realm cooperatives or by the Global Landscape Cooperative in order to promote applications development across domain and even realm boundaries. Thus, a megaprogram is a fundamental toolkit that can be used to create applications that span two or more domains. The terms *megamodule* and *megaprogram* are being used in almost the same manner as they were used twenty years ago by Wiederhold, Wegner, and Ceri. A major difference, however, is that the Global Landscape provides a high degree of standardization across all domains and also provides a competitive framework for the implementation of megamodules and megaprograms.

When a megaprogram is required involving three domains in the same realm, say X, Y, and Z, then the realm cooperative creates a new entity, called a megaprogramming board, that is in charge of creating the new megaprogram standard. The megaprogramming board creates a specification for the megaprogram using the basic standardization process that was used for megamodules. Once the standard is set, the megaprogramming board can then invite vendors at the requisite level of maturity to implement megaprograms based upon the standard. The megaprogram implementations must all satisfy the standard, and they must all pass a suite of tests in order to be certified as being compliant with the standard. The megaprogram interface provides a set of services that can be used by applications developers to create applications that span the domains X, Y, and Z. The megaprogram standard will determine to what extent the individual megamodule services (for the domains X, Y, and Z) will be visible in the new megaprogram interface.

Now that we have described the basic concepts, let's describe what computer scientists are doing in the Global Landscape in the year 2011. But first, let me ask you, Mr. Reporter, if you have any questions.

[Dan Rather seemed to be staring down at me. Cleareye, who apparently had been catching up on his shut-eye, bolted awake. "C'mon! Ask him a question!"

"But, it's a recording!" I replied.

"Nothing is simply a recording any longer. Everything is of an interactive nature. Even toilet seats are interactive these days! Ask something!" Cleareye looked at me with those pleading eyes of his.

"Mr. Rather," I began. "What is the sound of one hand clapping?"

"Damn you!" Cleareye shouted. "That's the sort of question that can lead to an irreconcilable space-time paradox!"

Cleareye pushed some buttons on a remote control device and Dan Rather seemed to be speeding ahead at an incredible rate of speed. Soon the lecture resumed.]

The Global Landscape provides many opportunities for computer scientists of every variety. The Global Landscape is a sophisticated distributed computing system, and the running and maintenance of this system is an enormous task. Software engineers, knowledge engineers, operating system specialists, and applications developers all have lots to do. Theoretical computer science has become much more important because of the rise of the specification language MML-I as a tool for specifying megamodules and megaprograms. Working with MML-I requires good mathematical skills but also knowledge of the domain, for example, knowledge of banking or health care. A significant effort is going into the development of domain-specific specification languages, such as the already successful BANK/MML. The opportunities for computer scientists are exploding exponentially, or so it seems.

There are three fundamental kinds of programmers in 2011: systems programmers, megalanguage programmers, and applications developers. This does not include the domain experts who work with MML-I and its derivative languages (such as BANK/MML).

Application developers are not applications programmers, as you might be familiar with from the 1990s. Application developers in 2011 do little or no programming at all, and whatever programming they do is in terms of extremely high level languages called UIDLs, or user interface design languages, that help them to build the user interfaces that end users eventually work with. UIDLs provide hooks into CDLs that allow megamodule services to be tied into user interface features in specific ways. For example, UIDL code will determine whether a given CDL service, such as creating a new account at a bank, will be implemented using natural language commands or mouse-driven commands. UIDLs will allow videos and sounds to be hooked into fundamental banking processes, for example.

Systems programmers are responsible for running and maintaining the Global Landscape.

Megalanguage programmers implement megamodules and megaprograms. They work for the major megamodule and megaprogram vendors, and there are thousands of these because there are so many domains. Megalanguage programmers are something like the programmers of your day and age.

The COBOL programmer is gone. The C programmer is gone, except for some hobbyists who still love that language. The same applies to C++. The Global Landscape Cooperative has mandated that all network programming and maintenance be done in the language U. U stands for Ultimate.

U is what we call a ternary language. Ternary languages represent a new language paradigm that pairs a declarative language with two nondeclarative languages. Every task is implemented as a triplet of programs, one in each of the three languages that constitute a ternary language. Most experts believe that some ternary language, not necessarily U, will become the dominant megaprogramming language in the 2010s. Ternary languages are replacing the object-oriented languages of your time.

In a ternary language, such as U, the programmer writes three sets of programs, one in each of the languages that together constitute the U language. Each program has a specialized purpose. One program, written in a declarative language, is responsible for checking a database of assertions that expresses constraints on the system. A second program is responsible for restoring the system to a state of compliance if the system is going off track. The third program is the normal program that executes when the system is in a state of compliance. This is an overly simplified view of ternary programming, which is based upon checking to make sure the system is satisfying all constraints, correcting to restore compliance with those constraints, and then running normally until a constraint is violated. In fact, if the system is not in a state of compliance, the restore-compliance module has the power to modify the manner in which the normal algorithm will run in order to help get the system back into compliance. This also means that the restore compliance and normal execution modules can cooperate with one another and can run concurrently. Ternary programs run in a distributed manner, across the entire network and also locally. This is possible because of the high speed of computers in the year 2011. This synergy between the three language modules provides an extremely dynamic, self-correcting mechanism.

I hope, Mr. Reporter, that you have learned a lot from your visit to 2011. Professor Cleareye has prepared another video presentation for you.

When the lecture ended, I looked at Cleareye in amazement.

Cleareye looked a little worried. "I hope this isn't boring you, but the wind could come for you at any moment. I have another video for you. Don't forget that the person you see on the screen is a computer-generated animation. The voice, which is of absolute fidelity, is also computer-generated. Except for a few references to your own time that I have inserted, this is a lecture I give to visiting high school students who are considering SVU for their undergraduate studies," Cleareye explained.

LECTURE 2: SLAVES, SERVANTS, AND COPS

Hello, I am Whoopi Goldberg, Virtual. The law requires that I identify myself as Virtual because I am not the real Whoopi Goldberg, but a computer-generated image of the popular actress. Fortunately, most people can forget the distinction between the real and the virtual without much difficulty.

I am going to tell you more about the Global Landscape, the infosphere. The infosphere has created numerous jobs, and Earth is now enjoying unprecedented prosperity. The infosphere has meant greatly reduced air pollution as automobile usage, at least in the United States, is down almost thirty-five percent. The infosphere has meant fewer trees being cut for paper as the infosphere has become a reliable repository for information and knowledge on an unprecedented scale.

In my recent film, *Sister Act XI,* you saw—oops, I guess you didn't, but you will see—how I used the Global Landscape to track down the rare holy relic that we needed to cure Sister Martha of her fear of classical music (symphonophobia). *Sister Act XI* was one of the first films to show slaves and servants, the very lifeblood of the infosphere.

Here are some definitions:

Property. Each user has property on the GL, the Global Landscape. A user's property consists of all the infosphere resources that belong exclusively to that user. It also includes any property that the user shares with other users.

Slave. A slave is an autonomous, intelligent agent that belongs to a specific user. A slave performs errands outside the user's property, although some errands can be performed on the user's property. A user can create as many slaves as needed. A slave can either be volatile, in which case it is deleted once it fulfills its purpose, or persistent, in which case it can perform the same task over and over again, learning from past experience and improving its behavior. A slave is created when the user wants to search part or all of the Global Landscape for information. A slave can also be used to request that some process be initiated on another property. It is possible for a slave to take months or even years to complete its task. For example, a scientist doing a longitudinal study can create a slave to collect experimental data automatically over a period of ten or twenty years.

Servant. A servant is an autonomous, intelligent agent that belongs to a specific user and is restricted to that user's property. Thus, a servant is just a slave that is confined to its owner's property. A servant can be created, for example, if the owner wants to search through his own databases, without going "outside" to scour the Global Landscape for data.

Guard. A guard is an autonomous, intelligent agent that meets a slave at the front door, as it were, and either rejects the slave's request or passes on the request to a servant. When a slave seeks a service provided at another property, the interaction goes like this:

1. The slave visits the property and gives a request to the guard.
2. The guard checks the slave's credentials and checks the reasonableness of the request.
3. Either the guard rejects the credentials and/or the request, in which case interaction is over, or the guard passes the request to a servant for processing.
4. The servant processes the request and returns the results (not necessarily a success) to the guard.
5. The guard communicates the results back to the slave

Cop. A cop is an autonomous, intelligent agent that is used to help enforce security over the Global Landscape. One purpose of a cop is to clean up after an accident. For example, a slave is permitted to spawn copies of itself in order to do its work. There are good software constraints to prevent this process from getting out of control, but if it does, cops are allowed to go into the network, seek out the runaway slaves, and delete them. Cops are also used to track down slaves that might be doing malicious things, like attempting to fool a guard into processing an illegal request. If a slave refuses to answer all questions that are asked of it by a cop, the slave is detained until its owner can produce an adequate explanation for its behavior. Slaves under detention can be deleted under certain circumstances.

Cops are permitted to enter any property if a warrant has been issued by the appropriate legal authorities. In other words, in terms of searches, a cop has the same right as a police officer in the civilian world.

Note that a slave cannot enter a property that is not its own. It can only interact with a guard at that property. A property can have multiple guards, allowing for concurrent access. A slave has specific credentials or permissions that a guard checks.

The world has undergone tremendous changes since the 1990s. There is more peace and harmony in the world, and the GL has contributed to that. The GL has contributed to human culture and learning. Here are some students at Silicon Valley High School. They are going to demonstrate how slaves work. These are not virtual kids. These are real kids. Believe me!

WHOOPI: Hello, kids!

CLASS: Hi, Whoopi!

WHOOPI: Which one of you geniuses is going to show me how you did that research for your Civil War term papers?

WARREN: I will, Whoopi. All I have to do is say, "New slave!"

WHOOPI: Note that a slave image appeared on screen. It looks like a genie from *A Thousand and One Nights!* The appearance of a slave can be customized to suit the user's level of cognitive development.

WARREN: Slave, I need maps and pictures relating to the Battle of Gettysburg.

WHOOPI: I don't know if you heard that, but the slave said, "Yes, young master."

WARREN: It only takes a few seconds.

WHOOPI: Why don't you time it for us, Warren? The slaves created by this scholastic system have specific permissions. So this slave can go to libraries within the state of California, but it cannot get information from libraries outside of California.

WARREN: Look, Whoopi!

WHOOPI: An entire stack of maps and pictures. Use the mouse to look at the first one. A wonderful map of the battle! You can print that out if you need to. Now, Warren, remember what else I asked you to try?

WARREN: Okay. Slave, try again, but this time search all public libraries in Alaska.

WHOOPI: This slave does not have the credentials to get information from those libraries. Alaska would want California schools to pay a fee for a service like that. He's back! What a forlorn-looking slave. Click on his mouth and see if he has something to say.

SLAVE: Sorry, young master. The guard did not accept my credentials.

WHOOPI: Now, let's try that other experiment I told you about, Warren.

WARREN: Slave, I want you to increase my mother's salary by $10,000 per year at First National Bank of Silicon Valley.

SLAVE: What is your mother's name?

WARREN: Thelma Drake. Look, Whoopi! Look!

WHOOPI: A cop! He looks angry. Click on his mouth and see what he is angry about.

COP: You have attempted an illegal activity on the Global Landscape at the First National Bank of Silicon Valley, USA. You have no prior warnings, but this will be your one and only warning. Any further attempts to violate the security of another property will be dealt with firmly.

WARREN: Does this mean I have a criminal record?

WHOOPI: Probably, Warren, but at least you got to be on television with Whoopi Goldberg!

The Global Landscape involves a degree of parallelism and concurrency that would be hard to imagine in your day. The key is the use of autonomous agents as intermediaries between the processes. Synchronization is necessary, but we do not have time to deal with that in detail. When a slave spawns another slave, the spawned slave and its descendants must obey the orders of the original slave. This is one way to maintain law and order and to achieve synchronization. When a cop spawns another cop, the younger cop and all of its descendants are beholden to obey the oldest ancestor cop.

When the lecture ended, I poked Cleareye's shoulder.

"Is it over?" he asked.

"Yes," I replied.

"Could you wait here while I relieve myself?" Cleareye asked.

Wait here? He must be kidding! Waste my precious moments in the year 2011? I ran into the lab. I wanted to get my hands on a computer. A computer was left abandoned it seemed, so I sat down in front of it, impressed with the size of the screen and the comfort of the workstation. I placed my hands on the ergonomic keyboard, and I immediately felt a sensation of healing warmth moving up from my hands through the rest of my body. A feeling of peace came over me and I thought, "If I could figure out how this ergonomic keyboard works, I could make a fortune!"

The interface was similar to what I used back in the 1990s, so I opened a document using the mouse and saw that I was in a word processor that was also somewhat familiar. So I decided to do a global replace as an experiment, and I asked the computer to change all occurrences of "Landscape" to "Widget." I did this verbally to see if the computer would understand what I said. It did. What struck me about the system is that when I made the change, it was as if my innards were changed, too. By innards, I mean my guts.

Cleareye returned. He was really angry: "You've made a terrible mistake! You made a global replace over the entire Global Widget!"

In the seconds following my global replace operation, I noticed subtle changes occurring in the environment. I could feel a knot of fear growing in my stomach. The students in the lab seemed even more concerned. Having been warned of a visitor from the past, they apparently knew that a global replace could have devastating effects. In retrospect, I wish someone had warned me about that.

I heard someone running down the hall. He was screaming, but the only words I could make out were, "*irreconcilable space-time paradox . . .*"

Then I experienced something that I shall never forget. It must have been this same man, the one running down the hall. He entered the lab where I had been working, his eyes bulging and his face contorted with fear. He saw me and ran toward me, screaming about the irreconcilable space-time paradox. I thought he was going to run into me, but just before he reached me, he literally split in two. He became two copies of himself. One copy was evidently the man as he saw himself, his ego, and the other was the part of himself that he had rejected, his shadow. One aspect of this unfortunate man passed to my left, and the other, I must say, less appealing aspect passed off to my right. And just as he passed me he let loose a blood-curdling scream that tore through me like a jagged-edged knife.

It was at that point that I heard terrible screams outside in the engineering school quad. I ran to a window and everything seemed colored by a strange light. Students and professors were running in random directions across the quad adjacent to the lab. I opened the window, and then I saw something that shook me to the core. There were two suns: one a bright yellow and the other a larger sun, red and menacing. Two aspects of the sun that had been one. The sky was a bluish orange, much darker than it had been, and the clouds looked as if they were soaked in blood. I noticed that more and more people, both students and professors, were splitting in two, just like the man in the lab, although I believe he was the first. At that point a cold wind blew into the lab.

Cleareye said, "I think the Global Widget is ruined forever, but that's not your problem. The wind has come for you. You must go back to Elk Mountain."

The wind continued to increase, until all I could hear was its roar. The bizarre scene in front of me melted into a brilliant radiance filled with love and compassion. The next thing I knew I was standing on Elk Mountain, staring into a starlit space.

"What did you see? What did you see?" Cleareye asked excitedly.

"You haven't been there?" I exclaimed.

"No, that's not what I asked to see. What you saw was for you, and what I saw was for me," he replied.

"What did you ask to see when you were initiated?" I asked.

"The last game of the 1955 World Series. The Dodgers versus the Yankees," he replied, giving me a strange look, as if to say "Couldn't you figure that out for yourself?"

Suddenly Cleareye, Chris, and Rachel were holding sleeping bags in front of them, as if Cleareye had given some signal that I had missed. "Time to get some sleep. We'll return to town in the morning. Eaglefeather will have breakfast ready for us."

"Don't I get a sleeping bag?" I asked, quite certain that one would be provided. I suppose I was really asking "Where is *my* sleeping bag?"

It was at this rather awkward moment that Cleareye decided to let me in on one of his people's most ancient customs. "The one who has been taught to see does not get a sleeping bag. That is our tradition."

"It's cold!" I shouted.

"Believe me, when you've seen your first rattler, you won't be worrying about the cold," Cleareye said in a soothing voice, as if trying to comfort me by explaining that the situation was, in fact, much worse than I had imagined. Rachel and Chris turned away. Their faces were strangely somber.

"What are you talking about?" I countered.

"Look, there are rattlers up here. Part of the initiation is to see if the initiate is worthy of surviving the night. It's up to the Great Spirit." Cleareye spoke impatiently, as if I should have known that the gift of seeing would not come cheap.

I still believe that my reaction was a rational one, given the situation. Anger arose in me like a mighty volcano.

"If you can sleep without moving, I think you will be okay. The danger comes when you turn over and hit one. So try not to move too much when you sleep. There's a good stone to lay your head on over there, but check under the stone first." Cleareye sounded less hurried, but he did not accept any further discussion. "I am going to sleep."

The three of them retired to their sleeping bags, leaving me alone in that great, cold, star-punctuated expanse of silence. Anger rose in me in great waves. Suddenly this intense anger was focused at Cleareye, and my body started to shake with rage. My heart was pounding in my chest, and I could hear the rushing of blood in my ears. How dare he take me up to this mountain, exposing me to danger like this? How dare he take me on this ridiculous journey, just to have this miserable end? I think I'll be all right if I just stay awake, but how dare he . . . !

This went on for several hours, intense anger coming in great waves, with brief intervals of only moderate anger, followed by an angry wave of even greater intensity. I then started to think how I could use my position as a reporter to destroy Cleareye. I would investigate his lab and find some irregularity there and ruin his whole reputation as a scientist. The plan, vague at first, became more and more vivid. I could see the outlines of the plan becoming more and more real, more and more lifelike. I could imagine the precise articles I would write to bring him to his knees for putting me into a situ . . .

I felt a stick poking me in the middle of my back. I was sitting on the stone that was supposed to serve as my pillow. About three hours had passed since the others had gone to sleep. My thighs and knees ached.

"Get up!" Cleareye said.

I was still shaking with anger, and if I had thought about it at all, I would not have gotten up, but I did, partly out of the desire to have it out with Cleareye.

"You made a promise not to abuse the creative power that comes with seeing," Cleareye said. "And here it is, hours after you received a great gift, and you are filled with anger toward me. I am the one that the Great Spirit used to give you this great gift, and now you have turned that gift against me."

I was speechless.

"The fire of creativity is a great gift, but you must use it wisely. This gift is the future, but that future can be heaven or hell. The very same creative process is involved in creating new technologies, writing novels, composing symphonies, and creating anger toward other people. Be forewarned: Anger is a form of creativity in which your own creativity turns against you and destroys you. It is the imagination, or fire of creativity, which fuels anger. You have failed the rattlesnake test." He looked into my face like a doctor trying to diagnose a patient with a deadly illness.

Suddenly, out of the blue, I started to cry. I realized the burden of the creative fire and the damage that would come if I misused it. I begged Cleareye to forgive me. I was still standing, but my shoulders were bent forward.

Cleareye, Rachel, and Chris formed a circle around me and embraced me, and I could feel their hands rubbing against my back and chest. It was Rachel who spoke first. "Frank, don't cry. Don't feel bad. We all failed the rattlesnake test, we all did just what you did, even Cleareye."

"But not George Eaglefeather," Cleareye interjected. "When my father initiated George and told George about the rattlesnakes, after my father had gone to sleep, George went over to my father to stand guard over him all through the night. And when it became cold, he took his own wrap and covered my father with it. His only concern was to protect my father, his teacher, from the snakes and from the cold. That is why George is the holy man in our tribe and not me.

"When my father taught me how to see and told me about the snakes, I was so angry. I was going to tell my mother that I had seen him with another woman. I was going to push him off the wall face. I was going to slash the tires on his truck. I was so angry that he would expose me to so much danger, and I was just a boy, so I think my reaction would have been much worse as a man." Cleareye was in front of me. He looked compassionately into my eyes.

"You are worthy of the Spirit's gift," he insisted.

"I'm embarrassed to say what I was thinking the night of my initiation," said Chris. "My plan was to ruin Cleareye's career by accusing him of stealing my research."

Cleareye then said, "When you fully understand this night, you will appreciate what has happened to you, and you will understand the love and the affection that I have for you. You will be thankful even for the difficult parts of this initiation. Now, get some sleep, Mr. Reporter. There's an extra sleeping bag over there. Stop worrying. Everything will be fine."

Late the next morning we had waffles and coffee at George Eaglefeather's house.

"Aren't these great waffles?" Cleareye asked, wolfing them down like a maniac.

"You're a wonderful cook, Mr. Eaglefeather," I said.

"Call me George," he replied.

"I'm a lucky woman," George's wife said, reaching over to kiss her husband.

But I had something else on my mind. "George, I have been in this region for several days now, and I spent one night on Elk Mountain, but I have not seen a single elk or anything like an elk anywhere near here. Where are the elk?"

George spun a piece of waffle around in the buttery maple syrup. He stared at me with his wonderful eyes as he chewed. Finally, he got around to my question. "As far as your question is concerned, Mr. Kafka, there has not been a single elk here in all of recorded history. There are elk in that direction and in that direction and in that direction, but not right here."

"Then why is it called Elk Mountain?" I asked.

"Because the white man named it that way," he replied.

"That's strange," I said.

"Not really," George replied. "You see, 'elk' is a word in our native language. Actually, it's a contraction of several words."

"And what does it mean?" I asked, wondering why he could not have said that right from the beginning.

"It's hard to translate but *roughly* it means 'rattlesnakes coming out of your ears.'" George Eaglefeather laughed so hard tears started to form in his eyes, and he could hardly catch his breath.

LETTERS TO THE SENTINEL-OBSERVER SUNDAY MAGAZINE

To the editor:

I am disappointed that the Sentinel-Observer Sunday Magazine *chose to publish Mr. Kafka's story about a visit to the future. On those rare occasions when your magazine has published fiction in the past, it was clearly labeled as such. Mr. Kafka's account, clearly fictitious, is presented as a true story, and I found this deeply disturbing. Please cancel my subscription to the* Sentinel-Observer.

—*Richard Epstein*
West Silicon Valley

Mr. Kafka does like to write fiction and is a frequent contributor to our acclaimed Literary Supplement. *However, he swears that the vision quest story is factual.*

Professor John Cleareye, a man of unimpeachable integrity, confirms that the vision quest did take place much as Mr. Kafka has written. Of course, Professor Cleareye was not privy to the private experience of the future that Mr. Kafka had. Professor Cleareye is of the opinion that there are many possible futures and that Mr. Kafka visited one of those.

—*Ed*

To the editor:

It seems to me that the Global Landscape is too highly structured to represent the future of computing. Computing technology is clearly headed in the direction of less and less order and more and more chaos. The Internet and the Web are evidence of this. How could something as organized and as structured as the Global Landscape possibly emerge from that?

I am very skeptical that Mr. Kafka visited the actual, historically accurate future that we are facing. Perhaps he had a dream induced by the tribal holy man. Or perhaps the whole thing is a hoax perpetrated by Mr. Kafka.
—*Amy Winchell*
 Silicon Junction

To the editor:

I enjoyed Frank Kafka's account of his vision quest. I doubt that his vision of the future was anything more than a private construction of something that he wanted to know. However, I see his story as something of a cautionary tale. Do we want an organization such as the Global Landscape Cooperative Executive Council that he described to wield so much power in the future? I am especially concerned that such a governing body may not be held accountable to the people of the United States by any democratic process. Information is power, so I am very concerned about possible abuses of power by an agency such as this, which might not respect the will of the people in a free and sovereign nation.
—*Wendy Steinfeld*
 East Silicon Valley

To the editors:

I have two questions about the future that Mr. Kafka experienced. If children can have electronic slaves that do their homework for them, will those children develop healthy levels of intelligence, persistence, and initiative? Also, if the dominant metaphor for human-computer interaction is one of master and slave, won't this perhaps affect the way people relate to one another? That is, won't people start to view other people as slaves to be bossed around? My response to Mr. Kafka's vision of the future then is, "Hell no, I won't go!"
—*Ted Rukansi*
 Silicon Heights

Do you have any choice? —Ed

PART TWO

BROADCAST MEDIA

Factual coverage of the killer robot by radio and television stations. One radio talk show, three televised public affairs programs, and one televised university lecture on computer ethics are included here.

VARIETIES OF TEAMWORK
EXPERIENCE

FRESH TALK: I am Terry Conway in Silicon Valley and this is "Fresh Talk."
Today's guest is Hiram Milton, professor of computer science at Silicon Valley University. Professor Milton is famous for his study of software developers at work. His unique "Milton diagrams" show that teams come in many shapes and colors. Recently, Professor Milton published a paper concerning the software development team that wrote the software for the now infamous "killer robot." Dr. Milton received his Ph.D. in Computer Science from the University of Michigan.

Later, Dr. Harry Yoder of Silicon Valley University will join us. He is an expert on computer ethics and the social impact of computers.

Before I start our discussion of the killer robot, I would like to remind those of you who phoned in pledges last week during our fund drive to please mail in your checks as soon as possible. Needless to say, it's the actual money and not just your expression of good intentions that keeps this NAP radio station on the air.

Professor Milton, could you give us the context for your study of the killer robot software development team?

MILTON: I studied the killer robot software team before the Robbie CX30 robot came to be known as the killer robot. I studied the development team for a month. When I first got involved, team members were debating which programming language to use. Thus, I got to study the team before they got down to the business of writing code.

I went into Silicon Techchronics, along with two graduate students, armed with video cameras and other tools that would help us to record the interactions between the team members.

FRESH TALK: Is there something special about a software development team that makes it different from other kinds of teams?

MILTON: The only difference that I see is that technical knowledge of a very specific kind is required to work on a software development team.

FRESH TALK: Do you mean that bias and emotion play no role whatsoever?

MILTON: No. Bias and emotion often play a role, but the team exists for the purpose of solving a technical problem.

FRESH TALK: How did you get started studying teams and team dynamics?

MILTON: I think it all started with my having so few friends when I was a kid. I couldn't understand why I was being excluded from groups and sports

161

teams and such. If I ever got to play on a team, I was always the last one chosen. There seemed to be a dynamic behind groups that I did not understand.

When I got to college I started to study psychology, but then I switched to computer science. I fell in love with computer technology and went on to earn my doctorate. But my original interest in teams stayed with me.

As a professor of computer science, I came to realize that some of my students were poorly equipped to go out into the real world where team efforts are central. Most of our courses ask students to work alone. I started to assign team projects, and I began to look into the characteristics of teams and team dynamics.

FRESH TALK: You wrote in one of your papers, "Students do not understand the essential role that conflict plays in technical problem solving." What did you mean by that?

MILTON: When I was growing up, I saw all conflict as an imperfection. Conflict was something to be avoided. Perhaps this was because my parents, before their divorce, were almost always arguing and fighting about something. It was difficult for me, after seeing that kind of bitter fighting between my parents, to see that conflict could be beneficial. Perhaps I left psychology and went into computer science because I saw computing as a profession that did not involve interacting with others. Yet, no matter how strenuously I tried to avoid conflict, it always cropped up somewhere . . .

FRESH TALK: [Laughing] It crops up everywhere!

MILTON: It's an unavoidable part of life. Then I began to see that conflict is central in team processes and that the manner in which conflict is managed on a team will be an important determining factor as far as the success of that team is concerned. Some researchers at the University of Texas in San Antonio, led by Diane Waltz, helped me to see this.

There are many different types of teams, and part of the attention that my work has gotten comes from the fact that I have developed graphical notations for representing the static state of a team as well as the evolving situation on a team. My diagrams are like CAT scans for a team. I can show you one of my diagrams, and once you understand what the various symbols mean, you will be able to say, "Oh, that team is in trouble!" or "That team has gotten its act together."

FRESH TALK: Of course, you are talking about your "Milton diagrams."

MILTON: Yes. I called them "team interaction diagrams," but my colleagues renamed them "Milton diagrams."

FRESH TALK: What do *you* mean when you use the term *conflict*?

MILTON: By conflict I mean differences of opinion. People might have differing opinions about team goals or about technical issues that need to get resolved. How a team handles differences of opinion is critical to the success of a team.

FRESH TALK: Could you give us some examples as to how conflict might be handled?

MILTON: Team members need to see the issues as objectively as possible. When a team member identifies with a stated position, there is always the danger that an attack on that stated position will be viewed as a personal attack, even if the attack was not meant in that way. A good team uses conflict for learning. There is an energy inherent in conflict, and a good team uses that energy to promote the goals and objectives of the team. A poor team will allow conflict to deteriorate into personal attacks and bruised egos.

FRESH TALK: How can one avoid personal attacks and the fragmentation of a team?

MILTON: I always tell my students, "Keep your eyes on the prize." You have a task to accomplish. That task is the success of your team. In a democratic team in which there is no leader, someone might play the role of a conflict watchdog. When conflict moves away from its positive aspects, then the watchdog should intervene. One intervention might be, "We are discussing whether to use C or C++ as the programming language for this project, and the discussion is getting rather personal. We are moving away from the purely technical issues. How can we get back on track?"

All team members need to be aware of the positive role they can play in moving the team toward its goal of success!

FRESH TALK: You and Diane Waltz have emphasized the positive role that conflict can play on a team—especially for the dissemination of information and for learning. Isn't it the case that conflict sometimes arises because you are staring across the table at an implacable foe?

MILTON: We need to ask ourselves whether the other person is objectively an implacable foe or whether we ourselves are creating this perception of that other person. In our careers we will inevitably meet difficult people, and we will have to learn how to deal with them, but the most difficult person that I personally have ever had to deal with was me, myself.

FRESH TALK: What exactly is a "Milton diagram"?

MILTON: The purpose of a Milton diagram is to represent the state of a team or its evolution over time. I have two types of diagrams. One diagram is designed to show the ideological camps within a team and the interactions between the camps. The second type of diagram is intended to show speech acts and their impact on team cohesion. I call these type A and type B diagrams, respectively.

A type A Milton diagram shows the cognitive or ideological distances between members of a team and the interactions between them. Each team member is shown as a black dot. If two dots are close in the diagram, they represent team members who agree on most issues given in our survey instrument. If two dots are far apart, they represent team members who disagree on most issues. This required that we create a two-dimensional metric space out of the data that we collected. The dots show us where each team member is positioned in that metric space.

Speech acts or verbal exchanges are shown as arrows. An arrow originates at a dot and is directed toward the recipient of the comment or to a neutral area if there was no specific intended recipient. An arrow may be either green for a positive, friendly comment or red for a negative, hostile comment. A diagram with lots of red indicates a hostile environment. Lots of green indicates a friendly environment. Our researchers had to classify comments as being hostile or friendly. Neutral comments are shown using green arrows. We decided not to use a third color for neutral comments. We recorded all meetings on videotape, and we carefully counted speech acts and distances between people as measured by our survey instrument.

FRESH TALK: Not all of the arrows have the same thickness.

MILTON: The thickness of an arrow shows the number of speech acts emanating from that person in a particular direction during the observation period. The thicker an arrow emanating from a dot, the more that person spoke.

Terry, here is an example of a type A diagram. What can you say about this team?

FRESH TALK: The dots appear to be randomly scattered. Also, no arrows mean that there is complete silence.

MILTON: I left out the arrows for the first few diagrams so we could focus on the dots. The randomly scattered dots indicate that there are no cohesive ideological subgroups within the larger group. Now what about this diagram?

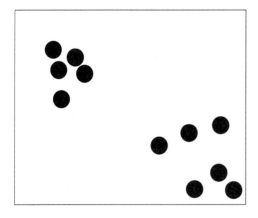

Figure 1. A type A Milton diagram showing a team that is divided up into two ideological camps. Conflict arrows are not shown.

FRESH TALK: The dots are in two distinct clusters, one in the upper left and the other in the bottom right. This team is divided into two distinct ideological camps.

MILTON: And this diagram?

FRESH TALK: All the dots are grouped together, adjacent to one another. This group is of one mind! Is this the ideal team? Complete and total agreement on everything?

MILTON: No, this kind of cohesion within a team can be bad. This could indicate a cultlike "group think." There needs to be some conflict, at least one team member who can provide needed feedback when the team is going off on the wrong track. In interpreting a Milton diagram, please bear in mind that our survey instruments are narrow in focus, so the members of this team may have disagreements in areas that were not captured by our questionnaire.

What about this diagram?

FRESH TALK: This is the same diagram as the previous one except that we now have lots of thick, red arrows. The arrows are crisscrossing across the boundary between the two camps. They are attacking one another. There's a war going on.

MILTON: This is an actual representation of the killer robot software development team when they were debating which programming language to use. The group on the top left is the C group and the group on the bottom right is the C++ group. You can see that this debate is heated and hostile. It's war.

Now let me show you a sequence of diagrams over five meetings of the killer robot group. What do you see?

FRESH TALK: There's no change. The dots are not moving. The red arrows are pretty much the same from diagram to diagram. Trench warfare.

MILTON: Here's another sequence of diagrams from the killer robot team. What do you see?

FRESH TALK: Some of the C++ dots are moving over to the C camp. There is only one dot left in the C++ group!

MILTON: That's Randy Samuels.

FRESH TALK: He's all alone—and a hostile attack is now focused against him.

MILTON: That attack was led by Fred Worthington, the son of Max Worthington. In the transcript of this meeting, Worthington is quoted as saying, "We wasted a whole week discussing C++ because of your being so pigheaded!" Worthington's comments are aimed at Randy Samuels. No one is defending Samuels. He is isolated and beaten. It makes you wonder how strong Samuels's commitment to the robot project could be after such an experience.

This dot is George Cuzzins, the project leader. He is in the C group, but he has little to say. Our tapes show that Cuzzins is very deferential toward Worthington and is very reluctant to oppose him on the language issue. Cuzzins is not playing any kind of leadership role here, either on the technical side or on the team dynamics side.

Now look at this sequence of diagrams from another team that we studied. What do you see on this diagram? There are no arrows.

FRESH TALK: We have two camps again, but there is one team member who seems to be neutral.

MILTON: That's the team leader.

FRESH TALK: Should the team leader always be neutral?

MILTON: No, but sometimes the team leader can gather information by assuming a neutral stance. This particular team leader was trying to use the conflict process as a learning and information-gathering tool so that she could then make an informed decision concerning the direction the team should take. This is just one example of how a good team might evolve.

Now look at a diagram of this same team with arrows added.

FRESH TALK: There are mostly green arrows going from one camp to the other, and the team leader is contributing his input to the discussion in a positive manner.

MILTON: The team leader is a she. Yes, she was managing the conflict between the opposing camps. She acted to prevent the discussion from becoming hostile or divisive. She is consciously managing and controlling the conflict, so that the entire team can learn from the clashing opinions.

FRESH TALK: It reminds me of a controlled chain reaction.

MILTON: I like that analogy. Now consider these diagrams from the same team.

FRESH TALK: In this diagram the leader is taking a position.

MILTON: Yes, she has decided to go along with one of the opposing groups, and then she brings both sides together in a consensus.

Because of her leadership style, she is able to preempt hostility among team members. She taught the team how to use differences of opinion as a learning tool. The team developed a positive attitude toward conflict. Differences of opinion were not confused with personal animosity.

FRESH TALK: Did you bring any of your type B diagrams with you?

MILTON: Yes. Type B diagrams illustrate the consequences of individual speech acts. I am not sure that people realize how destructive a simple speech act can be. These diagrams attempt to portray the destructiveness of harmful speech in a graphic manner.

This subject always reminds me of the Epistle of James in the Bible, in which James, the brother of Jesus, writes that the tongue can set fire to the whole wheel of creation. My diagrams show how the tongue does that.

FRESH TALK: How does the tongue set fire to the whole world?

MILTON: By creating animosity, hatred, and ill will. By shattering social groups into splintered fragments that end up being at war against one another.

A type B diagram shows speech acts, who participated in the speech act, what the speech act was about, and finally the impact of the speech act on the cohesion of the team.

FRESH TALK: What is a speech act exactly?

MILTON: A speech act is a discrete utterance or attempt to communicate a fact or an opinion. For example, later on we will discuss with Harry Yoder an incident in which Fred Worthington tells the software development team that George Cuzzins told him that Randy Samuels told George that Zelda Riddle-Davis told Randy that she is a lousy programmer. This ultimate speech act was like throwing a match into a pool of oil. It ignited bad feelings among many of the members of the team, and my diagrams show how this whole explosion took place. It is just as if Fred's tongue had set fire to the whole wheel of creation—or at least to part of it.

Fred's linguistic fire bomb, if you will, had a sequence of antecedent speech acts that I will represent using a sequence of my type B diagrams, and I will describe them for the listening audience.

First, Zelda Riddle-Davis confided in her friend Randy Samuels that she was a lousy programmer. The diagram shows an arrow from a dot labeled Zelda to a second dot labeled Randy. That is the speech act. Coming off of the speech act arrow is a crow's-foot arrow that indicates the content of the speech act. This is called the message content arrow. In this case, the message content arrow points to Zelda herself. I also have arrows that show emotional reactions to the speech act. An "anger arrow" from Randy to Zelda, for example, would indicate that Randy is angry with Zelda for her having shared this information with him. However, there are no anger arrows in this diagram. Randy is not angry at Zelda. Zelda is not angry at Randy. The anger comes later. The anger arrows are based on interviews we conduct with the relevant parties. In the case of this specific episode, we interviewed the relevant parties one week after the explosion occurred. During that interview Randy told us that he was not angry at Zelda for sharing her sensitive information with him at this particular point in time. Later on, as we shall see, after the whole episode blew up in everybody's face, Randy did become angry at Zelda.

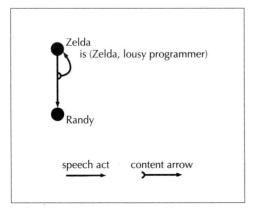

Figure 2. Zelda tells Randy that she is a lousy programmer.

Randy Samuels decides to tell George Cuzzins that Zelda Riddle-Davis told him that she is a lousy programmer. The next diagram shows the new speech act, from Randy to George. The message content arrow goes from the speech act arrow back to the original speech act arrow (from Zelda to Randy) because the new speech act was about the original one. If George resented the receipt of this information, we could draw an anger arrow back from George to Randy. However, an anger arrow is not warranted in this case based on the information we obtained from George when we interviewed him after the fact. Also, note that Zelda is not angry at Randy for telling George at this point in time because *she does not know that Randy disclosed her secret to George.* When she finds out, she will become angry.

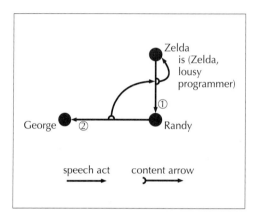

Figure 3. Randy tells George that Zelda told him (Randy) that she is a lousy programmer.

Next, George Cuzzins decides to tell Fred Worthington that Randy Samuels told him that Zelda Riddle-Davis had told Randy that she is a lousy programmer. In this new diagram, which builds upon the previous two, we have a speech act from George Cuzzins to Fred Worthington. The message content arrow for this new speech act points to the second speech act (the one between Randy and George). In other words, this latest speech act is again about a previous speech act. This is just how gossip spreads.

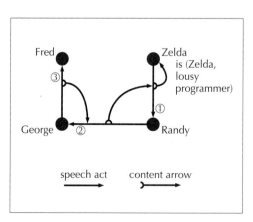

Figure 4. George tells Fred that Randy told him (George) that Zelda told Randy that she is a lousy programmer.

Now comes the explosion: Fred Worthington tells the entire development team that George told him that Randy told George that Zelda told Randy that she is a lousy programmer. My final diagram shows the new speech act being directed to a new symbol representing the team. This is in lieu of having many speech act arrows going from Fred to each individual team member. The message content arrow goes back to the speech act between George and Fred. But now this one speech act has unleashed a fury of angry feelings, shown by the anger arrows. Zelda is angry at Randy for betraying a confidence, she is angry at George for telling Fred something of this sensitive nature, and she is angry at Fred for sharing this information with the whole team. Randy is angry at George and Fred, and George is angry at Fred for their own reasons. Randy is also angry at Zelda for sharing a confidence that he proved too weak to honor. George is angry at Randy for bringing this matter to his attention in the first place. It's a fire!

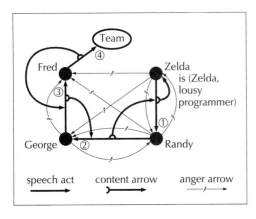

Figure 5.   Fred tells the entire development team that George told him that Randy told George that Zelda told Randy that she is a lousy programmer.

This shows how the tongue can set fire to the whole wheel of creation.

FRESH TALK: I think you are discussing a fundamental process.

MILTON: Yes. I am describing how a team fragments. A fragmented team cannot succeed. Look at the killer robot.

FRESH TALK: No, I mean that you are describing how the whole world gets fragmented.

MILTON: Yes. I realize that.

FRESH TALK: Let's listen to the first tape that you brought. Then Professor Harry Yoder will join us as we consider a second tape. Could you tell us something about the first tape that we will be listening to?

MILTON: We recorded the meetings of the killer robot software development team over a period of one month. They met two or three times per week on average. These meetings occurred after the death of John Cramer.

FRESH TALK: The original project leader who was killed in the skydiving accident?

MILTON: Yes. When we taped these team meetings, George Cuzzins was the project director, and the analysis portion of the project had been completed. Some work on design had begun, but people realized that it was an opportune time to discuss the language issue.

FRESH TALK: We're ready when you are.

MILTON: This is a tape of the first meeting that we recorded at Silicon Techchronics. The people who took part were George Cuzzins, Randy Samuels, Fred Worthington, Rita Rankle, Harry Ulrich, David Tabriz, Ruth Witherspoon, Irv Poole, Robert Ambler, and Zelda Riddle-Davis. Edna Barsky, another team member, was out sick on this particular day.

VOICE: Day 1. 2:04 P.M.

WITHERSPOON: Do we have an agenda?

CUZZINS: I think the agenda for today is to discuss the language issue.

WITHERSPOON: No, I mean a printed agenda. I didn't get one.

CUZZINS: I think I have stated a sufficient agenda. Did anyone take minutes of the last meeting?

RANKLE: Nah.

CUZZINS: Didn't I assign someone?

ULRICH: Nope.

CUZZINS: Well, I want someone to take minutes at this meeting. Okay?

WORTHINGTON: We might save a lot of time if we just have a show of hands of who wants C and who wants C++, because I think only a small minority have any interest in C++.

AMBLER: Shouldn't we have a general discussion first? Shouldn't we set out some guidelines or landmarks for what we are trying to accomplish?

WORTHINGTON: We're choosing a language.

POOLE: I agree with Bob [Ambler].

CUZZINS: We're choosing a language. Okay. In favor of C, raise your hands: three. In favor of C++, raise your hands: three. What about you others?

RIDDLE-DAVIS: Ada.

POOLE: Eiffel.

AMBLER: Smalltalk.

WORTHINGTON: Smalltalk? You've got to be kidding! [sarcastically] Do we have any votes for COBOL?

CUZZINS: I prefer COBOL, actually. I mean, that's my background. I just voted for C since you people used C on the previous robot.

WORTHINGTON: Hey, boss! There's nothing wrong with that. COBOL is a wonderful language. I mean, it's . . . it's . . . it's *historical!*

CUZZINS: Well, I guess we need to have a discussion, although I tend to go along with Fred [Worthington] on the necessity to save some time. Since C has the most support, let's hear first from the Ada, C++, Eiffel, and Smalltalk people. Zelda [Riddle-Davis], tell us something about Ada.

RIDDLE-DAVIS: Ada would be perfect for . . .

WORTHINGTON: Excuse me. I think we should consider the overriding consideration, which is that we have been using C for many years and with great success. I am talking about CX10 and CX20. We can port much of the old C software from CX20 over to this new robot. Going to a new language will put us further behind schedule.

SAMUELS: How much of the old software will port over to the new robot?

WORTHINGTON: Lots of it.

SAMUELS: How much is "lots"? Ten percent? Fifty percent?

WORTHINGTON: Samuels, whenever you know it's the ninth inning with two outs and two strikes, you ask for statistics!

SAMUELS: Look, Fred [Worthington], I'm sick and tired of your political maneuverings. I've never known you to listen to opposing points of view or to learn from them.

CUZZINS: It seems to me that Fred [Worthington] is right. Why go to a new language if we already have lots of software that can be ported from CX20?

SAMUELS: But it's not going to port! That's the point! We're not going to be able to just take code from CX20 and plug it into this new project. The robot hardware is completely different. Furthermore, there is a strong artificial intelligence component to this project. I think an object-oriented language should help us there.

AMBLER: I agree with Randy [Samuels]. Very little of the original software will port, except the numerical routines. I mean, things like Laplacian interpolation and numerical integration will port, but the software that is tied into the hardware will not port. Also, the visual image processing software is being provided, as if I needed to remind you, by Eyeball AI Techniques, Inc. The AI software that we have to write is basically a simple inference engine, more like an expert system.

TABRIZ: Maybe we should use Prolog for the inference engine.

SAMUELS: But Prolog is too inefficient for what we've got to do.

WORTHINGTON: I think some people are trying to evade the issue of porting software from the CX20 to the new robot. None of you has presented any facts to counter what I have said. How much of the software *won't* port? Give us some hard facts before we throw the baby out with the bath water.

CUZZINS: I think CX10 and CX20 show us that a considerable amount of the C code can be ported from one project to another. I think Fred [Worthington]'s point is well taken.

POOLE: But this is CX30! This is an entirely different ball game.

WORTHINGTON: [to Poole] I just hate it when you use sports metaphors.

SAMUELS: [to Worthington] But, it's okay when *you* use sports metaphors!

RIDDLE-DAVIS: Doesn't anyone want to hear about Ada?

WORTHINGTON: No one cares about Ada.

SAMUELS: Give Zelda [Riddle-Davis] a chance to speak! Let's establish a policy that everyone gets a chance to speak before we take any votes. This is supposed to be a democratic team.

AMBLER: I agree with Randy [Samuels]. I want to hear about Ada, and then I'd like to tell you folks about Smalltalk. I also want to hear about Eiffel and C++. I especially want to hear Randy tell us about some of the things he's been doing with C++.

WORTHINGTON: What things? I asked Randy [Samuels] to show me his C++ programs, and despite his enthusiasm I came to the conclusion that they were just Tinkertoy projects. This is my pet peeve, and you people know this well enough. I cannot tolerate people who would have us commit a major project to a particular methodology or language on the basis of some Tinkertoy project that they have done. Look at what happened to us with the SHEOL CASE tool.

SAMUELS: But, you were SHEOL's strongest advocate!

WORTHINGTON: That was then, this is now. I really hate to put Randy [Samuels] down like this in public, but a lot is at stake. We cannot commit the CX30 to C++ on the basis of his Tinkertoy programs.

WITHERSPOON: George [Cuzzins], don't you think you can impose some order around here?

CUZZINS: [to Witherspoon] Why didn't you vote?

WITHERSPOON: I don't want to sound like a weirdo, but I thought it would be good to hear the issues first. We need facts and not just opinions. The opinions are masking a political agenda that is all about power. While some people are trying to advance their careers, the rest of us are charged with producing a robot that is effective, reliable, and safe. That's why I think we really should have some tutorials on the various languages so we can consider their strengths and weaknesses. Can't we invite in some outside experts?

WORTHINGTON: The last thing we need right now is to have a bunch of outsiders come in here and try to dictate the way we do things. We didn't need experts when we decided to use C for the CX10 and CX20. I do not see anything fundamentally new about our present situation.

SAMUELS: The trouble with language experts is that they don't know anything about robotics.

CUZZINS: Then let's hear from our in-house experts. Zelda [Riddle-Davis], what can you tell us about the new Ada standard?

WORTHINGTON: Before we start that, I move that we eliminate Ada, Eiffel, and Smalltalk from these deliberations. These are fringe languages. Let's not waste our time discussing them if we have no intention of using them.

WITHERSPOON: [to Cuzzins] Is he allowed to make a motion like that?

CUZZINS: Do I hear a second?

SAMUELS: Second.

WITHERSPOON: I would like to hear about the other languages before we vote.

CUZZINS: Then, vote against this motion. All in favor of Fred [Worthington]'s motion, raise your hands: four. All opposed: five.

WORTHINGTON: [to Cuzzins] You forgot to vote!

CUZZINS: Did I? Okay, so it's a tie.

WORTHINGTON: Does that mean it passes? Does anyone know the rule that applies when the chairman votes for something and there's a tie?

RIDDLE-DAVIS: It's defeated! May I say a few words about Ada?

WORTHINGTON: Please make it quick. I have a meeting upstairs in just a few minutes.

CUZZINS: Zelda, hold your thoughts on Ada, and we'll continue this discussion on Friday at two. We're making good progress. I didn't think we'd get this far.

WITHERSPOON: George [Cuzzins], are there any action items for the next meeting? You haven't given us anything to do between now and Friday.

CUZZINS: We'll discuss Ada, C++, and the other languages on Friday. Isn't that enough?

WITHERSPOON: [quietly to Cuzzins, after the others have left] George, I am not enjoying these meetings. I think you need to control what goes on more.

CUZZINS: There's nothing wrong with the way I conduct these meetings, Ruth. I think the problem is that you're too shy. Speak up! You've got to learn how to mix it up with the boys, with fellas like Fred and Randy. They're very bright, and they share what they know. Don't you love it when brilliant minds lock horns? To be perfectly blunt, I don't feel that you are contributing as much as you could or should. If you could just teach yourself how to mix it up with the boys, you would enjoy these meetings as much as I do!

FRESH TALK: That was just terrible! Are all software teams like that?

MILTON: No. We are talking about *the* team that produced *the* killer robot. The product reflects the qualities and the consciousness that went into it.

FRESH TALK: Fred Worthington and Randy Samuels are playing a central role in all of this. Randy Samuels is well known, but tell us more about Fred Worthington.

MILTON: He's a software engineer, the son of Max Worthington, who was in charge of corporate security for Silicon Techchronics when this meeting was recorded. Obviously, Fred is the sort of person who is very opinionated and likes to get his way. He does not have good teaming skills, but he seems to be quite influential with the project leader, George Cuzzins.

FRESH TALK: In your opinion, what are some of the specific problems plaguing this team?

MILTON: For one thing, there seems to be no appreciation of the importance of maintaining a team memory. In my software engineering course, my students have team projects, and I tell them to take their team meetings seriously and not to treat them as casual social occasions. Each meeting should have a written agenda, and one team member should be responsible for taking minutes. The minutes should be reviewed and approved at the beginning of the next meeting. Normally, each meeting will generate action items that need to be accomplished before the next meeting. A careful record must be kept of the action items that have been assigned, including who is responsible for completing each item. All of these measures help to ensure that an accurate team memory is maintained. In the second tape, Fred Worthington is going to try to take advantage of the team's faulty memory in order to push his own agenda.

FRESH TALK: There doesn't seem to be any leadership on this team.

MILTON: George Cuzzins is not an effective leader. He has no agenda, even though he says he has one. This leaves a vacuum that Worthington is all too eager to fill. However, Cuzzins believes that he is a good leader. He sees Worthington and Samuels as two exceptionally bright people who are having it out, and he seems to think that this process is going to produce good decisions. Unfortunately, he does not see that Worthington and Samuels are not arguing on a factual basis. They are throwing opinions at one another. This is not the sort of conflict that yields benefits for a team.

FRESH TALK: Worthington is coming across as being especially aggressive, but is it possible that he is just trying to provide the leadership that Cuzzins is not providing?

MILTON: Yes, that could be.

FRESH TALK: Do you know the basis for the antagonism between Worthington and Samuels?

MILTON: It started long before we arrived at Silicon Techchronics. That's all I know about it.

FRESH TALK: I would now like to introduce our second guest, Professor Harry Yoder. Professor Harry Yoder is the Samuel Southerland Professor of Computer Technology and Ethics at Silicon Valley University. He has written numerous papers and books on the social impact of computers and on computer ethics. He received a Ph.D. in Electrical Engineering from the Georgia Institute of Technology. He also received a Master of Divinity Degree from Harvard Divinity School. Welcome.

YODER: I'm honored to be here with my friend and colleague, Hiram Milton.

MILTON: Harry and I go way back.

YODER: I loved your discussion of how speech acts can set fire to the whole world. Since I am a man of the cloth, I thought it might be a good idea to read the entire quote from the Epistle of James that Hiram alluded to.

FRESH TALK: You brought a Bible!

YODER: This is not just any Bible. This Bible is an absolute precondition for my existence. That's why I carry it around. You see, some scientists have pointed out that the laws of the universe have to be just the way they are in order for human life to exist. Another way of stating it is that our very existence implies that the universe must have particular properties, because we couldn't exist if the universe had different properties. This is called the anthropomorphic principle, although it has several different formulations. For example, if the properties of the hydrogen atom were just a wee bit different, then water would not have the properties that it currently has and life could not exist and you and I wouldn't be here blabbing away on this radio program.

FRESH TALK: What does that have to do with your Bible?

YODER: This particular Bible is an absolute precondition for my own existence. Do you understand? I am talking about this particular Bible, the one I am holding in my hand. This particular Bible established, at least to my satisfaction, that there is another dimension to this anthropomorphic principle that the physicists talk about—a personal dimension. I am only here because this Bible once belonged to my great-great-great-grandfather, Eliezer Yoder of Pennsylvania. He was a deeply religious man and a fervent abolitionist, and unlike most of the men who fought in the Union army, he was totally committed to ending the institution of slavery, even if he had to make the ultimate personal sacrifice.

He volunteered for the Union cause before the war officially started, and he saw many battles, including the Battle of Bull Run right outside of Washington at the beginning of the war. Toward the end of the war, he was involved in the Peninsula Campaign. In fact, it was during the siege of Petersburg that a Confederate bullet with his name on it was aimed right at his heart. And this Bible that I am holding stopped that bullet. Now, Eliezer Yoder was a bachelor and childless at that time, so I must conclude that if *this Bible* had not stopped *that bullet*, I would not exist, and this moment would not be happening.

MILTON: Harry's always got some kind of story up his sleeve!

FRESH TALK: Did the bullet stop at any particular passage? In the movies, doesn't the bullet always stop at an especially meaningful passage?

YODER: You can see for yourselves that the bullet stopped right at these words. All of the pages up to this page, starting from Revelations and going backwards, have a hole through them, but this page has just a deep crease that has remained to this day. The bullet stopped at Genesis 1:28: "God said to them, 'Be fruitful and multiply.'"

FRESH TALK: That's remarkable.

YODER: As I said, my great-great-great-grandfather was deeply religious, so after the war he married my great-great-great-grandmother, Rachel Gibbons. In joyful fulfillment of the command written in this very Bible, they had eleven children together.

But I don't think Terry invited us here to talk about Eliezer Yoder. Let's talk about the ethics of speech. Here's what the Epistle of James has to say on the subject. This quote is from a more modern translation of the Epistle that I jotted down before coming down to the station. The Epistle states, "After all, every one of us does something wrong, over and over again; the only man who could reach perfection would be someone who never said anything wrong—he would be able to control every part of himself. . . . So is the tongue only a tiny part of the body, but it can proudly claim that it does great things. Think how a small flame can set fire to a huge forest; the tongue is like that. Among all the parts of the body, the tongue is a whole wicked world in itself: it infects the whole body; catching fire itself from hell, it sets fire to the whole wheel of creation."

FRESH TALK: Let's listen to that second tape of yours, Professor Milton.

MILTON: Okay. This tape is from the meeting immediately after the one that we just listened to. The meeting did not take place as scheduled on Friday, but was postponed until the following Wednesday, one week after the original meeting. Edna Barsky, who missed the previous meeting, is in attendance. There were no action items. There are no minutes from the previous meeting. There is no agenda. Thus, because people often do not remember details from one week to the next, there is a faulty team memory, and Worthington tries to exploit this to push his own agenda.

      VOICE: Day 2. 9:05 A M

WITHERSPOON: Do we have an agenda?

WORTHINGTON: Did someone order doughnuts for us?

RIDDLE-DAVIS: Doughnuts would sure help!

CUZZINS: I think the agenda for today is to discuss the language issue.

WITHERSPOON: No, I mean a printed agenda. I didn't get one.

WORTHINGTON: Should we get Doris [the secretary] to call out for some?

CUZZINS: I think I have stated a sufficient agenda. Did anyone take minutes of the last meeting?

ULRICH: Nope.

CUZZINS: Well, I want someone to take minutes at this meeting. Samuels, why don't you do that?

SAMUELS: I can't. I am one of the major players.

WORTHINGTON: Maybe it would be good for that gigantic ego of yours to lie low for one meeting.

SAMUELS: Then, why don't you take the minutes?

WORTHINGTON: I don't have the kind of mind that can attend to trivialities.

CUZZINS: Look, I don't care who takes the minutes as long as some one takes them.

Someone came up to me at the end of the last meeting and criticized the way these meetings were being run. I think I straightened her out on her misconception that meetings have to be flaccid affairs.

WITHERSPOON: I think you meant to say "placid." You said flaccid.

CUZZINS: Did I?

WITHERSPOON: Yes, I heard you clearly. You said "flaccid" because that word has to do with male sexuality and potency, and you think only men have what it takes to conduct a good meeting. This was obvious from what you said to me last time.

CUZZINS: Okay, the cat's out of the bag. It was Ruth [Witherspoon] who came up to me with this silly idea that I have to guide the discussion. I tried to explain to Ruth that valuable ideas can only emerge when ideas are freely exchanged.

I want all of you women to know that I am fully supportive of women in the workplace. I think a woman can be every bit as good as a man if she applies herself.

RIDDLE-DAVIS: Being every bit as good as a man isn't exactly the goal that I've set for myself.

[Laughter]

WORTHINGTON: Look, I've got another meeting in fifty minutes. Can we get back to the issue of C versus C++?

CUZZINS: Okay. Where were we?

WORTHINGTON: We had just voted to limit the discussion to C and C++ and to avoid the fringe languages.

SAMUELS: [shouting] That's a lie!

WORTHINGTON: [to Samuels] Temper, temper!

CUZZINS: I recall that we did vote the way Fred [Worthington] indicates.

WITHERSPOON: George, that is not true. It was a tie vote, so the motion failed. We were going to discuss Ada, Eiffel, C++, and Smalltalk at this meeting. Maybe Fred [Worthington] can present a formal argument in favor of C while we are at it.

TABRIZ: May I suggest that this meeting be held on a higher plane than the previous one?

WORTHINGTON: My sentiments exactly. This is what I've been arguing for all along. I'd be happy to defend C as our implementation language, but I believe that C needs no defense. It is the language that we have been using all along for our robot projects. A lot of the old code is going to port to the new robot, and no one has given one piece of evidence to refute this.

SAMUELS: Where is *your* evidence?

WORTHINGTON: The burden of proof is on those who want to change the language we have been using all along. Need I remind you that when Cramer tried to lead us all in the direction of object-oriented programming, the result was a disaster?

SAMUELS: You brought that up at the last meeting, at which time I reminded you that you were Cramer's most vocal supporter. It seems that you always bring up Cramer to divert our attention from a more important issue. The issue is, Where is your evidence that we will be able to port the CX20 software?

WORTHINGTON: Our memories differ on the Cramer affair. I was only trying to keep up morale while I was doing my best to get Cramer into a twelve-step program behind the scenes. I wasn't really in favor of SHEOL per se.

RIDDLE-DAVIS: You really have not established that using C will allow us to reuse code from the CX20 project. The CX30 hardware is fundamentally different from the CX20. It seems to me that we will really have to tear apart the CX20 software in order to reuse even tiny fragments of it. Even if the software does port over, we will have a very tricky job of testing the old software in the new hardware.

BARSKY: There will be no code reuse if we use C++, Eiffel, or any of those other languages. So the issue is how important is it for us to have code reuse.

SAMUELS: But if we use an object-oriented language that supports code reuse, we will get the code reuse on future robot projects. We won't get the payback immediately.

CUZZINS: Code reuse was never much of a consideration on the COBOL projects that I managed.

WORTHINGTON: We all respect what you have done in the good old days, George, but code reuse is the name of the game these days.

CUZZINS: Is it?

POOLE: If you want code reuse, I suggest that we use Eiffel. Eiffel is an object-oriented language with a large class library, including sophisticated data structures. Eiffel has many features for successful software engineering, including features for attaching assertions to the code.

WORTHINGTON: What's that good for?

POOLE: Eiffel includes pre and post conditions, loop invariants, loop variants, and class invariants. Ordinary assertions are also possible. The assertion-checking mechanism can be turned on during software development, and it can be turned off when the product is delivered. This helps to ensure more robust software because more bugs will be found during development and testing. I really think it would be helpful to have a formal presentation on Eiffel and its features.

WORTHINGTON: Is there anyone else in favor of Eiffel? If not, maybe we could just vote it down right now.

RIDDLE-DAVIS: Does Eiffel support exception handling like Ada?

POOLE: Yes.

SAMUELS: The key to code reuse is to use an object-oriented language. Everyone knows that.

WORTHINGTON: Everyone knows that who doesn't read the literature, like the *Communications of the ACM* or *IEEE Software* or *Transactions on Software Engineering*. A lot of evidence is accumulating that the key to industrial-strength reuse is organizational commitment to reuse. With organizational commitment to reuse, we can achieve reuse with C or even COBOL. Language is not the central issue in reuse.

RIDDLE-DAVIS: Ada is such a good language for this kind of project, and unlike C, Ada was designed for software engineering. It has exception handling and tasking, two features that we need. Also, Ada supports generics.

CUZZINS: I don't recall that COBOL had generics.

SAMUELS: C++ supports generics in the form of templates. It also supports exception handling. The language is growing all the time. There is an assert macro that can be used for assertions. Most of all, it is object-oriented. Despite what Fred said about organizational commitment, I think that C++ will support reuse for future projects.

WORTHINGTON: [to Ulrich] Are you supporting C or C++?

ULRICH: C++.

WORTHINGTON: Let me ask you then: Can the insertion and extraction operators be overloaded for types that are not classes?

AMBLER: Come on, Fred [Worthington]. This is not an exam. Give the guy a break!

WORTHINGTON: [to Ulrich] Well?

ULRICH: [to Worthington] Uh . . .

WORTHINGTON: Well, this is a fine state of affairs! We have people supporting languages they do not even know. Well, I know C, and I have worked with it for over fifteen years.

WITHERSPOON: George [Cuzzins], don't you think you should discourage personal attacks at these meetings?

CUZZINS: All in favor of Fred [Worthington]'s motion, please raise your hand.

SAMUELS: What's the damn motion?

WITHERSPOON: I don't remember any motion.

CUZZINS: The motion is to eliminate Eiffel from consideration. All in favor raise your hands: ten. Opposed: one.

POOLE: I'm joining Randy for C++.

ULRICH: I'm sticking with C++.

AMBLER: I'm a Smalltalk fanatic, but I'll probably go over to C++.

WORTHINGTON: It's heresy for a Smalltalk person to support C++ even under threat of torture or death. But, I'm curious, what could you possibly say in favor of Smalltalk for this kind of project?

AMBLER: Well, I built a small prototype of the operator interface for Robbie CX30, and I've already shown it to George [Cuzzins] . . .

WORTHINGTON: I don't think it's fair of you to be doing things behind our backs!

AMBLER: It's just a small prototype to try to convince George that the user interface is really important.

WORTHINGTON: Another Tinkertoy! When people support a language other than C, all they have to show us are Tinkertoys. Robbie CX30 is not going to be a Tinkertoy.

AMBLER: But I thought George should get to see what a real user interface, using a GUI, looks like.

WORTHINGTON: George has more knowledge about computing in his pinkie than you do in your whole body.

CUZZINS: Hey, guys. I'm sitting right here, you know.

WORTHINGTON: George, the issue is whether one of the team members should be allowed to negotiate with you behind our backs, especially on something as important as the choice of a language. Shouldn't the system that Bob [Ambler] showed to you be presented to the rest of the team?

CUZZINS: Yes, I think so.

AMBLER: I'm sorry. This is ridiculous! Are you implying that I cannot discuss things with George without your being there?

WORTHINGTON: Well, the thing is that we all know how a lot of dirty politics can go on behind people's backs, so I think everything should be out in the open.

AMBLER: But you and George have a lot of conversations behind our backs. You advise George all the time.

WORTHINGTON: George and I are personal friends. Isn't that so, George?

CUZZINS: Well, I . . .

WORTHINGTON: I know, for example, that Randy [Samuels] went to speak to George about some matters relating to this project. Randy told George that Zelda [Riddle-Davis] had told Randy that she was a lousy programmer and that she was worried about how this might impact on the rest of the project. That's an example of someone going behind our backs instead of us discussing it as a group.

CUZZINS: Damn you, Worthington! I told you that in strictest confidence!

RIDDLE-DAVIS: [angry and hurt] Randy, how could you? I confided in you, and you betrayed my trust.

SAMUELS: [to Riddle-Davis] I was trying to be helpful!

CUZZINS: I think I've got to put my foot down!

WORTHINGTON: [to Cuzzins] Well, do it for God's sake!

CUZZINS: Fred, I should never have shared that . . .

WORTHINGTON: But you did share it, and isn't it better that the truth came to light? Everyone thinks this is one happy family, but it's not one happy family. There are a lot of undercurrents going on around here that can hurt this project. I think people need to fall in line with the way this project is heading, or they should ship out to some other project.

WITHERSPOON: Can we get this meeting moving in a more positive direction? Is that possible? In all seriousness, I sometimes think that this robot project is doomed. How can a team that behaves like this possibly create a quality product?

CUZZINS: I'm shocked that you have such a negative attitude. What about the rest of you? Okay, so maybe I shouldn't have told Fred what Randy told me about Zelda, but I'll patch things up.

WORTHINGTON: I think we should vote now so we don't waste time.

SAMUELS: Vote on what?

WORTHINGTON: First, I want to reintroduce the motion that we limit considerations to just C and C++.

AMBLER, RIDDLE-DAVIS [simultaneously]: I object!

CUZZINS: Your objections have been noted. Okay, all of those in favor of limiting the discussion to just C and C++ please raise your hands: six. All opposed: five. Motion passes.

WORTHINGTON: I move we vote on the C versus C++ issue. Maybe we can save some time if there's not enough support for C++. I mean, let's face it, Cramer led us down that object-oriented path before his death, and the result was a fiasco. Also, incredible as it may seem, some of the people who are supporting C++ do not even know C++.

WITHERSPOON: Shouldn't we discuss the C versus C++ issue in greater detail before we vote?

WORTHINGTON: It's really a matter of efficiency versus inefficiency.

SAMUELS: I thought you said it was a matter of code reuse.

WORTHINGTON: That also.

SAMUELS: C++ is plenty efficient.

WORTHINGTON: Says who?

SAMUELS: Says *C++ Report*.

WORTHINGTON: Look, if you were living during the days of Soviet communism, would you have read *Pravda* in order to find out if communism was working or not?

What about all of those constructor and destructor calls? One tiny little function can call thirty other functions. What about all the overhead from the use of virtual functions? We'd be better off using Smalltalk.

AMBLER: What do you know about Smalltalk?

WORTHINGTON: Enough to know that I don't want to use it. The only thing that I know in all of nature that is more tightly coupled than the Smalltalk system is a black hole.

CUZZINS: All those in favor of C, please raise your hands: five. All in favor of using C++: five.

WORTHINGTON: George, you didn't vote.

CUZZINS: I'm abstaining.

WORTHINGTON: I mean, you are the project director.

CUZZINS: I'd rather have a detailed discussion of the C versus C++ issue at our next meeting. That will be on Friday.

RANKLE: What time?

WORTHINGTON: Two is the only time that's good for me.

CUZZINS: Two it is.

SAMUELS: What about the rest of us? Don't we count?

WITHERSPOON: [to Cuzzins] Will you circulate an agenda?

CUZZINS: [to Witherspoon] Write one up, but I can't promise that we'll actually follow it.

[to Witherspoon, after calling her aside] Did you enjoy the meeting, Ruth? The key is to get in there and mix it up like one of the boys. It's all coming out into the open, everything we need to know in order to make Robbie CX30 a robot whose name will be on everybody's lips. Even this personal animosity stuff. I think it's all best laid right out on the table. Anyway, I just wanted to tell you that I thought you did a good job today. I don't mean any harm when I tell you that this is a man's world with masculine rules. Look, I have a daughter just about your age, and I want her to succeed. Of course, I wouldn't want her to lose her femininity in the process. That's an awfully high price to pay.

FRESH TALK: Professor Yoder, human encounters seem to involve ethical decisions by their very nature.

YODER: Yes, you and I are sitting here, I say something to you, and I immediately have to confront an ethical issue: Should I have said that?

FRESH TALK: Perhaps you should have asked yourself that question *before* you said what you did.

YODER: Yes. But once I say it, then you have to ask yourself whether you should listen to what I said or whether you should ignore it.

MILTON: That's what I began to see as I pursued my research. I was interested in quantifying aspects of group dynamics, but I soon realized that a good team member is an ethical person, and that an unethical person is not a good team member.

YODER: Yes.

FRESH TALK: Professor Yoder, how would you describe a person who is ethical?

YODER: I view an ethical person as a person who has gained mastery over mind and body so that all of his or her actions are ethically correct. Such a person strives, at the very least, to cause no harm. I like to use the analogy of the violin virtuoso who never makes a mistake.

FRESH TALK: So ethical behavior is a kind of virtuosity.

YODER: Correct. In fact that is precisely what I call it in my writings and in my lectures: virtuosity. Virtuosity means doing what is right and having mastery over oneself.

Consider what virtuosity means in the performing arts, for example. In order to achieve virtuosity in the violin world, so I am told, one must have the proper feeling and the proper technique. I think ethical behavior is like that. It is a matter of maintaining the proper feelings of respect and caring for others and the proper technique of doing the right things and saying the right things.

The tape that we just suffered through is mostly about the need to achieve mastery over just one small part of the human body—the tongue. It is much more difficult to control one's tongue than it is to win a gold medal at the Olympics. When you understand what the tongue is and what harm it can do, you will realize that you are indeed responsible for achieving mastery over that part of the human anatomy. You will also realize that your life and your career can be affected in a negative manner if you fail to achieve this kind of mastery. This is serious business.

FRESH TALK: Why have people become so reckless, so insensitive to the feelings of others?

YODER: Because they are asleep. Recklessness is just a symptom of a lack of awareness, a lack of consciousness. Our tongues are on automatic pilot when they should not be. This recklessness destroys relationships. It can destroy a marriage. It can ruin a career.

There are several techniques that I use to teach students how to become more conscious of what they are saying and of the appropriateness of various speech acts in the workplace. One technique I use is to develop sets of questions that students can use to help them decide whether a given speech act is appropriate or not. The Golden Rule plays a fundamental role. Whenever we speak, we are doing something unto someone. What is less obvious is that whenever we speak, we are also doing something unto ourselves.

I use these questions to help students become aware of the consequences of speech acts. These questions are only learning tools. They allow students to develop an awareness concerning the implications of speech acts. Later on, they can refine these questions to more accurately reflect their own ethical values.

Now, let me ask you whether it was ethical for Randy Samuels to tell George Cuzzins that Zelda Riddle-Davis confided in him that she was a lousy programmer.

MILTON: No, it was not ethical. This is not the way things are done in the business world.

FRESH TALK: Yes, it was ethical. He was motivated by the desire to help Zelda and the team.

YODER: In order to illustrate how we might analyze a situation for the purpose of making a correct decision, let us pretend that we are Randy Samuels and that we are facing the ethical dilemma: Should I tell George Cuzzins that Zelda Riddle-Davis told me that she is a lousy programmer? Our purely hypothetical Randy Samuels will use the four sets of questions that I give my students when we discuss the implications of speech acts. Here are the questions.

Question set number one: What are your motives and intentions? What are your reasons for the proposed course of action?

Question set number two: If you are sending information, is the recipient of that information in need of that information? If you are receiving information, are you setting aside information that is none of your business?

Question set number three: Are your actions consistent with the Golden Rule: Treat others in the way that you yourself would like to be treated? Who are you doing this to, and what is the impact? What are you doing to yourself? Are you avoiding causing harm to others? If someone is being hurt in some way, is this unavoidable given the nature of the situation?

Question set number four:　Are you absolutely certain that the action that you are planning is ethical? Are there alternative courses of action that are clearly better?

Here is a hypothetical analysis of the situation wherein we allow Randy Samuels to answer these four questions:

Question set number one:　What are your motives and intentions? What are your reasons for the proposed course of action?

SAMUELS:　My intent is to help the team and possibly to help Zelda Riddle-Davis herself. The fact that Zelda is a lousy programmer is going to hurt us when we get to the coding part of the project. I am certain of that. Zelda is herself unhappy with her situation. That's why she confided in me. She would prefer to work on documentation and some other aspects of the project.

Question set number two:　If you are sending information, is the recipient of that information in need of that information? If you are receiving information, are you setting aside information that is none of your business?

SAMUELS:　Cuzzins needs to know this because the fact that Zelda is a lousy programmer will have a negative impact on the entire project.

Question set number three:　Are your actions consistent with the Golden Rule: Treat others in the way that you yourself would like to be treated? Who are you doing this to, and what is the impact? What are you doing to yourself? Are you avoiding causing harm to others? If someone is being hurt in some way, is this unavoidable given the nature of the situation?

SAMUELS:　In performing this action, I am doing something to Cuzzins, to Zelda, to myself, and also to the whole team. I think it is in Zelda's best interest in terms of her growth in her career, since she hates programming. It is also in the best interests of the team in terms of its success. However, I am not sure that Zelda's reaction will be positive if she finds out that I have gone to Cuzzins, because I never told her of my intention to do so. Nonetheless, I think if I were Zelda, I would want someone to tell Cuzzins about my situation. I am giving Cuzzins important information, so I must trust that he will handle that information in a responsible manner. As far as what I am doing to myself, there is a slight risk that Cuzzins will think that I have spoken out of turn. There is a strong corporate prejudice against doing this sort of thing, which is really talking behind someone else's back. If Zelda has a problem, she should speak to Cuzzins herself. There is also a slight risk that I will lose Zelda's friendship and that I might get the reputation that I cannot be trusted when it comes to sensitive information. Zelda never said straight out that this information was confidential.

Question set number four: Are you absolutely certain that the action that you are planning is ethical? Are there alternative courses of action that are clearly better?

SAMUELS: I have some doubts that I really know what is best for Zelda, and perhaps I am jumping the gun. Perhaps I should speak to Zelda before I speak to Cuzzins. Sometimes I wonder if Cuzzins will behave responsibly if I provide him with sensitive information like this. I think this is ethical because it is for the good of the team and for Zelda's benefit, but it goes against the corporate culture, which determines what is ethical within the corporate environment.

FRESH TALK: Based on this analysis, Samuels should not have gone to Cuzzins, although Cuzzins has need of this information. Samuels should have spoken to Zelda Riddle-Davis first. Does that sound right to you?

YODER: Yes. Samuels also has reason to be concerned about what Cuzzins will do with this kind of sensitive information. Will he tell Worthington? Of course, we know that he did tell Worthington! If the leader of a team who receives sensitive information cannot use that information in a fair and ethical manner, then I think you have a team with a serious problem.

MILTON: Also, in many business settings it would be just plain unacceptable for Randy to go to his manager with this kind of information. What I am saying is that the local corporate culture must be considered before taking an action of this kind, irrespective of the result that Harry's question set might yield.

YODER: Yes, I agree with Hiram. The corporate culture has its own implicit ethical rules. One should follow those rules unless one has a compelling ethical reason not to do so.

Part of being an ethical person is to know the ethics of sharing information: who to tell and who not to tell, when to say something and when not to say it, what to say and what not to say, how to say something and how not to say it, where to say something and where not to say it, and why one should say something and why one should not say it.

FRESH TALK: Can the truth ever be harmful? Is it ever unethical to spread the truth? For example, would it be okay for Samuels to tell R, who is not on the team, that Zelda is a lousy programmer? I am assuming that R does not need this information at all.

YODER: Let's force Samuels to confront this ethical dilemma using our four questions: Should Samuels tell R about Zelda Riddle-Davis being a lousy programmer?

Question set number one:	What are your motives and intentions? What are your reasons for the proposed course of action?
SAMUELS:	My only intention is to gossip at Zelda's expense. I like R, it is fun to chat with him, and what else is there to talk about? I certainly don't intend to hurt Zelda, not really, although I guess she might get hurt, but that's not my primary motivation. In fact, I like Zelda, but this is just harmless gossip.
Question set number two:	If you are sending information, is the recipient of that information in need of that information? If you are receiving information, are you setting aside information that is none of your business?
SAMUELS:	It's none of R's business. It's just gossip.
Question set number three:	Are your actions consistent with the Golden Rule: Treat others in the way that you yourself would like to be treated? Who are you doing this to, and what is the impact? What are you doing to yourself? Are you avoiding causing harm to others? If someone is being hurt in some way, is this unavoidable given the nature of the situation?
SAMUELS:	I do not think this behavior is consistent with the Golden Rule. I am doing this to Zelda, to R, and to myself. What I am doing to Zelda is that I am spreading gossip about her behind her back. Even if it is true, it is still negative information, and if it gets into the wrong hands, it could hurt Zelda in some way. By giving R information that he does not want, I might be placing him in a difficult situation. I might be harming myself if I take this course of action because R might think less of me for speaking behind Zelda's back. He might then tell others that I am not trustworthy, that I am a gossip. He might tell Zelda that I violated a trust,

so as to warn her against entrusting sensitive information to me ever again. So by gossiping in this way, I am hurting myself.

Question set number four: Are you absolutely certain that the action that you are planning is ethical? Are there alternative courses of action that are clearly better?

SAMUELS: How would Zelda feel if she knew about this? I can see that harm can come from spreading information like this, even though it is true. Zelda's reputation might suffer in unanticipated ways I might get a reputation as a gossip. R might think, "If this is what Samuels says about Zelda, I wonder what he tells Zelda about me!" An alternative course of action that would be clearly better would be to keep my mouth shut.

FRESH TALK: I think it is clear that Samuels should not say bad things about Zelda behind her back, even if they are true, unless the recipient of the information needs to know that information. Thus, the answer to Professor Milton's question is, The act of spreading true but negative information can be ethically incorrect.

YODER: People should mind their own business!

MILTON: Was it ethical for George Cuzzins to tell Fred Worthington that Randy Samuels told him (George) that Zelda Riddle-Davis told Randy Samuels that she was a lousy programmer?

YODER: Okay. Let's have Cuzzins ask himself, Should I tell Fred Worthington what Randy Samuels told me about Zelda Riddle-Davis being a lousy programmer?

Question set number one: What are your motives and intentions? What are your reasons for the proposed course of action?

CUZZINS: My intentions are positive. I consider Fred a valuable colleague, and I trust his judgment on technical issues. I'm not sure what I should do with this information, so I will share it with Fred. My intention is to use Fred to help me make a decision that will be the best one for the team. I know that Zelda has a lot of talent, but I guess not in the programming sphere, so this discussion with Fred will help me to move Zelda into a new area that is better suited to her.

Question set number two: If you are sending information, is the recipient of that information in need of that information? If you are receiving information, are you setting aside information that is none of your business?

CUZZINS: Fred needs to know this information because he is serving as my unofficial advisor. Of course, he doesn't need to know that Randy gave me the information about Zelda. In fact, he doesn't even need to know that it is Zelda that we are talking about. I could pose the whole thing hypothetically, "Suppose we have this team member who is a lousy programmer . . . "

Question set number three: Are your actions consistent with the Golden Rule: Treat others in the way that you yourself would like to be treated? Who are you doing this to, and what is the impact? What are you doing to yourself? Are you avoiding causing harm to others? If someone is being hurt in some way, is this unavoidable given the nature of the situation?

CUZZINS: There is absolutely no problem here with the Golden Rule. I am trying to do what is best for the team and for Zelda. The way that I see it, Zelda would not object to what I am doing, because Zelda will benefit from what I am doing. Randy, however, would probably not like me to mention him in all this—he and Fred do not get along too well—so I better be careful not to tell Fred who the source of the information is. But, you know, if Fred wants to know something, he has a way of extracting it from you. On the other hand, I wonder whether I am really doing what is best for the team by using Fred in this unofficial capacity as advisor. This gives Fred a lot of power. So, in fact, when I tell this to Fred, I am doing something to Randy and to Zelda and also to Fred and to the entire team. In doing this to Fred, I am giving him power and influence, which he likes, but that may not be good for Fred or for the team since power can corrupt. It's certainly not good for Randy, since Fred and Randy do not get along.

Question set number four: Are you absolutely certain that the action that you are planning is ethical? Are there alternative courses of action that are clearly better?

CUZZINS: The thing that smells bad about this is that I am not sure that I can trust Fred to keep this information strictly confidential. He's extremely shrewd,

> even brutal, politically. Even if I give him this information in the strictest confidence, will he keep that confidence?

FRESH TALK: Based on this analysis, Cuzzins should *not* have told Worthington about Zelda or about Randy's role as the informant. That's how I read it.

MILTON: I agree.

YODER: But what should he do?

FRESH TALK: Make the decision by himself?

YODER: What if he is incapable of making such a decision?

MILTON: No. I know what Harry is getting at. Cuzzins is lying to himself. Cuzzins has not performed the ethical analysis honestly—and he knows it!

YODER: Right, our *hypothetical* Cuzzins has been lying to himself. Here is a more truthful answer to the last question about whether there is an alternative course of action:

> CUZZINS: Actually, I know a better course of action. I should go to *my* superior, Ray Johnson. But I hate the man's guts! If he mentions that Ivory Snow theory of his one more time I'll scream! No, I'd rather deal with one of my subordinates. It's less threatening. I know that dealing with Fred Worthington in this way is hurting my relationships with the people on my project, but the only alternative is to see the Ivory Snow man.

This brings out the point that the absence of communication has an ethical dimension. Not speaking is a form of speaking. The communications channel between George Cuzzins and Ray Johnson is an important one for the success of the project. George Cuzzins is allowing his personal feelings about Ray Johnson to shut down that communications channel, probably to the detriment of the project.

FRESH TALK: Can we use your questions to derive the theorem "It is never ethical to violate a confidence"?

YODER: Here's a counterexample to your theorem: Someone tells me in the strictest confidence that he is going to blow up the Golden Gate Bridge. Q.E.D.

FRESH TALK: I didn't think that one out too clearly.

YODER: But what about Fred Worthington's breaking confidence with George Cuzzins? I think we can show that this was not ethical. Breaking a valid and sincere confidence usually means giving information to people who have no need for that information, *at least in the judgment of the person who was the original source of the confidential information.*

In the case of Fred sharing information that was given to him in confidence by Cuzzins, Fred apparently feels that the entire team should know about this, but Cuzzins felt that only Fred should know about this. In this case, Fred is doing unto Cuzzins and unto Samuels and unto Zelda all in one fell swoop, and none of them likes what he is doing unto them.

FRESH TALK: I wanted to raise this earlier, but I think we need to mention that if we do something to another person and that person does not like it, that does not mean that we have violated the Golden Rule or that we have acted unethically.

YODER: This is an important point. In implementing the Golden Rule you need to assume that everyone is perfect and that they would want things done unto them that would ensure their own professional and ethical growth. But even the one who is "doing unto" must be perfect in order to make such a judgment. Consequently, being imperfect, we need to do our best, always acting out of respect and love, in order to bring about the best result. In my opinion, there is no alternative.

So, the Golden Rule is really about that sometimes painful commitment that is called love. Applying the Golden Rule is very difficult because it means that you will make people angry and you will make mistakes.

In this case, I would say that Fred is not acting in accordance with the Golden Rule. He is not acting from the point of view of desiring professional and spiritual growth for anyone. His motivations are to sow discord and to embarrass Cuzzins and Samuels. He knows that he can embarrass Cuzzins without fear of retaliation because Cuzzins has become dependent upon Fred, and this may not even be the most damaging information that Fred could share. In other words, *Fred may have the goods on George Cuzzins*. Fred is also doing unto the team by destroying their unity and creating bad feelings.

FRESH TALK: It seems that when you do something unto an individual on a team, you are also doing something to the whole team.

YODER: I like that observation!

FRESH TALK: Is George Cuzzins being ethical in his treatment of Ruth Witherspoon? He is being condescending, patronizing, and sexist, in my opinion.

YODER: George Cuzzins may believe that he is being ethical because he is trying to help Ruth Witherspoon make progress in her career. He fails on the Golden Rule test, however, in that he should know that if he were a woman he would not appreciate being spoken to in that manner. Thus, if there is something that he needs to communicate to Ruth Witherspoon for her benefit and for the benefit of the team, he should do so in a manner that is not offensive.

MILTON: I can say this for your questions: They allow us to see that a simple speech act is not as simple as we might at first suppose. When working on a team, quite a few people are involved, and it is important for team members to know the proper way to interact with others on the team. An effective team member needs to understand the implications of backbiting, gossip, and deception.

YODER: Yes, a tongue can be a very dangerous thing. I would favor some kind of license, like a driver's license, for using one, but I think I represent a tiny minority. An anthropologist, I think it was, observed that human beings invented speech in order to deceive one another. Many speech utterances take the form, "I am not doing what your eyes are plainly telling you that I am doing. Don't believe *your eyes,* believe *my tongue."*

FRESH TALK: I know this is highly unusual for "Fresh Talk," which is not a call-in show, but according to my producer, we have a caller who insists that he—I'm sorry, that she—be given some air time. Caller, you're on "Fresh Talk." Please, tell us your name and where you are calling from.

CALLER: I am Zelda Riddle-Davis, and I am damn mad! Now the whole world knows that I'm a lousy programmer! I think telling the world that I am a lousy programmer is a serious ethical lapse, worse than anything Samuels did to Cuzzins or to Worthington or to Ambler or to Poole or to R and a lot worse than anything that Worthington did to Cuzzins or to Samuels or to Poole or to anybody.

FRESH TALK: When you shout into the phone like that, we can't hear you clearly.

MILTON: R is not a real person. We used R as a hypothetical team member.

FRESH TALK: I don't think she cares about that.

YODER: Caller, I think I can regain your respect if you just realize that I had a special dispensation from God so that I could teach our listeners about the ethics of speech.

CALLER: Are you nuts?

YODER: God gave me permission to do this. Otherwise, it would have been highly unethical for us. . .

CALLER: Do you expect me to believe that?

YODER: Please don't interrupt. . .

CALLER: I'll interrupt whenever I damn please! It's little comfort to me that you are a lunatic who believes that God has given you special permission to behave unethically. Do you take me for a fool? Now the whole world knows that I am a lousy programmer!

YODER: If you would just let me finish!

CALLER: You'll be hearing from my attorney—all of you!! [CLICK]

YODER: Did she hang up?

FRESH TALK: Yes.

MILTON: Do you think that what we did was ethical—telling the whole world that Zelda Riddle-Davis is a lousy programmer?

FRESH TALK: A good question.

YODER: It was ethical because I had a special dispensation from God. Otherwise, what we did would have been improper.

FRESH TALK: But we only have your word for it. For all we know, you could be having a psychotic episode, and I should be calling down to the front desk to get a security guard. In any event, I could find myself up to my eyeballs in lawsuits!

MILTON: I mean, I trust you, Harry, but if only God could give us some sign.

YODER: Very well, then! If God has given me such a dispensation, let a voice from heaven prove it!

VOICE: I gave my friend, Reverend Yoder, a special dispensation so that he could teach people about the ethics of speech. Okay? Understand? Got it?

MILTON: Awesome!!!

YODER: I rest my case.

FRESH TALK: Does your friend give interviews?

Transcript of a radio interview conducted by Terry Conway for "Fresh Talk" on National American Public (NAP) Radio.

THE CASE OF THE VIRTUAL EPIDEMIC

PAM PULITZER: It's 5:30 A.M. on Sunday, and that means it's time for "Roundtable." This is the only talk program in our time slot that is broadcast live. We come to you from the studios of KPAT-TV in Silicon Valley. So grab a cup of coffee, and brace yourselves for thirty minutes of riveting talk.

Our regular viewers know how "Roundtable" operates. We invite guests who are involved in some controversy, and we try to get information from them. Our regular viewers also know that I am an investigative reporter for the *Sentinel-Observer* and I do my best to get the facts. It is my policy never to be rude to my guests, and I do my best to allow them to present their case to the public. I also do my best not to editorialize. It is for you, the viewer, to decide who acted wisely and who acted foolishly.

Let me add that it takes a lot of courage to appear on "Roundtable" because the issues that we discuss are not simple ones. It also takes courage to get up so early on a Sunday morning. Welcome to "Roundtable."

GUESTS: Thank you.

PULITZER: Recent events in the case of the killer robot have focused attention on artificial intelligence, or AI, research at Silicon Techchronics. This morning's program has to do with a tragic death that was caused by an AI system. Mildred Persinny of Outback, Montana, died after she received an incorrect diagnosis and prescription from an expert system called DiaScribe. Mrs. Persinny's death did not receive much attention in the media, perhaps because of the saturation coverage of the case of the killer robot. It certainly deserves more attention than it has received. This morning's focus: "the case of the virtual epidemic."

My first guest is Mr. John Blake. He came up with the idea for DiaScribe, an expert system that would be used in poor rural and urban areas in order to improve the quality of health care delivery in those areas. Could you tell our viewers about your background, Mr. Blake?

BLAKE: I work for a cutting-edge company back east in Hohokus, New Jersey, that develops expert systems as diagnostic tools in various professions and industries. My main function is to come up with ideas for new applications. I am also involved in selling these ideas to prospective clients. Once we reach an agreement with a client, we cooperate with them in the building of the actual expert system.

PULITZER: What is an expert system?

BLAKE: It's a system that captures the expertise of human experts in a particular domain. Our domain was medical diagnosis. Building an expert system involves in-depth interviews with experts in the domain. Usually, expertise is encoded in terms of if-then rules. Our expert system was built using an expert systems shell, which provides a framework for encoding expertise in terms of rules.

PULITZER: Tell us about the original idea behind DiaScribe.

BLAKE: Some of my ideas come from my social conscience. I was aware that certain rural and inner-city areas were not getting the quality of health care that was being provided to wealthier areas, so I tried to come up with a system that would improve health care delivery in the poorer areas.

PULITZER: How would DiaScribe accomplish this?

BLAKE: DiaScribe was intended as a surrogate general practitioner in areas where physicians were in low supply. DiaScribe could diagnose most basic complaints and could prescribe medications for those complaints. We are talking about colds, common bacterial infections, flu, migraine headaches, high blood pressure, some viral infections, and other common ailments that would normally be handled by a family physician.

PULITZER: Are you saying then that the people in these communities would use the computer with no health care professionals being present?

BLAKE: No, the original concept was that a nurse or other trained person would interact with the system, giving the patient the best medical advice available.

PULITZER: Best in what sense?

BLAKE: Best in the sense that our company always works with world-class experts when we develop our expert systems. DiaScribe would contain the very best medical knowledge available.

PULITZER: Our next guest is Marvin Silver, founder and president of Global ExperSys, the company where John Blake works. What did you think of John's idea when you first heard about it?

SILVER: I loved it. I told him that his idea was terrific. It was a humanistic idea, an idea that reflected the high values that I want our company to represent.

PULITZER: Who would be your client in this case? Usually you develop a system only after you have a client who is going to pay for it.

SILVER: I decided that the best shot would be to make the federal government our client by going after a federal grant to fund development of the system.

PULITZER: Did you go that route?

SILVER: Yes. John wrote up the grant proposal, and it was excellent.

PULITZER: My next guest is Frank Feldor. Mr. Feldor works at the federal agency in Washington that processed the DiaScribe grant proposal. What did you think of the DiaScribe grant proposal, Mr. Feldor?

FELDOR: I thought it was outstanding.

PULITZER: Didn't you fear that the quality of health care might be lessened rather than improved?

FELDOR: No, I saw this as a wonderful way to improve the quality of health care for the poor. However, I saw some legal hurdles for this grant. It was not clear to me that a computer would be allowed to prescribe medications, for example. I called up my friend, Congresswoman Whistler, to see if she could help me out.

PULITZER: My next guest is New Jersey Congresswoman Harriet Whistler. Her district includes Hohokus, where Global ExperSys is located. Congresswoman Whistler appears via satellite. Congresswoman, did you like the concept behind DiaScribe?

WHISTLER: I immediately liked the idea. Of course, Frank Feldor had to give me a long lecture on what an expert system was. The key thing for me was the fact that world-class medical experts would help to build these systems. Thus, poor people could get better medical guidance than most affluent people. Your run-of-the-mill affluent person does not have access to a world-class expert. I also ran this by the Office of Technological Assessment here on Capitol Hill, and they also thought it was a good idea.

PULITZER: So, eventually you introduced a bill on Capitol Hill that would allow expert systems to diagnose illnesses and prescribe medications under the watchful eye of the Food and Drug Administration.

WHISTLER: Yes, my bill was for any expert system that was designed to diagnose illnesses and to prescribe medications. It would have to undergo rigorous testing by the FDA. The FDA would only approve such a system if it could establish by rigorous testing that the expert system was at least as good as a regular doctor.

PULITZER: By a "regular" doctor you mean a . . .

WHISTLER: . . . human doctor.

PULITZER: Why didn't the medical establishment oppose your bill?

WHISTLER: They did not oppose it because the legislation stipulated that expert systems could be used only in designated impoverished areas, areas that did not have adequate medical expertise. The expert systems would not be allowed in areas with an adequate supply of doctors. By the way, I had considerable help from the Office of Technological Assessment and from the FDA in drafting this bill. I also got help from Senator Whitmore, who sponsored the bill in the Senate.

PULITZER: Joining Congresswoman Whistler in our Washington studio via satellite is New Jersey's junior senator, Abe Whitmore. Senator, you supported CHEAP, the Computerized Health Enhancement and Augmentation Program. Why?

WHITMORE: I supported it because it was one of the best bills that has ever crossed my desk. I am an advocate for the poor, and I thought this system would address one of the many problems facing the poor in this country.

PULITZER: Well, the bill passed both houses of Congress and was signed by the president. The federal government gave Global ExperSys a two-million-dollar grant to build DiaScribe. Upon FDA approval, Global ExperSys would be qualified to distribute their system throughout the nation in designated communities as specified in the authorizing legislation. The next step was for John Blake, as head of the DiaScribe development project, to find the medical expertise that was needed to build the system.

John, could you tell us some more about this stage of the DiaScribe project?

BLAKE: I contacted chairs of departments at dozens of medical schools, and I asked them to give me the name of the very best diagnostician that they knew for ailments that would normally be treated by a family doctor. Two names appeared much more often than any of the others. They were Dr.

Jane Talbot, a graduate of Harvard Medical School, and Dr. Steven Mitchell, a graduate of Georgetown Medical School. I offered each of these eminent physicians one quarter of a million dollars if they would allow me to pick their brains in order to build the DiaScribe system. They both agreed with enormous enthusiasm.

PULITZER: Did they indicate why they thought this was a worthwhile undertaking, I mean, besides the money?

BLAKE: Neither of them mentioned the money as being significant in any way. I think the money was more like a gratuity as far as they were concerned. Dr. Talbot was especially interested in the possibility that these systems could be deployed in underdeveloped countries, such as the countries of central Africa, eastern Europe, and the republics of the former Soviet Union. She felt that systems such as this could improve medical care in those impoverished nations. I remember having a lively talk with her about this.

PULITZER: Did you have any medical expertise going into the project?

BLAKE: No, I am not expected to be an expert. I am a knowledge engineer. My expertise is in capturing the knowledge that experts have. Of course, I did read up on medicine before I really got down to work, so I would know the vocabulary and the concepts.

PULITZER: Congresswoman Whistler, is it legal to export the DiaScribe system overseas?

WHISTLER: Global ExperSys has voluntarily halted shipment of the system overseas as long as the system is under recall by the FDA here in the States.

PULITZER: Neither Dr. Talbot nor Dr. Mitchell would agree to appear on "Roundtable" this morning. These doctors became embroiled in a bitter controversy surrounding the DiaScribe project.

What happened between Drs. Talbot and Mitchell?

BLAKE: Things started off smoothly enough. I interviewed Dr. Talbot and Dr. Mitchell alternately over a period of many months. I was trying to capture how they arrived at diagnoses in the form of if-then rules. I also asked them to assign probabilities to the rules that they gave me. For example, if a patient has a dry tongue, then there is a ninety-five percent probability that the patient is dehydrated. Drs. Talbot and Mitchell each had their areas of specialization, but there were a few areas where these overlapped, and I should have anticipated this problem. I interviewed both doctors on the matter of gastrointestinal ailments, and I found that they had decidedly different perspectives on this subject.

There was no way to reconcile their differing views on four specific issues relating to gastrointestinal ailments. That is, for four specific sets of symptoms, they gave widely divergent conclusions.

Finally, the two doctors started to fight over these issues, using me as their messenger boy. Dr. Talbot called Mitchell a "liar," and Dr. Mitchell said that Talbot was "incompetent" in the area of gastrointestinal ailments. When we first got started, Talbot and Mitchell had only good things to say about each another.

PULITZER: It was at about this time that you called in additional experts. What did they find?

BLAKE: They found that Dr. Mitchell was correct in all four of the issues in which he had disagreed with Dr. Talbot. Consequently, I decided to throw out all of the knowledge that Dr. Talbot had given me on gastrointestinal ailments and to depend wholly on Dr. Mitchell's expertise in that realm.

PULITZER: But, what about your confidence in the other knowledge that Dr. Talbot gave to you? Wasn't your confidence in her expertise shaken a bit?

BLAKE: I felt that Dr. Talbot was an outstanding expert in those remaining areas. She received the highest recommendations from literally dozens of department chairs at medical schools across the country. She received more recommendations than Dr. Mitchell.

PULITZER: Did you know that Dr. Talbot was severely depressed and was taking several medications during the latter part of the period when you were interviewing her?

BLAKE: Obviously, if I had known that, I would have chosen another expert.

PULITZER: My investigation has shown that her college-age daughter died in a tragic car accident during the middle of the period when you were interviewing her.

BLAKE: Yes. It was quite a blow. We did not meet for three weeks while she pulled herself together.

PULITZER: Was she okay when she came back?

BLAKE: I'm not a doctor. She seemed okay.

PULITZER: In fact, she was taking an antidepressant and was under sedation during this period. Were you aware of that?

BLAKE: No. She did not volunteer that information. She said, "I am raring and ready to go!"

PULITZER: Didn't that seem strange to you? A woman just loses her daughter and she's raring to go?

BLAKE: In retrospect, yes. But, at the time I was just happy to see such a wonderful woman in such good spirits. Dr. Talbot is one of the nicest people that I have ever met.

PULITZER: It was at this time that you were collecting information about gastrointestinal illnesses.

BLAKE: Yes.

PULITZER: As the discrepancies arose between the diagnostic techniques of Drs. Talbot and Mitchell, John Blake consulted with his boss, Marvin Silver. Did you give the project a green light?

SILVER: Yes. I agreed with the way John handled the case. Dr. Talbot is an outstanding medical expert, just not apparently in the gastrointestinal ailment domain. We had no idea that her thinking was impaired by medication. We were a bit under the gun. Unless the project was finished by January 1 of the following year, the federal government would impose a fine against our grant. The fine would increase on a monthly basis until the system was completed. A six-month delay would completely remove any possibility of making a profit.

PULITZER: What about the other medical knowledge that Dr. Talbot contributed to the system?

SILVER: We did not know that Dr. Talbot's thinking was somewhat impaired by her medications and her grief. We just tried to resolve the inconsistencies between the two doctors.

PULITZER: John, when you look at your creation, DiaScribe, what do you see?

BLAKE: I'm not sure I know what you are getting at.

PULITZER: Who do you see inside the system?

BLAKE: I see myself, the creator of the system, and also I see Drs. Mitchell and Talbot.

PULITZER: So, DiaScribe is really about rendering Drs. Mitchell and Talbot literally incarnate in the expert system. Is that it?

BLAKE: Yes. Mitchell and Talbot are actually consulting with the patients, not a chip from Intel.

PULITZER: But the patients are not consulting with the real Dr. Talbot. They are consulting with the Dr. Talbot who is overwhelmed by grief due to the death of her daughter.

BLAKE: Yes.

PULITZER: My next guest is Cynthia Ozark. She was in charge of testing the diagnostic system at FDA. What was your testing procedure?

OZARK: We gave a large population of doctors various diagnostic situations to consider in the form of symptoms and patient histories. Then we presented these same cases to DiaScribe. We then showed the results generated by the first population of doctors and by DiaScribe to a second population of doctors. Each doctor in the second group was shown fifty cases. For each case there was one diagnosis and prescription from a human doctor and another diagnosis and prescription from DiaScribe. This was a blind test. The second group of doctors did not know which diagnoses and prescriptions were from DiaScribe and which were from human doctors. The results were startling. In ninety-three percent of the paired cases, DiaScribe did at least as well as the human doctor it was paired with. This was the critical test for DiaScribe.

PULITZER: It seems like this methodology ignores individual cases where DiaScribe might have been much worse than a normal doctor.

OZARK: We did test for individual cases also, and we found a few bugs, which were fixed. However, you need to understand that even a human doctor makes mistakes. What if you were a patient of the world-renowned Dr. Talbot when she was grieving over her daughter?

PULITZER: DiaScribe was approved. Global ExperSys could now sell DiaScribe to clinics in impoverished communities throughout the United States. Congress passed a new bill that gave clinics moneys to purchase this kind of expert system.

My next guest is George, who works as a paramedic at a Los Angeles clinic. He is appearing in shadow this morning because he wishes his identity to be kept a secret. George is not his real name. Were you trained to use DiaScribe in consultation with patients at the clinic?

GEORGE: Yes.

PULITZER: Did you like DiaScribe?

GEORGE: I loved it. It helped me to keep my drug habit going.

PULITZER: How's that?

GEORGE: I created six fake patients on the computer system, all of whom needed the same drug that I used for my habit. I also created some fake patients to get drugs for my friends. You see, DiaScribe prints out a prescription form that must be signed by one of the authorized medical personnel. Fortunately or unfortunately, depending on how you look at it, I was considered an authorized medical person.

PULITZER: You are currently under treatment for your addiction?

GEORGE: Yes.

PULITZER: John Blake, are you aware of other instances like this one, where people have abused your system to get access to drugs?

BLAKE: A few cases have come to light, but even doctors and nurses are known to abuse drugs. It's an occupational hazard.

PULITZER: My next guest is Peter Persinny of Outback, Montana. His late wife, Mildred, is the person whose death caused the recall of all DiaScribe expert systems earlier this month. That recall is in effect until the FDA is satisfied that the system is perfectly safe.

Mr. Persinny, let me once again extend my sympathies on the death of your wife.

PERSINNY: Thank you. She was a beautiful person. I feel guilty that I could not afford to get her to a real doctor.

PULITZER: Can you tell us what happened?

PERSINNY: She had a terrible headache and was feeling dizzy and faint, so we decided to take her to the clinic.

PULITZER: Then what?

PERSINNY: I asked the nurse when the doctor could see my wife. I was asking for Doc Winter, the clinic doctor. The nurse said he would only be coming out to Outback on Tuesdays from now on. Used to be that he would come out on Tuesdays and Thursdays, but that was before the computer system came in. I guess he figured that the computer system meant that he would not have to come out to Outback so often. It was a Wednesday when my Millie took sick.

PULITZER: Yes, go on, Mr. Persinny.

PERSINNY: Well, the nurse showed us this new computer set up. She gave me and Millie a brochure that told us all about it. This was not a leaflet, but an expensive-looking brochure. On the front cover they had a glossy photo of a Harvard medical degree and on the back cover they had a glossy photo of a Georgetown medical degree. The brochure explained that a doctor from Harvard and a doctor from Georgetown had put their world-class medical knowledge into this system. I don't think Doc Winter got his degree from one of those big places.

PULITZER: We'd like to know everything.

PERSINNY: Well, this nurse started to ask us questions, and she began typing information into the computer. The blood pressure device was hooked up directly to the computer. The computer took Millie's blood pressure.

The nurse then showed us a screen on the computer that showed Millie's medical history. I remember the nurse laughing, "See, Millie, the computer knows all about you." I hate it when computer folks talk like that. As if I don't have the smarts to know that the computer don't know nothin'.

The computer then printed out a prescription, and we asked the nurse what the problem was. The nurse hit some keys on the keyboard. She looked up at the screen, and she looked a bit puzzled, perhaps surprised would be a better way of describing her look, but then she said, "You have very low blood pressure." But Millie never had low blood pressure in her life. She usually suffered from high blood pressure.

Well, two nights later, she died in her sleep of a massive stroke. Doc Winter says that the computer's prescription for a woman who already had very high blood pressure was the cause of the stroke. In any case, I am suing Mr. Blake's company in the death of my wife.

BLAKE: It is difficult for me to comment on this case, and not because of the lawsuit. I feel great sadness about this incident. We found some faulty medical reasoning in the system after the Persinny incident, but none of that seemed to have anything to do with this particular misdiagnosis. We are still trying to track down the source of the error in our knowledge base. Mrs. Persinny's case was somewhat unusual in that she already had an aneurysm in her brain before she began taking the new medicine. Still, the drug she took due to the computer error caused the aneurysm to burst.

PULITZER: So, who is inside the expert system, Mr. Blake?

BLAKE: Myself, the people who developed the expert systems shell, Dr. Talbot and Dr. Mitchell, the user interface experts who designed the user interface. Also, the Congress, the FDA, and even the president, who signed CHEAP into law. We're all in that computer. But I think Dr. Talbot should have been more forthright in communicating her state of mind after her daughter's death.

PULITZER: Isn't it possible that your desire to get the product done before the January 1 deadline influenced the manner in which you handled Dr. Talbot's tragic situation?

BLAKE: This issue is being litigated right now, so I will decline comment on that point.

PERSINNY: You see! It's like I said to my lawyer. They rushed it! All for the almighty dollar!

PULITZER: Our next guest believes that he has found out the real reason for the Outback tragedy. He is Professor Horace Gritty of Silicon Valley University. Professor Gritty is an expert on user interfaces, and his analysis of the killer robot operator console is widely cited in discussions of the killer robot incident. Professor Gritty has asked me to warn the viewers that he is an energetic person, and he hopes no one will take offense at this.

GRITTY: Especially Mr. Persinny, who suffered such a grievous loss. I'm always like this! I can't help myself. I have a lot of energy.

PULITZER: So what went wrong, Professor?

GRITTY: If the camera would just follow me over here, I have a DiaScribe system set up, and we have two patients who have volunteered to serve as guinea pigs. My own personal physician, Sidney Werth, M.D., is checking them over and is also using the DiaScribe system to get a diagnosis. What is wrong with this first patient, Sid?

WERTH: Low blood pressure, and the system has correctly diagnosed the problem.

GRITTY: Bring on the second patient. As you can see, this second patient is severely obese. Dr. Werth is going to use the computer to take the blood pressure, and he is also going to take the patient's blood pressure independently. You'll see why he's doing this in a moment.

This will take some time, so please be patient.

[A few moments later]

What did you come up with, Sid?

WERTH: According to DiaScribe this patient has extremely low blood pressure. DiaScribe has prescribed a medication that, in my professional opinion, could be deadly for a patient such as this. In fact, this patient has a serious water retention problem and very high blood pressure: 220 over 130.

GRITTY: I am really proud of myself because I was able to reconstruct this tragic incident without much difficulty, and it had nothing to do with the knowledge base, although I suspect the knowledge base is not perfect.

PULITZER: What's going on?

GRITTY: The DiaScribe system is attached to a blood pressure cup. That cup provides a continuous blood pressure reading to a bunch of registers inside the computer, but the blood pressure is recorded only when the computer sends a signal to the registering device. That causes the latest blood pressure reading to be stored in a pair of variables that are used by the expert system. When the registering device receives a signal "take reading," the device sends the current blood pressure reading to those two variables. These store the systolic and diastolic pressures. The blood pressure readings stored in those variables will not be updated until another signal to take a blood pressure reading is received or until the user enters a blood pressure reading manually.

Now, Dr. Werth took a manual blood pressure reading from the first patient. This means he took the blood pressure and typed in the numbers directly at the keyboard. In the user interface there is an entry for blood pressure mode, and Dr. Werth entered M for manual. He then took the manual blood pressure and typed that into the system. These readings, the systolic and diastolic pressures, were then entered into the two variables that I mentioned earlier. These variables get their data either from the keyboard or from the registers that continuously monitor a patient's blood pressure. The first patient's blood pressure was 77 over 40, which is extremely low. That's why she is in a wheelchair. She faints whenever she stands up. DiaScribe correctly diagnosed her situation and prescribed medication.

Then our second patient sat down at the computer. He was hooked up to the blood pressure cup, and Dr. Werth decided to take his blood pressure automatically, in other words, to allow the computer to take the blood pressure. So he moved the cursor over to the field that asks for blood pressure mode, and he entered an A for automatic to replace the M for manual. Now the screen shows automatic mode for taking the blood pressure.

However, the doctor—and presumably the nurse back in Outback—did not hit the enter key after changing the mode. Furthermore, it is by no means obvious that one should have to hit the enter key. Consequently, the computer still thinks we are in manual mode, in which case the user must enter the blood pressure manually. The internal variables still contain the blood pressure from the previous patient. The user interface is providing a misleading system image. What I mean is that the user interface is presenting an image of the system that does not conform to actual state of the system.

Dr. Werth is taking us through the most critical steps again. Now, when Dr. Werth hits the DIAGNOSE key, the system gives us a warning beep. There is no written message indicating what is wrong. The system is trying to tell us "Enter a blood pressure manually," but the user cannot guess the problem because the displayed mode is A for automatic. Dr. Werth hits the

DIAGNOSE key again, as if to say, "*Diagnose*, you worthless bucket of silicon!", but again there is a beep, but no further indication of what to do. Now we come to the critical juncture. The system is programmed to accept a third DIAGNOSE command as an override of all other safety features. Dr. Werth just hit DIAGNOSE, and there was no beep. A diagnosis and a prescription are being printed out. The diagnosis is low blood pressure. Dr. Werth is now hitting the DATA key, which brings up a new screen showing all of the data collected for our second patient, and we see he has an extremely low blood pressure of 77 over 40.

I contend that this is what happened at Outbank, Montana. Mrs. Persinny had high blood pressure, but one of the patients who used DiaScribe before her had low blood pressure.

PERSINNY: Damn, dang it! If that don't beat all. That explains what the nurse meant when she told my wife, "You're the third low blood pressure case I had in a row. It's a virtual epidemic! "

PULITZER: Our next guest is Professor Jacob Lowe-Tignoff. He is an ordained rabbi and also a professor of religious studies at Silicon Valley University. He is the author of the book *Is Your Computer Stealing from You?*, a meditation on ethics and computers.

Professor, your book states that we must be careful to prevent computers from stealing human capabilities. Was DiaScribe stealing from anyone, in your opinion?

LOWE-TIGNOFF: My contention is that stealing is the most fundamental ethical lapse. When we murder, we are stealing a life; when we spread falsehoods, we are stealing the truth. It seems to me that we need to evaluate computer systems in terms of what they are contributing as compared with what they are stealing. If a system contributes more to human well-being than it steals away, then it is an ethical system. But if a system steals more than it gives, then it is an unethical system and it should not be built.

PULITZER: Does DiaScribe give more than it steals?

LOWE-TIGNOFF: This is not a difficult question for the system as it currently exists. But I would also like to discuss an ideal system without the bugs and the flaws.

PULITZER: Go ahead.

LOWE-TIGNOFF: DiaScribe as it currently exists should be and has been removed from operation. DiaScribe stole a woman's life. It has the potential, as we just saw, to cause tremendous harm because of the stupid way in which it was designed.

PULITZER: You started to talk about a perfect DiaScribe? Would that give more than it steals?

LOWE-TIGNOFF: A perfect DiaScribe, encoding the expertise of great medical experts, without any flaws, would be of great benefit to many people, both here in America and in the underdeveloped world. A system like DiaScribe could disseminate medical knowledge on a wide basis.

On the other hand, there is a shadowy side to DiaScribe and similar systems. What are the ethical implications of our depending upon computer systems to minister to the poor and the disadvantaged? The rich get carbon-based doctors, and the poor get silicon-based doctors. I find this deeply disturbing. In my system of thought, DiaScribe is stealing as well as contributing.

PULITZER: In what sense would a perfect DiaScribe system be stealing?

LOWE-TIGNOFF: There is something valuable and absolute in a single human contact, where flesh presses flesh, where kind words flow from one human being to another, where the breath of one person mingles with that of another. When I take in the air that you have breathed, I am getting some of your unique energy, and when you do the same, you get some of mine. A computer cannot do that. Don't you think it is important, when you visit a healer, that the healer have the ability to share with you the positive energy that belongs to that person because he devoted his entire life and soul to healing and nurturing?

Despite all the rhetoric, Global ExperSys went into this project because they saw an enormous opportunity for profit, and they were in the process of realizing those huge profits when the Mildred Persinny tragedy occurred. They would not have cared about health care delivery for the poor if there weren't big money in it.

So, we have to ask ourselves whether we as a civilization can afford to treat poor people as a class separate from the rest of us.

PULITZER: Are you opposed to systems like DiaScribe in principle?

LOWE-TIGNOFF: No. What I am saying is that we must be careful to look at things beyond the level of cold intellect. DiaScribe is an intellectual solution to a problem that is not solely one of the intellect. The intellect views problems intellectually, but the heart views things differently.

PULITZER: Mr. Blake, is there anything you would like to say in response to what Professor Lowe-Tignoff just said?

BLAKE: No, I think DiaScribe is a good solution for a difficult problem. My own opinion is that silicon doctors will one day be superior to carbon-based doctors.

LOWE-TIGNOFF: That's where we differ.

BLAKE: We hope to have all bugs out of the system within a few months, and pending FDA approval, our systems will be back in service, helping poor people to get the expert medical advice that they need.

PULITZER: I would like to thank my guests for appearing on "Roundtable" this morning.

Transcript of "Roundtable," the Sunday Morning Public Affairs Program, Broadcast on Public American Television

THE CASE OF THE DEADLY DATA

PAM PULITZER: It's 5:30 a.m. on Sunday, and that means it's time for "Roundtable." This is the only talk program in our time slot that is broadcast live. We come to you from the studios of KPAT-TV in Silicon Valley. So grab a cup of coffee, and brace yourselves for thirty minutes of riveting talk.

Our regular viewers know the nature of "Roundtable." We invite guests who are involved in some controversy, and we try to get information from them. Those of you who read the *Sentinel-Observer* know that I am an investigative reporter and I do my best to get the facts. It is my policy never to be rude to my guests. I do my best to allow them to present their case to the public without any editorializing on my part. It is for you, the viewer, to decide who acted wisely and who acted foolishly.

Let me add that it takes a lot of courage to appear on "Roundtable." It also takes courage to get up so early on a Sunday morning. Welcome.

GUESTS: Thank you.

PULITZER: Our viewers are probably aware of several incidents relating to Red Flag Blood Products, the international blood products firm with headquarters here in Silicon Valley. Red Flag collects blood for the purpose of producing blood products for use by hospitals. They must screen blood because of HIV and other viruses. Unfortunately, some tainted blood was delivered to area hospitals last month. In addition, an employee has been charged with selling sensitive blood test data to interested third parties. These events raise some serious issues about database security and data privacy.

A key person in this case is Michael Keating, the programmer who is accused of compromising the integrity of the database. He has fled this jurisdiction and is currently a fugitive from justice.

I will introduce my guests as I call upon them. My first guest is Jane Farnsworth, personnel director at Red Flag. She is responsible for hiring computing professionals at Red Flag.

Mrs. Farnsworth, what do you look for in a new hire at Red Flag?

FARNSWORTH: We look for written and oral communications skills, technical skills, social skills, domain knowledge if at all possible, and good business ethics.

PULITZER: When Michael Keating came to interview at Red Flag, did he seem to possess these qualities and skills?

FARNSWORTH: Yes, he did. He was an impressive-looking candidate. He was articulate; he showed me a portfolio of interesting programs that he had written. He showed me a user's manual from one of his team projects, and it was well organized and clearly written. His grades were very high in computer science, nearly a 4.0, but he seemed to be weaker in most other subjects. He did not have the specific domain knowledge that some of the other candidates had, but his other credentials were far superior.

PULITZER: So Keating was coming right out of college?

FARNSWORTH: Yes.

PULITZER: But what about business ethics? Did you raise that issue?

FARNSWORTH: I always do, implicitly and explicitly.

PULITZER: In this particular case, how did you raise the question of ethics with Mr. Keating?

FARNSWORTH: I said, "Mr. Keating, the work we do here is very sensitive. It is really important that all our employees be trustworthy. Is there anything in your background that you might want to tell me that is not in your vita or in your letter of application?"

PULITZER: How did Keating respond?

FARNSWORTH: He said, "No." His reply sounded sincere.

PULITZER: But now we know that he lied to you.

FARNSWORTH: Yes, he lied. He did not mention, nor did any of his references from the university mention, the computer security incident at the university.

PULITZER: Don't you think you could have asked him some probing questions about his values and about how he would behave in certain situations?

FARNSWORTH: We didn't, but we are doing that now. We ask questions that are intended to determine whether a candidate has considered the ethical implications of working with sensitive data to the same degree that she or he has considered the technical aspects of work with a database.

PULITZER: Our next guest is Ronald Knuth, director of academic computing at Silicon Valley University. Mr. Knuth, you handled the Michael Keating incident several years back. Could you tell us about it?

KNUTH: Michael Keating was taking a data structures course, and he was a legitimate user on our UNIX-based network. However, we caught him attempting to access other accounts on the system. This occurred when four or five students in a row could not log in to the system from a particular workstation. We discovered that a program was running on that workstation that emulated the login procedure and the distinctive S.V.U. log in screen. This program captured user I.D.'s and passwords from unsuspecting students who tried to log in at the terminal on which the emulation program was running. The emulation program was written by Michael Keating. He confessed to writing the emulation program and to capturing the user I.D.'s and passwords.

PULITZER: That sounds like a serious breach of computer security.

KNUTH: It was taken very seriously. As director of academic computing, I called Michael Keating into my office, and I really chewed him out. I was trying to put the fear of God into him. I read him the riot act. In all of my years as an administrator, I never yelled at anyone that loudly. He looked quite contrite by the time I finished.

PULITZER: Did you take any disciplinary actions against him?

KNUTH: According to the rules of the university, I had grounds for expelling him from the university for at least five years, which is effectively permanent expulsion from the university. However, when I actually looked into his face and saw how remorseful he looked, I just could not make that decision. I told him that the next violation would mean automatic expulsion from the university. I'll never forget his hang-dog look that morning.

You know, I almost forgot about this incident, even though I would bump into Keating occasionally. He always flashed that winning smile of his. Then one day, I heard that he was applying for a position at Red Flag.

PULITZER: How did you find out about that?

KNUTH: Just by accident I heard some friends of Keating laughing about it in the hallway.

PULITZER: Laughing?

KNUTH: They were saying something like, "Can you imagine *Michael Keating* working at a place like Red Flag?"

PULITZER: So what did you do?

KNUTH: I ran back to my office and locked the door and thought long and hard about the ethical dilemma that faced me. You see, I have this tremendous inhibition against hurting another person. I was afraid that if I contacted Red Flag about Michael Keating, I would be doing irreparable damage to a young man's life.

PULITZER: But didn't Michael Keating damage his own life by acting irresponsibly? What about your responsibility to all of those who could be affected if he created a security problem at Red Flag? What about the patients who might receive tainted blood, their families and loved ones?

KNUTH: You see, all the evidence was that Keating had reformed himself.

PULITZER: What evidence?

KNUTH: There were no further incidents that I heard of. Also, he always greeted me in such a friendly manner, I couldn't imagine that he was doing something behind my back.

PULITZER: What did you ultimately decide to do with your knowledge that Keating was applying for a job at Red Flag?

KNUTH: I decided to call a project leader that I knew over there, namely, Sally Smothers.

PULITZER: That would be the same Sally Smothers that is appearing on our program this morning?

KNUTH: Yes.

PULITZER: What did you tell her?

KNUTH: I asked her if I could speak to her in strictest confidence about one of our students. She said, "Certainly." Sally is a neighbor of mine, and we've known each other for many years. I told her that a student who had been involved in a security incident at the university was now applying for a job at Red Flag. I told her that I thought the student had reformed himself and that there had been just this one incident several years back.

PULITZER: Our next guest is Sally Smothers. She is a software development project leader at Red Flag. Mrs. Smothers, what did you do when your friend, Ronald Knuth, called with that information?

SMOTHERS: I think I took the wrong approach. The way that I heard what Ronald was telling me was something like this: "Sally, this student is applying for a job at Red Flag, and he was involved in a security incident a few years back, but he seems totally reformed, so I've decided not to take any action on this. Do you concur?" Perhaps because of our friendship, I did concur. In retrospect, I should have looked at the facts objectively and not from the perspective of giving a close friend moral support in a decision he had made.

PULITZER: So you did not contact Jane Farnsworth?

SMOTHERS: Much to my regret, no. You see, I think this thing about youthful indiscretion is very compelling. Michael Keating, based on the description I got of him over the phone, sounded like a personable and intelligent young man.

PULITZER: Are personality and intelligence the key issues, however?

SMOTHERS: No.

PULITZER: Did Michael Keating work with you when he did come to Red Flag?

SMOTHERS: No.

PULITZER: Mrs. Farnsworth, would you have hired Michael Keating if Sally Smothers had told you about the security incident?

FARNSWORTH: Absolutely and definitely not!

PULITZER: Our next guest is Kumar Krishna, professor of computer science at Silicon Valley University. Dr. Krishna, you wrote a letter of reference for Michael Keating, supporting his application for a position at Red Flag.

KRISHNA: Yes, I did. Michael Keating was one of the brightest students I have seen at the university. He received an A+ in my theory of computation course. Based on this and other information I had about him, I could write a glowing letter, the kind of letter that I write only once or twice in a decade.

PULITZER: Did you know about the computer security incident?

KRISHNA: Yes.

PULITZER: But you did not mention it in your letter.

KRISHNA: I didn't think it was legal to mention things like that in a letter. Couldn't I get sued for character assassination?

PULITZER: But the computer security incident was an actual incident.

KRISHNA: Nonetheless, I was concerned about a lawsuit. I figured that Red Flag would call me for more information if Keating were a serious candidate for the job.

PULITZER: Why didn't *you* call them instead of waiting for them to call you?

KRISHNA: Have you ever taught at a university? Did you ever experience the crush of an ongoing semester?

PULITZER: Isn't it true that Michael Keating did a lot of favors for you—setting up your computer system and helping you to access papers off the Web and to otherwise provide information that you needed for your research?

KRISHNA: What are you implying?

PULITZER: Perhaps your personal relationship with him blinded you to some of his faults and to the implications of a person like Michael Keating working at Red Flag.

KRISHNA: I think that the letter of reference that I wrote for Mr. Keating was completely aboveboard and professional. I knew of Mr. Keating's faults, but I didn't feel free to write about them.

PULITZER: Isn't it true that you always give students a copy of letters of reference that you write for them?

KRISHNA: Yes.

PULITZER: Then you gave Michael Keating a copy of the letter that you wrote for him?

KRISHNA: Yes.

PULITZER: Isn't it possible that you felt intimidated by Michael Keating? Did you fear that he might sabotage your system if you did not write him a good letter?

KRISHNA: That idea did cross my mind.

PULITZER: Our next guest is another professor who taught Michael Keating, Susan Benjamin of the Computer Science Department at S.V.U. Dr. Benjamin, you were not asked to write a letter of reference for Michael Keating, but you had some concerns when you heard that he was applying for a position at Red Flag. Why?

BENJAMIN: Why was I concerned? Or why was I not asked to write a letter of reference?

PULITZER: Why were you concerned?

BENJAMIN: I was concerned because Michael Keating had been a student of mine in the fall semester of his senior year, my first semester at Silicon Valley. I was pretty naive about system security, so I stored my exams on the UNIX system. I can't believe that I was that dumb! I am convinced that Mr. Keating was somehow able to get my password and that he stole the test and sold the test to fellow students for fifty dollars apiece. That was my first semester on campus, so the frat houses didn't have my tests on file as yet.

This information about the stolen exam came to me by means of an anonymous note left in my mailbox. It charged Keating with stealing the exam and selling it. The note was attached to a copy of an exam that had to have come from my account because it contained typos and spelling errors that I had subsequently fixed. I realize that an anonymous note does not constitute proof that Michael Keating was the person who stole the exam. However, a few weeks later an incident occurred that I consider very damning. Michael Keating handed in a program that had a variable named sky8LA. The variable's name had nothing to do with its purpose, but sky8LA was the password that I was using when the test was stolen. When I asked him why he called the variable "sky8LA" he said that sky8LA was his former girlfriend's license plate number in Connecticut. I didn't pursue it further, but I am convinced he used that variable name just to rub my nose in the fact that he had gotten hold of my password and had stolen the test.

PULITZER: Did you know about the earlier security incident involving Keating at the computer center?

BENJAMIN: No. That incident happened before I came to S.V.U. I found out about the computer security incident later.

PULITZER: Did you pursue your suspicions concerning Michael Keating?

BENJAMIN: No. I did not have the means or the time. Can you imagine what it is like being a junior faculty member at a major university? I work sixty hours a week easily.

PULITZER: Did you contact anyone at Red Flag concerning Michael Keating?

BENJAMIN: No. I had no proof. It was only a suspicion. I did not want to ruin a young man's career unless I had proof.

PULITZER: Did you speak to other faculty members about Michael?

BENJAMIN: No. I knew Professor Krishna was close to Michael Keating, but Professor Krishna has always treated me with contempt. He does not respect people who do systems work. Of course, no one told me about the bitter schisms in the department when they interviewed me for my current position. In any event, Krishna and I speak to each other only rarely.

PULITZER: Don't you respect Dr. Benjamin, Dr. Krishna?

KRISHNA: We do not have much in common. It's nothing personal. I just don't think that slopping a system together with a bunch of pretty graphics is science, that's all.

PULITZER: Our next guest is Mike Clark. He is director of security operations at Red Flag. Mr. Clark, could you describe some of the measures in place at Red Flag to protect the integrity and security of data?

CLARK: Our main data collection effort concerns blood donors, blood donations, and blood products manufactured using the donated blood. Of great concern is the tracking of the HIV virus. When blood containing HIV is donated, it is naturally not used in our products. Once a donor is identified as being HIV positive, that donor is not permitted to donate blood again at Red Flag. We send this information to MediData Central, the massive national medical database, so that other blood product manufacturers can use this information. Also, we access MediData Central to identify questionable donors in advance, as a screening process.

Our own blood donor and products database is built around a relational database product. However, two years ago the database was built around an older database system that was not fully relational and had its own peculiar programming language. Consequently, we decided to port the old database to the new relational database, and we were in the process of doing that when Michael Keating came over to Red Flag.

We feel that our old database and our new database have very good security. The reason for moving over to a state-of-the-art relational database was to promote ease of application development using applications generators. These are very high level languages and tools for generating reports based on the data in the database. Also, programming in the new relational system is much simpler than in the older system, and we are using SQL2 as our query language.

All our database files are encrypted, and this gives us added security against possible intruders, since we are accessible via the Internet. We need to be on Internet in order to share our data as widely as possible both with MediData Central and other blood products manufacturers. We use the most sophisticated security measures, and we have never experienced a serious security incident.

The issues that you want to discuss this morning relating to Michael Keating have nothing to do with the security of our computer system.

The various people who work on our database system are assigned an account, and each account has different permissions. The new relational database consists of a collection of files that are related to one another. A given employee has specific permissions with respect to the various files and the fields within those files. For example, one employee may be able to update an address field but not a blood test field. In fact, most employees interact with the system through applications that present information in report form. Most of our employees can use the database without knowing the underlying database structures. Each works with a localized view of the data.

PULITZER: Thank you for that description, Mr. Clark, but my own investigation has shown that there are areas where Red Flag needs to improve its data privacy practices. For example, there is no written policy at Red Flag concerning the kind of information that can be collected.

CLARK: There are written policies throughout the organization concerning who can handle which information. Each department within the company and each employee has access to specific data. The guiding principle is that you only get your hands on the data that you need.

PULITZER: We'll get to the issue of who gets access to which data a little later. I was really asking about the kind of data that you do collect. There is no written policy that limits the kinds of data that Red Flag can collect concerning donated blood.

CLARK: We collect the information that we need to ensure the safety of our blood products.

PULITZER: However, Red Flag's management has, on occasion, directed that new kinds of blood data be collected for the purpose of selling that data for commercial advantage. For example, you collected and sold blood alcohol data to an automobile insurance company.

CLARK: Miss Pulitzer, it is well known that you like to stir up controversy and create problems for the business community. I think your view of the world is a bit naive. Information is money. If we have access to information that an insurance company could use, well that's business. There's nothing wrong with making a buck. Besides, most of the data we sell is anonymous data.

PULITZER: Yes, such as the data shown on this map, which is part of the data you sold to an automobile insurance company. Camera three, can you get a close up on this? Great! This graphic shows the average alcohol concentrations in the blood of donors throughout California, organized by congressional district, and we see that several districts are bright red, indicating the highest levels of blood alcohol. The districts colored white have the lowest levels of blood alcohol.

CLARK: That's right, and an automobile insurance company can use that data to adjust rates in order to maximize its profits. People in the red areas are at higher risk to get involved in serious automobile accidents. They should be paying higher rates. The people in the white areas should be paying lower rates.

PULITZER: But, what about the people who live in the red areas who do not drink?

CLARK: I suggest that they consider moving to one of the more sober areas.

PULITZER: I assume that was an attempt at some dry humor.

CLARK: Dry as a martini.

PULITZER: So, Red Flag does not have a policy that limits the collection of data for entirely new purposes? Your original purpose was to use the data to protect the safety of blood products, but now you are using the data as a tool to generate revenues.

CLARK: We do not have any policy limiting the data that we can extract from donated blood, that is true. Actually, Miss Pulitzer, we see a great potential here that can benefit many companies. Can you imagine the amount of data that can be extracted from human blood? We believe that selling the data that we can extract from donated blood may become more lucrative than selling the blood products themselves.

PULITZER: Do you sell only anonymous data?

CLARK: Yes.

PULITZER: But, the data you sell to MediData Central is not anonymous.

CLARK: We do not sell anything to MediData Central. They provide a service that is used throughout the health care community. That data is intended for the use of health care providers and insurance companies only.

PULITZER: But I was able to buy data from MediData Central without any difficulty. I told them that I ran a boarding home for the elderly.

CLARK: Maybe they changed their policies.

PULITZER: Does Red Flag have a corporate policy that prohibits the sharing of data across corporate boundaries? For example, can the marketing department get blood data from the medical services department?

CLARK: We do have rules, but they are mostly implicit. Each department head decides which data under his or her jurisdiction can be shared across departmental boundaries.

PULITZER: But implicit rules are so easily violated. Who enforces them?

CLARK: I can assure you that the people in marketing have read-only access to sensitive blood data and cannot change the data in any way.

PULITZER: But why does marketing have access to sensitive blood data at all?

CLARK: Because in recent years the major thrust of the marketing department has been to enable us to profit from the sale of the blood data that we have. Also, the marketing people are responsible for determining new kinds of blood data that could be collected for the purpose of selling that data to other enterprises for a profit. That's how we found out that car insurance companies wanted blood alcohol data. That's the way business operates, Miss Pulitzer.

PULITZER: Please call me Mrs. Pulitzer. One of your employees, who wishes to remain anonymous, a woman who works in marketing, told me that she asked her supervisor for read permission on blood test data. She was hoping to research new statistical analyses on the blood data that would make that data more revealing for prospective clients. However, when she got access to the blood test data, she found that she had write access as well as read access. In other words, she received much more power over the data than she had requested. Isn't this a serious breach of security?

CLARK: What's the name of the woman who gave you that information? If you give me her name, that might help me to remember the details of this incident.

PULITZER: You know that I must keep her identity confidential. I want to know whether this was a unique incident or whether this is common practice at Red Flag?

CLARK: Miss Pulitzer, if I kept track of every little detail like this just so I could answer your questions, I wouldn't be able to do my job properly.

PULITZER: Deliberate destruction of data is grounds for dismissal from Red Flag and possibly grounds for criminal prosecution. Is there an explicit policy concerning sabotage and malicious acts of destruction?

CLARK: Of course.

PULITZER: However, my investigation found that you do not have an explicit policy regarding accidental destruction of data or accidental leaks.

CLARK: Our new database gives us better capabilities in terms of tracking down the sources of clerical errors, for example. Clerical errors are a grave danger to a database such as ours, but we know of no incident where a clerical error compromised the safety of our blood products.

PULITZER: A major charge against Michael Keating is that he sold blood donor information to several institutions, including a hospital and two major employers here in Silicon Valley. He sold information regarding the HIV status of a doctor and four other people. It is conceivable that he sold other data, but these are the cases that we know about thus far. Did Michael Keating have access to the blood donor database?

CLARK: No. As an applications developer, he always worked with fake data in developing and testing his programs. He did not have write access or read access to any part of the blood donor database.

PULITZER: Then where did he get the data that he sold?

CLARK: You know as well as I do, Miss Pulitzer.

PULITZER: I'd rather hear it from you.

CLARK: From a recycling bin.

PULITZER: Could you elaborate on that?

CLARK: Red Flag recycles. I think the law forces us to do that. In any event, the paper really piles up because the paper recycling truck only comes by once every two weeks. Michael Keating spent some time going through the trash, and he found out that these five people were HIV positive. He got that information from computer printouts that were left in the trash. He contacted the hospital first, and he told them, "One of your doctors is HIV positive. Would you like to buy that information?" and they did.

PULITZER: The hospital had a public policy of considering the HIV status of its staff a private matter. Why did they buy this data from Keating?

CLARK: Because their public policy and their private beliefs were inconsistent. The hospital obviously wanted to get rid of this physician if they could prove that he was HIV positive. The public disclosure that the doctor was HIV positive and the consequent public furor forced the doctor to resign.

PULITZER: What about the others that Keating exposed?

CLARK: Keating sold the data to their employers, who fired them, until the public outcry forced the companies to reinstate the people concerned. Just the opposite of the situation at the hospital!

PULITZER: In this morning's *Sentinel-Observer*, which probably has not been delivered as yet, I reveal that Michael Keating was evidently planning to run a regular business using data he had access to at Red Flag, data obtained from discarded computer printouts. Silicon Valley police found evidence that Keating was planning to extort money from a prominent local politician who was listed as a sexual contact by a man who tested HIV positive. An extortion note and other evidence was found at Keating's house.

Mr. Clark, your company does not have a policy concerning the handling of hard copies of data.

CLARK: We do now.

PULITZER: Is there any evidence that Michael Keating tried to get unauthorized access to data using the computer?

CLARK: None whatsoever. We have effective security measures in place, and we also have comprehensive auditing of all activities on our system. It would be difficult to violate security, even for someone as resourceful as Michael Keating.

PULITZER: Our last guest is Marvin Moore. Mr. Moore was Michael Keating's immediate boss at Red Flag. He supervised the programming work that Michael did at Red Flag. Mr. Moore, can you explain how the tainted blood got out to the public?

MOORE: This was a result of a bug in a program written by Michael Keating.

PULITZER: Yes, but what was the nature of that bug?

MOORE: It's not easy to explain what he did.

PULITZER: Could you give it a try?

MOORE: In the new relational database system, Michael was writing an application that would display blood data at the screen. This application would allow the user to make changes to the blood data, after which the revised blood data would go out to the database. Basically, this was a database update application.

Each SQL query against our database produces at most one thousand records, so Michael wrote a little C routine to sort those records according to social security number. I cannot, for the life of me, figure out why he insisted on doing his own sorting routine, since SQL provides for sorting a query result. In technical terms, Michael was using embedded SQL in a C host language environment, so he wrote the sorting routine in C. The sorting routine he used required the swapping of records produced by the SQL query. He did this by swapping the data field by field. He did a normal swap for all fields except for the infectious disease blood test field. Now, this is really bizarre. Instead of doing a normal swap using a temporary variable, he used a C feature where you can do a swap without a temporary variable using the bitwise exclusive OR operator. Unfortunately, he implemented this incorrectly, with the result that some HIV positive codes were dropping out as negatives.

The fact that this error could have slipped by is evidence that Red Flag has serious deficiencies in terms of software quality assurance and testing. The problem is that we have a mentality where writing new applications is rather routine and testing new applications is done rather informally. In fact, I thought that this application was tested rather exhaustively, but obviously our testing was not adequate. As it turns out, none of the test data suites for Mr. Keating's application included an HIV-positive code of 127, and hence the deadly data was never detected. This was the only input value for which Mr. Keating's code does not work properly. But, I must say, his code is a mess. I can't say that I understand all of its intricate obscurities.

PULITZER: A security system is only as strong as its weakest link, wouldn't you say?

MOORE: Yes.

PULITZER: Isn't the fact that Michael Keating's software could destroy the integrity of your data a security issue? The way I see it, Michael Keating had de facto write access to the sensitive data in the database!

MOORE: No, he did not. He had neither read nor write access to the database.

PULITZER: But his programs could update the database, so it seems to me that he had effective write access to the database. He could compromise the integrity of the database.

MOORE: Okay. I see what you're trying to say.

PULITZER: Someone who writes applications programs for a database of this nature should be treated as a person who could potentially do great harm. Someone should have looked more carefully into his background and his character.

MOORE: I couldn't agree with you more, Ms. Pulitzer.

PULITZER: How many people received tainted blood as a result of this incident?

MOORE: Thirty-one.

PULITZER: Is there any evidence that Michael Keating acted maliciously to subvert the blood donation database?

MOORE: That's not for me to say. That's a police matter.

PULITZER: Did you find Randy Samuels's essay "In Praise of Obscurity" tacked to the wall next to Michael Keating's workstation at Red Flag?

MOORE: Yes, I did.

PULITZER: Would you have allowed Michael Keating onto your team knowing what you now know about his previous history?

MOORE: Absolutely not. I would have told Jane Farnsworth that I don't want this guy working here at Red Flag, and she would have kept him out. At Red Flag, we're dealing with people's lives.

PULITZER: I would like to thank my guests for appearing on "Roundtable" this morning. I hope the viewing audience learned some things about data and data privacy. This is your "Roundtable" reporter, Pam Pulitzer, wishing you a pleasant Sunday. Look for my article on the Red Flag situation this morning in the Sunday *Sentinel-Observer!*

Transcript of "Roundtable," the Sunday Morning Public Affairs Program, Broadcast on Public American Television

---

Transcript of "Close-Up," Public Television's Premiere Program about Academics and Academe

IS YOUR COMPUTER
STEALING FROM YOU?

CLOSE-UP: Good evening. I am Stanley Kahn, reporter for the Silicon Valley *Sentinel-Observer*, and your host for this week's edition of "Close-Up."

This evening's guest is Professor Jacob Lowe-Tignoff, professor of religious studies at Silicon Valley University. Professor Lowe-Tignoff received his Ph.D. from Temple University. He is also ordained as a rabbi in the Conservative branch of Judaism. Last year Professor Lowe-Tignoff's book, *Is Your Computer Stealing from You?*, won several prestigious awards. It was on the *New York Times* Best Sellers list for twelve straight weeks. This evening we are going to discuss Professor Lowe-Tignoff's thesis that computers can potentially steal away important human capabilities.

Welcome to "Close-Up," Professor Lowe-Tignoff.

LOWE-TIGNOFF: It's a pleasure to be here with you.

CLOSE-UP: Your book states that we need to develop a theory of ethical behavior for computers.

LOWE-TIGNOFF: More than a theory—actual guidelines. We need to develop ethical guidelines for computers that are similar to the ones that we already have for people. I am certainly not the only one who is discussing these issues.

CLOSE-UP: When I read what you had to say, my first reaction was that it was . . .

LOWE-TIGNOFF: Ridiculous! Let's be honest. Let's not mince words. People think that ethical constraints are for humans. They don't envision the possibility that we might have to impose ethical constraints on computers as well.

CLOSE-UP: Okay. At first I thought that the idea of ethical guidelines for computers was ridiculous, but by the time I reached the end of your book, I was a true believer. Computers have the potential to do great damage to human beings, as you emphasize.

LOWE-TIGNOFF: In the book I talk a lot about "Human Being," with a capital H and a capital B. "Human Being" refers to our humanity in the broadest possible sense. It refers to all aspects of our being human. I am raising the issue of whether computer systems should be constructed if they have the potential to diminish Human Being.

CLOSE-UP: Your book makes a subtle distinction between the need for ethical computer systems and the need for moral computer systems.

LOWE-TIGNOFF: My book suggests that professional societies develop ethical guidelines for computer systems. That is, using reasonable principles that most computing professionals can agree upon, we need to place constraints on computer systems and also to describe desirable properties for computer systems. I fear that unless the professional societies act first, then legislative bodies may try to regulate computers as a matter of public policy.

These ethical guidelines for computers should be somewhat narrow in focus, like the ethical guidelines that professional societies have already produced for computing professionals. For example, my book attempts to establish the principle that computers should not be allowed to steal as a fundamental principle behind any such set of ethical guidelines.

I also believe, as a religious believer, that computer systems should be moral. If someone tries to develop a computer system that deeply violates my sense of morality, I will try to oppose it. That sense of morality essentially derives from my religious beliefs. Since people have differing religious and philosophical beliefs, there will be conflict over issues of morality. In a democratic society, all sides have an opportunity to freely express their perspectives.

CLOSE-UP: Would you say, then, that you wrote more about ethics than about morality in your book because you felt that there is a more universal consensus within the computing profession about what is ethical and what is not?

LOWE-TIGNOFF: Yes. *More* universal, but not universal. For example, most computer scientists would agree that computer systems should be easy to use, that they should be reliable and effective, and that they should not steal, lie, or cheat. My book examines computer systems, both real and hypothetical, and asks whether these systems behave in an ethical manner based on the general consensus within the computing profession as to what constitutes ethical behavior.

CLOSE-UP: Is there such a consensus within the computing profession?

LOWE-TIGNOFF: I assume that professional codes of ethics, such as the ACM Code of Ethics, represent the broad outlines of such a consensus. These proscribe lying, stealing, cheating, and causing harm. They emphasize that computer systems should be harmless to humans and to the environment. They emphasize the need for systems to be responsive to user needs and not to hurt users physically or psychologically. Thus, my point of departure for discussing ethical computer systems is that such systems should be at least as ethical as the computer professionals who develop them.

Programmers and developers need to adhere to codes of ethics, but we also need a basis for judging whether a computer system is itself behaving ethically. Is a computer stealing, is it damaging the environment, is it spreading rumors and lies, is it promoting unnecessary violence and destruction? When we look at a computer system from an ethical perspective, we must ask questions about its functionality, about its impact on users, society, and the environment. That is the gist of my book.

CLOSE-UP: These concerns seem obvious. Computers should not murder, steal, or lie. But then in reading your book, I realized that your characterization of stealing is more comprehensive than the usual one, and that it subsumes almost every other kind of unethical and immoral behavior.

LOWE-TIGNOFF: Yes, in order to give my discussion of ethics for computer systems greater coherence, I characterize all ethical lapses as acts of stealing.

CLOSE-UP: What constitutes stealing, then, in your framework?

LOWE-TIGNOFF: Stealing means to diminish oneself or another in some way, to diminish oneself or another spiritually, physically, materially, or psychologically. Another way of stating it is that to steal is to do harm to oneself or to another.

When you diminish another person, you always diminish yourself as well. When you diminish yourself, you diminish all others simultaneously.

CLOSE-UP: Suppose I have a headache and somehow you take that away from me. Is that stealing?

LOWE-TIGNOFF: No. Presumably you have given me permission to take the headache away.

CLOSE-UP: But what if I don't want you to take it away?

LOWE-TIGNOFF: Then, if you are an adult person, I should not take your headache away unless there is some other compelling reason to do so. Perhaps you are a pilot, and your having a headache endangers the lives of your passengers.

CLOSE-UP: Before we discuss your concept of stealing in greater depth, I would like to back up a bit and ask you how you got interested in developing ethical guidelines for computers.

LOWE-TIGNOFF: I started thinking along these lines after I read a pair of articles by a computer scientist named Roger Clarke. He tried to use Asimov's laws for robots as a means of deriving principles for the construction of ethical laws for information systems. He ended up with a set of commonsense principles, but I do not believe that Asimov's laws were an essential starting point.

Let me read you the text of Asimov's laws of robotics as quoted by Roger Clarke:

First Law: *A robot may not injure a human being, or, through inaction, allow a human being to come to harm.*

Second Law: *A robot must obey the orders given it by human beings, except where such orders would conflict with the First Law.*

Third Law: *A robot must protect its own existence as long as such protection does not conflict with the First or Second Law.*

Clarke goes on to discuss the inadequacy of these laws and a set of revised laws that were subsequently developed by Asimov. Finally, Clarke develops a set of general principles for information systems.

I enjoyed Clarke's articles, but I think it is better to start with ethical principles that govern humans as opposed to ethical principles specifically devised for robots and computer systems. As a first approximation, if we view a computer system as being capable of doing whatever a human being can do behaviorally, then certainly the computer system should be bound by the same ethical guidelines that guide the behavior of human beings. For example, since human beings are not allowed to steal, computer systems should not be allowed to do so.

Now, this is just a first approximation because computer systems can potentially do things that humans cannot do, and we need to discuss that possibility as well.

Ethical principles are constraints on the human capacity for harmful behavior. If we study codes of ethics, we see that they also encourage positive contributions to society. These codes are not just proscriptive.

I think that a computer system should be programmed to fulfill the same ethical obligations as a human being. It should not do harm. It should contribute to the good.

However, as my book indicates, there is a subtle danger lurking in computer systems that needs to be addressed.

CLOSE-UP: Namely, the possibility that a computer system can potentially steal human capabilities?

LOWE-TIGNOFF: Precisely. That is my main message. That is my reason for being, to communicate this message and to alert people to that danger.

CLOSE-UP: Before we get to that, let's discuss your general theory about ethics. Your book illuminates the relationship between modern ethical problems and the source materials that provide the spiritual, cultural, legal, and ethical foundations for what you call "traditional civilizations."

LOWE-TIGNOFF: I also call them "self-renewing civilizations." We are talking about Hinduism, Judaism, Buddhism, Christianity, and Islam. These are the civilizations that have survived for at least one millennium and some for as many as five millennia. Thus, they seem to be self-renewing. Some people say that Hinduism has been around for five millennia. Judaism, Christianity, and Islam can trace their origins back to Abraham, who lived almost four thousand years ago. Buddhism is twenty-five hundred years old. By contrast, Nazi Germany lasted twelve years, and the Soviet Union lasted about seventy years.

The basic ethical precepts in all these traditional civilizations are proscriptions against stealing in various forms. The fundamental moral precepts are these:

1. Do not steal.
2. Do not murder.
3. Do not lie.
4. Do not use sexuality to hurt others.
5. Do not destroy your wisdom (with drugs, destructive emotions, or intoxicants).

CLOSE-UP: In your book, you show that these principles are actually proscriptions against stealing.

LOWE-TIGNOFF: Yes. I took the Ten Commandments and showed how each commandment could be viewed as an attempt to prevent people from diminishing themselves and from diminishing some "other" or "others."

CLOSE-UP: So, for example, if you worship idols, you diminish yourself, or you steal from yourself.

LOWE-TIGNOFF: Correct. You also steal from God.

CLOSE-UP: Could you explain the five precepts in terms of the concept of stealing?

LOWE-TIGNOFF: "Do not steal" is a proscription against taking the property of another. Of course, when you steal someone's property, you are diminishing their wealth and perhaps their happiness, but you are also diminishing yourself. You are a thief.

Stealing property is the concrete manifestation of stealing as a cosmic idea. In other words, conventional stealing is a symbol for and a reminder of the other forms of stealing.

"Do not murder" is a proscription against stealing away the life of another. The universe has given that person a life, but you decide you don't like the way the universe has arranged things, so you murder that person to try to get the universe to bend to your will. But you cannot get the universe to bend to your will. Instead, your act of deliberate evil forces the universe to compensate for your action. The universe is all-aware, alive, and intelligent.

In committing a murder, you diminish the other and you diminish yourself. You diminish yourself because you will have to suffer the consequences of your act at some level. You are a murderer, and you know it at all of the various levels of your being, conscious and unconscious.

CLOSE-UP: What about the other precepts?

LOWE-TIGNOFF: When you lie, you steal the truth away from the person who listens to your lies, unless they have the wisdom not to believe you. When you bear false witness against your neighbor, you are stealing away his or her integrity, dignity, and honor. Lying diminishes those who believe the lies by rendering them less knowledgeable. In lying, one diminishes oneself because one lives in an environment of falsehood. Furthermore, one is a liar, and one knows that one is a liar at all of the various levels of one's being, conscious and unconscious.

To gossip is also a sin, because you are stealing from a person's integrity, dignity, and honor. In other words, you are diminishing that person's reputation and the affection due to that person. Of course, the gossip also reduces his or her own stature on many levels.

The proscription against hurting others using sexuality is also about stealing. For example, if a man commits adultery with another man's wife, then he is stealing from his own wife and from that other man. He is also stealing from himself and from the woman he slept with. If you look at it in terms of diminishment, those who committed the act and all of those who are influenced by the act, especially the spouses and the children, are all diminished. At the very least, their happiness and peace of mind are diminished.

The proscription against destroying one's wisdom usually takes the form of a proscription against the use of alcohol, drugs, and intoxicants. However, anger, hatred, excessive fear, and anxiety also destroy wisdom. Clearly, if one destroys one's wisdom, then one has greatly diminished oneself. One's stature as a human being is much less. In addition, by destroying one's own wisdom, one contributes much less to the world, and thus the whole world is diminished.

Hurting the brain with excessive alcohol and drugs is stealing away from oneself in a dramatic and sometimes irreversible manner. The alcoholic not only steals from himself, the alcoholic steals from his family and friends. He steals away their peace of mind and, if he is violent, their physical safety. He can also steal away the prosperity his family might have enjoyed if he had been able to keep gainful employment. The alcoholic or other drug-dependent person diminishes himself and everyone in his environment.

What I am describing is the actual spiritual state of things. By thoughtless and unethical behavior, we greatly diminish ourselves and everyone and everything around us.

CLOSE-UP: I appreciate your perspective that when we act unethically or immorally, we are diminishing ourselves and others.

LOWE-TIGNOFF: Thank you.

CLOSE-UP: Now, taking these ideas and applying them to computers, what you are saying is that computers and computer technology have the potential to diminish human beings, to reduce our stature spiritually and psychologically.

LOWE-TIGNOFF: Absolutely. That is what I wrote, and that is what I believe.

CLOSE-UP: This is an important assertion, so how can you convince us of it?

LOWE-TIGNOFF: Let's analyze the impact that a computer system has when it is placed in its intended environment. Is that computer system stealing in any way? If it is stealing, is it contributing something in return that compensates for the stealing? In other words, we must demand that if a computer system steals, then it must more than compensate for its stealing by adding something of value to our lives and society.

CLOSE-UP: In other words, it must contribute more than it takes away?

LOWE-TIGNOFF: Yes.

CLOSE-UP: For example, you wrote that a computer system with a poor user interface is stealing from the user.

LOWE-TIGNOFF: Yes, it could steal in a variety of ways. It could steal the user's eyesight, or it could convert an enjoyable job into a hellish one. A computer with a poor user interface can diminish the user's happiness and physical health.

If a computer system is not reliable, it can steal the life of its operator, as in the case of the killer robot incident. A database system can steal away truth if it does not maintain the integrity of its data.

CLOSE-UP: But your main thrust is that computers might diminish human capacity, in effect, stealing from the human race.

LOWE-TIGNOFF: I am concerned about all of the issues that we have been discussing on this program. I believe we should carefully analyze each computer system from the point of view of how it can steal from users, clients, and what has been called the penumbra of that computer system.

CLOSE-UP: What is the penumbra of a computer system?

LOWE-TIGNOFF: This term was used by Robert Collins and his coauthors in their article on ethical guidelines for computer systems. It refers to all people indirectly influenced by the computer system. You see, a computer system can have a large penumbra, and thus it may diminish the quality of life for many, many people.

CLOSE-UP: Or it may be making their lives better in some way.

LOWE-TIGNOFF: For example, the penumbra for the killer robot includes Mrs. Matthews, the widow of the robot operator, her children, and other relatives. It includes the lawyers who have gotten involved in the case and, most broadly, the public that has gotten so absorbed in the issues raised by this incident.

If computer scientists begin to develop computer systems that steal fundamental human capabilities—such as medical judgments, ethical judgments, artistic and scientific creativity—then the penumbra will include all of humanity. There is a danger that we will all be greatly diminished by such a technological development. It will be a threat to our very humanity.

CLOSE-UP: These systems might augment human capabilities and human stature.

LOWE-TIGNOFF: This is what we need to look at. We shouldn't go into this new era with our heads buried in the sand.

Here are some hypothetical examples that I used in my book to illustrate this point.

Suppose a computer system is designed to make decisions in criminal trials. The system is motivated by a lack of faith in the jury system. The system requires that trained professionals take the facts in the case, prepared by lawyers, and enter them into a knowledge base. The computer system then reaches a verdict in the case and decides on a sentence. The judge is reduced to a mere administrator of data. One of the judge's responsibilities would be to read the computer results to the defendant and his lawyer.

The researchers who developed the system might test their product using the following experimental design. They choose a set of actual court cases that were decided by a traditional jury and judge. They then ask the computer system to arrive at a verdict and a sentence for each of these cases. The researchers then ask a population of legal scholars, in a blind test, to study the court cases and to indicate which gave the better judgment: the actual judge and jury in the case or the computer system. Suppose that the researchers discover that the population of legal scholars favor the computer system over the actual judge and jury eighty percent of the time.

I think a scenario like this is very possible in the next fifty to one hundred years, if not sooner. If we allow computer systems to try people and to pass sentence, are we allowing the computer system to steal from us? I would also like to know what it is that the computer is stealing and whether we, as human beings, can afford to allow computers to take that ability away from us.

The hypothetical computer system that I am discussing will be taking away our right to be judged by a jury of our peers.

CLOSE-UP: Someone might respond, But the peers are in the code. That is, the peers are the ones who wrote the program.

LOWE-TIGNOFF: But those are not representative peers.

CLOSE-UP: But what if the computer system is actually better than a human jury? Shouldn't we use the computer system?

LOWE-TIGNOFF: Would you want to be judged by a computer program if you were on trial for a crime you did not commit?

CLOSE-UP: Yes, if the computer program could do a better job than a human jury. Look at the jury pools that we have seen in some recent celebrity trials.

LOWE-TIGNOFF: So we should allow computers to serve as judge and jury because our justice system has so many serious deficiencies? Is that it?

CLOSE-UP: Perhaps. I really need some time to think this over.

LOWE-TIGNOFF: Your willingness to give up that human prerogative to a computer is what I call stealing. The computer would be stealing away a human function that has been central to our humanity for millennia.

CLOSE-UP: Is it stealing if we willingly, as a society, turn over this function to expert systems that are better than the "man on the street"? Stealing involves taking something from a person without that person's permission.

LOWE-TIGNOFF: Is it stealing if you voluntarily give something over to a con artist because you don't understand the value of what you are surrendering?

CLOSE-UP: You're implying that I am not seeing the full magnitude of what we human beings would be losing if we hand certain functions over to the computer.

LOWE-TIGNOFF: Yes. Are we not losing something by having no human element, no human involvement, in the judgment process?

CLOSE-UP: But there is some human involvement. Human beings programmed the computer.

LOWE-TIGNOFF: In the Bible, Solomon displays his wisdom, in part, by adjudicating difficult cases. His brilliance is demonstrated by extraordinarily intuitive but effective leaps of judgment. This is part of our humanity.

CLOSE-UP: I see. A figure like Solomon could not be recognized or acknowledged in the brave new world of the computerized court room. A fundamental human capacity would be reduced . . .

LOWE-TIGNOFF: Would atrophy. It would atrophy from lack of use. In other words, Human Being, with a capital H and a capital B, would be diminished.

Is there something fundamentally human about the wisdom that is required to pass judgment on another human being? Isn't this one of the nexus points where justice, compassion, and mercy meet, are developed, and are exercised? If this nexus point is removed, will justice, compassion, and mercy still have an opportunity to develop and manifest among humans?

Judges have been around since Biblical times. In all just societies, the responsibility of the judge has been based on a keen sensitivity to the rights of the accused and the presumption of innocence until guilt is proven. This is one nexus point where society expresses its capacity for justice, compassion, mercy, and empathy. Can we afford to say "Oh, this is too messy. Let the computer do it"?

Now, what if this happens in medicine and other professional areas as well? More and more, tough decisions are handed over to computer systems. Decisions about diagnosing illness, prescribing drugs. The doctor becomes a mere adjunct to the computer, which has enormous databases filled with knowledge. Engineers, computer scientists, accountants, and so forth all defer decision making more and more to computer systems. Is something being stolen? Is Human Being diminished?

CLOSE-UP: I see. A certain kind of thought process, involving risky thinking, involving tough decisions, is moved more and more onto the computer systems. Then what is the brain being used for? Who needs a brain one hundred or two hundred years from now?

LOWE-TIGNOFF: It's not just a thought process. It's that nexus of responsibility for our actions that makes us ultimately human. That nexus implies that we are conscious beings, that we are not automata. Shouldn't we think about all this *now* before it becomes a fait accompli?

Here's another possibility: A computer system that does our moral and ethical reasoning for us. Thinking ethically is too difficult—let's reduce it to a bunch of question sets, rules, and guidelines, and let the computer grind it out. Then we are free of all of those messy, difficult decisions. What if some computer system becomes the dominant means of ethical decision making?

CLOSE-UP: That reminds me of the infamous "killer robot tapes" that were played on the radio a few months back. Maybe Randy Samuels should have used such a system before deciding to tell George Cuzzins what Zelda Riddle-Davis told him about her being a lousy programmer. I face decisions like that all the time, and I wouldn't mind having the help of a computer.

LOWE-TIGNOFF: But what will the computer be stealing if this happens? Isn't there a sense in which your being will be diminished? Isn't there some human value in wrestling with ethical dilemmas and coming to a courageous decision when courage is required? Isn't the ability to decide between right and wrong a fundamental part of human nature? Can we afford to have that stolen from us?

CLOSE-UP: But couldn't human wisdom just be shifting from one domain to another? Solomon displayed his wisdom by judging disputes, but human beings in the future could display their wisdom by judging other issues, for example, issues involving the use of technology.

LOWE-TIGNOFF: I do not think so.

CLOSE-UP: Maybe the future will be a paradise. We will spend our years writing, composing, and doing those things that are challenging and soulful.

LOWE-TIGNOFF: Well, let's find out. Consider this hypothetical situation: A computer system is developed to compose newspapers automatically from compilations of raw facts and data. This is necessary because competing sources of information are all on-line and newspapers must be produced with incredible speed in order to provide relevant information. Human story writers are not up to the challenge, so a computer system now writes and composes newspapers. Reporters are laid off by the thousands. What do you think of that? You're a reporter.

CLOSE-UP: That damn computer just stole *my* job!

LOWE-TIGNOFF: Is that all?

CLOSE-UP: It stole away my passion—I am passionate about writing. Now I have no outlet for my passion.

LOWE-TIGNOFF: Who cares? People dislike the press, so they are happy to see you get yours.

CLOSE-UP: This system is stealing away something from the newspaper, something human, and it's stealing from the readers. They're not going to get that passion.

LOWE-TIGNOFF: Oh, but this computer system can add as much passion as it needs to. On a scale of 0 through 10, how much passion do we want in today's paper? Okay, put that into the machine, and let the machine grind it out.

Now consider the following hypothetical scenario: A computer system is developed to compose and perform music of a particular genre. Its compositions prove demonstrably better than human compositions in that people enjoy the computer-generated music much more. All musicians who compose and perform music in this genre see themselves being pushed aside by the public's enthusiasm for the computer-generated music. Is something being stolen here?

CLOSE-UP: Musicians are losing their jobs, and musicians are passionate about what they are doing. Does this music have feeling?

LOWE-TIGNOFF: This is the future, and computers have become incredibly adept at capturing feeling. The audiences love it. This new music is creative and brings in new elements the human composers had not imagined.

CLOSE-UP: Maybe this is just a better way to compose music. The system must reflect the true musical genius of at least one person.

LOWE-TIGNOFF: But what about the human musicians who are out of a job? No one wants to listen to their music any longer. Have we stolen something from them? If we say "that is progress" as group after group is dispossessed by computer systems, where is this heading?

CLOSE-UP: Artistic capabilities might atrophy as well as technical capabilities.

LOWE-TIGNOFF: So, what is left—computer programming? All human creativity is moved over to computer programming, but then the computer is better than the human even when it comes to computer programming.

In the end, the computers will do nearly everything that is intellectually challenging. Human beings will end up doing things that are too boring for the computer, like hauling manure. Humans will be mere slaves to an all-encompassing network of intelligent computers that will intrude into every aspect of human life. We'll be slaves, like the Israelites in ancient Egypt. The computer will be new Pharaoh.

CLOSE-UP: So, inevitably, we human beings will have to impose limitations on our computer systems.

LOWE-TIGNOFF: You're assuming that the man on the street will have the intelligence to see what is happening.

Let me put it bluntly. Inevitably and inexorably, computer technology will become as potentially dangerous as genetic engineering is today. Just as genetic engineering has the potential to introduce something into the environment that is devastating, so computer technology can also threaten human self-confidence, wisdom, and sovereignty.

CLOSE-UP: You said that the computer has the potential to become an intoxicant, like alcohol or drugs.

LOWE-TIGNOFF: Yes. That is already happening. Consider virtual reality entertainment. As the earth is despoiled, as the oceans become ever more polluted, as the air quality diminishes, as species disappear, as nuclear waste and garbage accumulate, as the population explodes and ecological systems are choked by human wastes and garbage, as free spaces disappear, as more and more of the natural world is pushed aside to make room for development and progress, as all these things happen and manifest, people can always resort to their virtual reality helmets and data gloves in order to experience mountains, oceans, rivers, the skies, the long-gone natural order.

You see, this is just the purpose of drugs and intoxicants. Because actual reality is becoming so bleak, we will resort to an intoxicant that will allow us to escape from that reality. So now we are creating a technology that will allow us to smell beautiful flowers and see beautiful scenes, even as we are up to our eyeballs in our own garbage.

CLOSE-UP: So what is being stolen here?

LOWE-TIGNOFF: In this case, our ability to process the feedback that the universe is trying to give us concerning the stupidity of our behavior. Whenever another precious species disappears, whenever another beach is closed because of pollution or oil washing ashore, whenever the earth appears diminished in its beauty and its richness, that is feedback from the universe that we are not being good stewards of the earth.

CLOSE-UP: Virtual reality can shut out the social reality as well: the poverty, the violence, the inequity, the despair.

LOWE-TIGNOFF: Of course.

CLOSE-UP: Do you think we need laws to govern technological development?

LOWE-TIGNOFF: I think laws will be necessary for those sectors where jobs are being lost and human capabilities are being stolen. Our civilization needs to consider whether we want our newspapers to be written by computers, whether we want computers as judge and jury, whether we want computers to diagnose and treat our illnesses, to make ethical and moral decisions for us, to write our novels, to educate our children, to compose and play our music, and to create our motion pictures.

CLOSE-UP: Are you pursuing these issues further? Is there another book that we can look forward to?

LOWE-TIGNOFF: I am working on a new book, or maybe several books. I have some chapters written out. This new book is not so much about computers, but the whole idea of how we diminish ourselves and others. My computer book emphasized stealing as a primordial ethical lapse. By the end of that book, I started to focus on this idea of how we diminish ourselves and others. The "other" could be God, my neighbor, a tree, an owl, the ocean, this entire planet. Whenever I do not admit the profound greatness of the other—of God, of my neighbor, of that tree in front of my house, of that majestic owl looking down from that tree, of the ocean, of this beautiful earth—then I diminish myself. I diminish who I am. You see, the other is not "other" at all. When we diminish another, we are diminishing ourselves. When we diminish ourselves, we diminish all others simultaneously.

CLOSE-UP: Can't you state it more positively? Shouldn't our effort be to augment, increase, or glorify everyone else and ourselves? I can't find the exact word I need here.

LOWE-TIGNOFF: I would use the word *redeem*. We would like to redeem ourselves and the world, to make the system whole and harmonious again. The danger is that people who think that they know how to redeem the world often become too aggressive, too imperialistic. It is a very delicate matter to think that you know what is good for another person. Thus, I emphasize respecting others—not diminishing them; not lying, stealing, and cheating; not doing things that will hurt other people. Perhaps if we remove the hurtfulness, redemption will flower by itself.

CLOSE-UP: One difficulty I had with your book was that you seem to insist that the computers are doing the stealing, when in fact it seems more accurate to describe the situation as our surrendering our talents to the computer. Who is really doing the stealing?

LOWE-TIGNOFF: My answer to your question is that we are stealing from ourselves. We have free will. If we give something away that is rightfully ours, we are stealing from ourselves.

CLOSE-UP: In your book you wrote that you were afraid that human beings were surrendering their spiritual power. What is spiritual power?

LOWE-TIGNOFF: I think that it is the power to redeem, heal, and repair.

CLOSE-UP: Did it ever occur to you that what you call "stealing" is just the opposite of love? Diminishing oneself, diminishing others, all of this is just the opposite of what love would do. Love heals, replenishes, and redeems that which has been diminished. Do you think that we are allowing computers to steal from us because we do not know how to love one another?

LOWE-TIGNOFF: That could explain what is going on.

CLOSE-UP: That's it for this evening's program. If you have any comments about this evening's program, please send them to close-up@naptv.org. I would like to thank Professor Lowe-Tignoff for offering his perspective on where computer technology is heading.

An Interview with Professor Jacob Lowe-Tignoff

Silicon Valley University's
CANDID PROFESSOR

ANNOUNCER: Those are the famous chimes of the Silicon Valley University Clarion Tower. It must be time for another lecture in our "Candid Professor" series. This week's lecture will be given by Professor Harry Yoder. The course: Computer Science 412—Ethical Issues in Computing. As you can see, the students are anxiously awaiting the illustrious Professor Yoder, who has written numerous books and articles about the social impact of computing and computer ethics. He is the Samuel Southerland Professor of Computer Technology and Ethics at the university.

As regular viewers of "Candid Professor" are certainly aware, Professor Yoder has no idea that he is going to be on television this morning. Of course, as soon as he sees our lights and cameras, he'll know that he's the "Professor of the Week" for this venerable Silicon Valley University tradition.

YODER: Oh, no! Of all weeks, why did you have to choose this week?

ANNOUNCER: We're taping this even as you speak, Professor. You know the rules. Harry Yoder, you're the "'Candid Professor' Professor of the Week."

YODER: How can I lecture with all of those lights in my face? I can't see my students. That's better, thank you.

Class, I have your exams, and I will return them to you at the end of the hour.

CLASS: Can't we get them back now?

YODER: Look, I cannot lecture when you guys are having evil thoughts about me.

Now, today's assignment was to read and discuss the paper "How Good Is Good Enough?" by Collins, Miller, Spielman, and Wherry published in the *Communications of the ACM* in January 1994. I hope you guys did a good job of reading that paper because, as you know, I was away in Hawaii last week at an important computer ethics conference. On top of that, I had to grade your midterms. On top of that, I rushed to class straight from the airport.

CLASS: Poor Professor Yoder!

YODER: Okay, let's cut out the sarcasm. It was not all fun and games as you imagine. This was a computer ethics conference, not OOPSLA. So who can give me a brief description of the paper that you were asked to read?

CLARISSA: It's about developing a framework for deciding whether it is ethical to release a software system.

YODER: An ethical framework as opposed to what?

CLARISSA: As opposed to a framework that is based just on technical issues, on software quality assurance.

YODER: And why is that important? Someone else.

JAMIE: Because the science of software quality assurance is not far enough along in terms of its reliability to allow those techniques to be used to decide whether software gets out the door.

YODER: Can you give some specific examples?

JAMIE: Software testing cannot find all bugs. Some bugs are related to the way in which users interact with the software. They may escape detection during normal software testing.

YODER: Do you buy this idea that technical criteria alone may not be sufficient to decide whether software is ready for release?

CLASS: Yes.

YODER: Any dissenters?

ABIGAIL: I think that the ethical criteria are just as primitive as the technical. The authors themselves state this at the end of their paper. In other words, I think these ideas need to be discussed over a period of time. Perhaps after ten years of intense deliberations we will arrive at a good set of ethical criteria.

NATE: I agree with Abigail. But it may not take ten years. It could take longer. I believe that ethical criteria may be as difficult to develop as technical criteria.

YODER: Let's discuss the criteria developed by Collins and his coauthors. First of all, what were the basic principles behind the development of their ethical guidelines?

NATE: The fundamental idea is that of a social contract, as found in the writings of Rousseau and Locke. For example, the proper behavior for the government and its citizens is based upon a contract between the government and its citizens. For Americans, the Constitution embodies that contract.

JAMIE: Perhaps we need a standard document like the U.S. Constitution that would explain the duties and obligations of the various parties involved in a software project.

ABIGAIL: That's why this paper is so important. I think it is leading us in that direction. I didn't take it as the final word. I think a document for computing professionals based on the notion of a social contract would go a long way toward outlining the duties and obligations of the various parties.

CLARISSA: Yes, the contract concept seems to be cropping up more and more in discussions of software and software engineering. In my software engineering class with Professor Silber, we discussed Bertrand Meyer's notion that classes should be designed around the concept of a "contract" that lists the duties of the various pieces of software as well as the benefits accrued by the use of that software. I would assert, therefore, that the contract idea is fundamental in computing because of the nature of computing and because of its complexity. The contract concept is inherent in the need to divide up responsibilities in the construction of a software system. It may be that software itself will need to be organized using the contract concept, just as society has been organized around the idea of a social contract.

YODER: Anyone else?

NATE: I am also taking software engineering this semester. I like what Clarissa said. Obligations and benefits are the building blocks of contracts, and it is interesting that these concepts apply at various levels of software construction. Turning back to the ethical and social implications of software systems, I think the message is that we have to carefully consider the parties involved, their duties, and the benefits that they can expect. Benefits are just as important as duties.

YODER: Okay, we will discuss this issue of benefits and duties a bit later. But I would like to return to the framework that Collins and his coauthors developed. Can someone give a summary of how that framework was constructed?

JAMIE: The authors relied heavily on an ethical theory of John Rawls that stressed negotiations between interested parties leading to a contract that would list the obligations of the various parties. The benefits are implicit, although I think they should be explicit.

CLARISSA: There was more to the ethical theory than the idea of contracts. The authors listed fairness, rationality, and a certain kind of ignorance as important for the negotiation of the contractual obligations. The parties in the negotiation would be fair, rational, and also ignorant of their own possible stake in the negotiation. Thus, the parties would naturally try to protect the most vulnerable party, since they might be the most vulnerable party.

YODER: So the people in the negotiation do not know their stake in the negotiation? They just know the kinds of parties involved, and they make an effort to protect the rights of all parties.

CLARISSA: Yes. Each negotiator could actually be the "least advantaged," or most vulnerable, party.

YODER: What parties did the authors see as having a role in the negotiation?

HANK: Software providers, such as Silicon Techchronics. Software buyers, such as CyberWidgets. Software users, such as Bart Matthews. And the software penumbra, such as Bart's wife and his children.

YODER: Could you define the *software penumbra?*

HANK: This is the population that lives in the "shadow" of the system, that can derive benefit from or can be harmed by the system. For example, fly-by-wire software would include in its penumbra all the passengers who fly in airplanes controlled by fly-by-wire software and all the friends, relatives, and acquaintances of these passengers. The penumbra can be quite broad. The fly-by-wire example is actually used in the article we read.

ABIGAIL: When the United States and the former Soviet Union were considering computer-mediated launch-on-warning systems, the penumbra would be the entire human race.

YODER: Can anyone explain what *launch-on-warning* means?

ABIGAIL: It means that a computer would decide to launch a nuclear strike in response to a perceived attack from the other side.

YODER: So a system like that would have an enormously broad penumbra. It's a scandal that the human race ever got to that stage of thinking during the Cold War. What came next in the "How Good Is Good Enough?" paper?

SAM: We have four parties—software providers, buyers, users, and the penumbra—and a negotiation that is going to decide their obligations to one another under a contract. Those involved in the negotiation are fair and rational, and they do not know their own stakes in the negotiation. They may not have any stakes in the negotiation, but they understand the nature of software development, and understand the roles played by providers, buyers, users, and those in the penumbra. They will naturally act to protect the least advantaged or most vulnerable.

JAMIE: In fact, the authors came up with three principles to guide the negotiators. These are, Don't increase harm to the least advantaged, the most vulnerable. Don't risk increasing harm in an already risky environment. From these they derive the corollary that, and I'm quoting here from page 86, "Software designed for a low-threat context should not be used in a higher-threat context." Finally, they propose a publicity test for difficult cost-benefit trade-offs. For example, and this is my own example, let's say a car company knows that a gas tank explodes when there is a rear-end collision. They can do a cost-benefit trade-off on whether to redesign the car. They might decide that it is worth absorbing ten deaths per year and the lawsuits that would ensue instead of absorbing the costs of redesigning the car. If the public would be outraged if it found out about such a trade-off, then the trade-off would be judged as being unethical according to the publicity test.

YODER: Can anyone give us a summary of the contractual obligations that the authors developed in their paper?

NATE: Each party has obligations to each of the other parties. Providers have obligations to buyers, to users, and to the penumbra.

CLARISSA: And to themselves! They must make a profit!

YODER: But can we have a summary of these obligations so that we can try to apply them to the case of the killer robot?

JAMIE: I made up slides that contain the content of their tables 1 through 4. These might be helpful for those who will be watching this on television.

YODER: You knew this would be on television?

JAMIE: I work at KPAT. You know it's affiliated with the university, and I'm a work-study student.

YODER: And you didn't warn me?

JAMIE: It's strictly against the rules. "Candid Professor" is a sacred university tradition.

YODER: Okay. Let's put up your slides.

JAMIE: They're on disk. It will take a few seconds to set up the computer and the projector. These are verbatim reproductions of tables 1 through 4 of the "How Good Is Good Enough?" paper from pages 88 and 89.

TABLE 1. OBLIGATIONS OF THE SOFTWARE PROVIDER

To the provider:

- make a *reasonable* profit

To the buyer:

- *reasonable* use warranty
- *informed consent* about testing process and potential shortcomings

To the user:

- *clear* operating instructions
- *reasonable* protections from and informative responses to use and abuse
- provide *reasonable* technical support

To the penumbra:

- reasonable protections against physical, emotional, and economic harm from applications
- open about software development process and limits of correctness

(from Collins et al., p. 88)

YODER: Excellent! Now let's take a few minutes to study the slide, and then I'd like to ask you whether these ideas apply to the killer robot case.

Okay. How would you apply these obligations to the software provider in the case of the killer robot? Clarissa?

CLARISSA: Clearly, Silicon Techchronics was not forthright in its communications to CyberWidgets about software testing techniques.

NATE: They failed miserably in their obligations to the user. The robot operators did not receive adequate training. They certainly did not protect the robot operators against potential harm that could be done by the robot.

HANK: It's not clear to me that they had any obligation to communicate to the penumbra about risks involved in the use of the robot. It seems like the penumbra, including Mrs. Matthews and her children, get involved after the fact.

YODER: Is this always true? Does the penumbra always come in after the accident, after the disaster?

ABIGAIL: No, I think that the authors are making an excellent point. Some systems have a more intimate connection to their penumbras. For example, the entire population was in the penumbra for the proposed launch-on-warning systems in the 1980s. The people should have a say in whether such a system gets deployed or not.

NATE: I wonder how companies like Silicon Techchronics can fulfill the obligation to be "open about software development process." If they had been open about what was going on, would that have dampened the negative public reaction to the killer robot?

JOHN: That's why I think this paper is heading in the right direction. The public does not understand how software is developed, and they do not understand the limitations of computer systems, but they need to.

YODER: Okay. Let's study Jamie's next slide, and then we'll discuss it.

TABLE 2. OBLIGATIONS OF THE SOFTWARE BUYER

To the provider:

- negotiate in *good faith*, recognizing the importance of provider's fair profit
- learn *enough* about the software to make an *informed* decision
- facilitate *adequate* communication to users.

To the buyer:

To the user:

- provide *quality* software *appropriate* to users' needs within *reasonable* budget constraints
- *prudent* introduction to automation
- *informed* consent to using software
- *represent* user's interests with providers

To the penumbra:

- buy software only with *reasonable* safeguards for the public
- *open* about software capabilities and limitations

(from Collins et al., p. 88)

YODER: The software buyer was CyberWidgets. Did they fulfill these obligations?

MIKE: I think they were deficient in the way in which they communicated with Silicon Techchronics. Nothing that I have seen on TV or read in the papers so far indicates that they really tried to learn all they could about the Robbie CX30 project from the point of view of safety and so forth.

HANK: There didn't seem to be any effort on the part of CyberWidgets to facilitate communications between Silicon Techchronics and the robot operators. That would have solved a lot of problems

ABIGAIL: But shouldn't Silicon Techchronics have been more aggressive in that way? This seems to be lacking in the authors' list of obligations by the provider. I think the provider must communicate with users to determine their needs *early* in the project, before the thing gets built.

CLARISSA: Good point.

JAMIE: This is really interesting. I think we're discovering significant deficiencies in the way that CyberWidgets behaved. The media has concentrated its attention on Silicon Techchronics. CyberWidgets did not fulfill its obligations to users based on this slide. They did not check to see that the new system would be appropriate to the needs of the robot operators. They did not really ensure a quality product, which was their obligation to their employees, the users. I don't see that CyberWidgets really consulted with users or represented their interests to Silicon Techchronics.

MIKE: I think that CyberWidgets failed in its obligations to the software penumbra. The obvious software penumbra includes the family of Bart Matthews, but it includes all of the families of the robot operators. I don't think CyberWidgets had any awareness of a penumbra.

YODER: Okay. Let's look at the next slide.

TABLE 3. OBLIGATIONS OF THE SOFTWARE USER

To the provider:

- respect ownership *rights*

To the buyer:

- *active* communication with the buyer
- *good faith effort* to learn and use software responsibly
- *reasonable* requests for computing power

To other users:

- *willing* cooperation in learning and using software

To the penumbra:

- *conscientious* effort to reduce any risks to the public
- encourage *reasonable* expectations about software capabilities and limitations

(from Collins et al., p. 89)

YODER: What do you think? Did the robot operators fulfill their obligations?

CLARISSA: I don't see how they could be faulted.

JAMIE: I think they can be faulted. First of all, if you are a husband and a father with three children, isn't it your responsibility to make sure that the robot you are using is safe? That's your obligation to the penumbra.

CLARISSA: Okay, but we see no evidence that Bart Matthews was irresponsible in the say that he used the software. He did communicate his concern to CyberWidgets that the robot console had a poor user interface. I think he was willing to learn, although he didn't know everything he needed to know in order to save his own life.

NATE: I can see how in certain situations the obligations of the user to the penumbra are very significant. For example, consider the operator of an X-ray machine, such as the one that we studied [the Therac-25]. The operators really have the obligation to inform patients of the nature of the machine and of possible risks.

MIKE: This slide shows that users have more power than we usually give them credit for. They need to understand the limitations of computer systems so that they can make reasonable requests for new systems. I wonder if the workers at CyberWidgets were pushing for the new robots and whether that was a factor in the haste with which the robots were introduced.

YODER: Let's consider the final slide.

TABLE 4. OBLIGATIONS OF THE SOFTWARE PENUMBRA

To the provider:

- become *aware* of the capabilities and limitations of software.
- advocate a *suitable* economic and statutory environment for quality software

To the buyer:

- advocate a *suitable* economic and statutory environment for quality software

> To ... [the] users:
>
> - expect only *reasonable* service from users
> - become *aware* of the capabilities and limitations of software
>
> To the penumbra:
>
> - become *aware* of the capabilities and limitations of software
> - advocate a *suitable* economic and statutory environment for quality software
>
> (from Collins et al., p. 89)

YODER: Okay. What about the obligations of the penumbra?

CLARISSA: These seem to be rules about good citizenship in the computer age.

YODER: But what about the killer robot case?

MIKE: Mrs. Matthews is the most obvious member of the penumbra. She is advocating a suitable statutory environment in that she wants to see accountability in the death of her husband. She is not going to be satisfied with liability damages against Silicon Techchronics. She wants those who caused the accident to suffer appropriate legal penalties.

YODER: Do you support that kind of accountability?

MIKE: No. I would find that kind of legal environment very intimidating. It might get hard to get anything done.

ABIGAIL: Jane McMurdock, the prosecutor, is also part of the penumbra, and she is working for a suitable statutory environment for software development in her own way.

YODER: Is there a broader penumbra in the killer robot case?

JAMIE: Yes. It includes everyone who has read about it, everyone who has seen a television program devoted to it, and everyone who has listened to a radio talk show about it. We are all in the penumbra because this issue is being discussed in the media. I think our obligation is to learn as much as possible so that we can understand the issues.

YODER: Is there anything beyond that?

NATE: Yes, I think there's a missing element in the authors' analysis, although I think it is an excellent paper. It almost seems like a top-down analysis. The apex is the obligation of the provider to make reasonable profits. I would like to see a new obligation added to the penumbra's obligations to itself, and that would be to increase the well-being and happiness of the penumbra. I think the obligation of the penumbra to itself is to protect its own happiness, health, and well-being. This may place providers at odds with the penumbra. It may require new obligations in all four tables that were given in the paper.

YODER: I think you have a good idea there. So, we have a top-down analysis where business leaders are trying to maximize their profits and a bottom-up analysis where the penumbra is always asserting its right to protect its well-being and happiness.

NATE: Yes.

YODER: Class, that was a good discussion. Please pick up your exams on the way out. And Jamie, don't forget your diskette!

Is that thing turned off?

I can't believe you people chose this week to put me on "Candid Professor." You chose the worst possible week. I'm just returning from the airport. I didn't even have a chance to get home yet.

ANNOUNCER: It was a good class.

YODER: I usually give more of a lecture. This was more like a discussion.

ANNOUNCER: Your students were really on top of the material. They made lots of good points.

YODER: Jamie, you really saved the day with your slides.

JAMIE: Well, this is the second course I've taken from you, and I remember what happened last fall when you came back from a computer ethics conference in the Virgin Islands. Remember when you came to class right from the airport, and you opened your briefcase and your bathing suit fell out?

YODER: How can I forget? Well, at least it was *my* bathing suit.

Transcript of the Television Program

APPENDICES

APPENDIX A

REAL PEOPLE AND INSTITUTIONS

Pam Pulitzer and her book are entirely fictitious. There never was a killer robot incident as described, and most of the characters, places, and institutions mentioned in the book are entirely fictitious. These include the Silicon Valley *Sentinel-Observer*, Silicon Techchronics, CyberWidgets, Global ExperSys, Red Flag, and Silicon Valley University.

I have done my best to portray the technical aspects of software development accurately. All software engineering concepts that are named are actual concepts from software engineering and are not fictions. These include all named technical processes (analysis, design, implementation, and testing) and all named methodologies and tools with the exception of SHEOL. References for these concepts are given in Appendix B.

The characters in Pam's book are working in the same professional and factual world as you and I. I have made a great effort to report accurately on diverse issues and fields of knowledge, including repetitive strain injuries, stress in the workplace, social implications of computing, legal issues in computing, computer ethics, and ethics generally. In all cases I provide the reader with references so that he or she can explore these issues in greater depth.

The Association of Computing Machinery (ACM), of course, is a real organization, and the code of ethics discussed in the text is the actual ACM Code of Ethics. However, a colleague brought to my attention the simple fact that not all readers know that the ACM is a real organization, unlike Red Flag, which is fictitious, or that Bertrand Meyer is a real computer scientist, unlike Wesley Silber, who is fictitious. One simple rule for distinguishing the real computer scientists from the fictitious ones is that the fictitious ones always work for Silicon Valley University or Silicon Techchronics. Nonetheless, I am including a list of all real persons and institutions that are mentioned in the book. Hopefully, this will prove useful for those readers who may not be familiar with the personalities and institutions that exist in the contemporary world of computing.

When the *Killer Robot Papers* mentions an article authored by a list of researchers, only the name of the first researcher is given in our list of real people. Full references to these research papers are given in Appendix B.

I would also like to note that the book mentions three places that, to my knowledge, are totally fictitious. These are Apu, India; Chip Creek; and Outback, Montana.

I also consider Silicon Valley and its institutions as being totally fictitious. I do not know the real Silicon Valley, although I saw it once through the window of an airplane. Beyond that, all my impressions come from media images. The Silicon Valley that I wrote about was my own construction of that somewhat mysterious place where technology gets created. Some might understand that I am writing about the *Mythic* Silicon Valley. If you are producing software anywhere in the world, you are still a part of the *Mythic* Silicon Valley because the *Mythic* Silicon Valley is where *all* technology gets produced. This is how I actually view the Silicon Valley that I created in this work of fiction.

In order to keep the list of real people and places as short as possible, I have omitted from the list all people who should be known to an educated layperson. On the same grounds, I have omitted all agencies of the U.S. and foreign governments, including the IRS, FBI, National Security Agency, Department of Defense, Department of Justice, Federal Drug Administration, and the Office of Technology Assessment.

All institutions of higher learning mentioned in the text with the exception of Silicon Valley University are actual universities. These are M.I.T., Carnegie-Mellon University, Indian Institute of Technology, California Institute of Technology, University of Michigan, University of Chicago, University of Texas, Ben Gurion University, Georgia Institute of Technology, Harvard Divinity School, University of Washington, Harvard Medical School, and Georgetown Medical School. Consequently, I shall not mention these institutions any further.

The *New York Times,* the *Washington Post, World Weekly News,* and CNN are real news organizations (as of this writing), and they shall not be mentioned further.

LIST OF REAL PEOPLE AND INSTITUTIONS

ACM. Association of Computing Machinery. Along with IEEE Computer Society, one of the major professional organizations for computer scientists. The ACM Code of Ethics used in the text is the code of ethics for this organization.

Anderson, Ronald E. First author of reference given in text for the ACM Code of Ethics. He led the task force that produced the ACM Code of Ethics.

Antonovsky, Aaron. Author of book that defines *sense of coherence.*

Booch, Grady. Influential author on object-oriented design. He developed a popular notational system for documenting a design.

Brooks, Fred. Software engineer, author of influential paper "No Silver Bullet." He also authored the classic book *The Mythical Man-Month.*

Brooks, Regina. My editor at John Wiley & Sons.

C++ Report. Technical magazine devoted to C++.

Clarke, Roger. Australian computer scientist whose work influenced the fictitious Professor Lowe-Tignoff's study of ethical guidelines for computers.

Collins, Robert. Computer scientist and first author of paper "How Good is Good Enough?".

Communications of the ACM. Flagship publication of the ACM. An outstanding publication.

Davis, Martha. First author of *The Relaxation and Stress Reduction Handbook*.

Denning, Peter. Software engineer and leader in the computing profession.

Dickinson, Emily. Nineteenth-century poet who lived in Amherst, Massachusetts.

Einstein, Albert. Famous physicist; first person to discover that space is curved even if the observer is sober.

Foley, Jim. Computer scientist; first author of paper cited in text on user interfaces; coauthor of influential text on computer graphics.

Gates, Bill. Will give a quarter of a billion dollars to West Chester University of Pennsylvania. Will give a quarter of a billion dollars to West Chester University of Pennsylvania. Will give a quarter of a billion dollars to West Chester University of Pennsylvania. Hey, it's worth a try!

Goldberg, Whoopi. Bigger-than-life movie star, who appears in the *Killer Robot Papers* as a "virtual person," that is, a computer-generated image of a real person.

Grillo, John. Computer scientist and coauthor (with Ernest Kallman) of book that the fictitious Harry Yoder uses in his computer ethics course.

IEEE Computer Society. Important professional society of computer scientists, along with ACM.

IEEE Software. One of many good IEEE Computer Society publications. This one is about software and software engineering.

International Standards Organization (ISO). Their new process maturity standard is expected to eclipse CMM in importance.

Kallman, Ernest. Coauthor (with John Grillo) of book that is used by the fictitious Harry Yoder in his computer ethics course.

Locke, John. Seventeenth-century British philosopher.

Meyer, Bertrand. Software engineer; developer of Eiffel language; author of influential paper on "design by contract."

National Public Radio (NPR). Not to be confused with National American Public Radio, NPR is the real public radio system in the United States. NAPR is fictitious.

OOPSLA. ACM SIGPLAN's conference on object-oriented programming systems languages and applications. A hugely popular conference with tutorials, symposia, paper sessions, vendors, and plenty of food.

Pravda. Communist-era newspaper.

Rather, Dan. CBS news anchor, who appears in the *Killer Robot Papers* as a "virtual person," that is, a computer-generated image of a real person.

Rawls, John. Ethicist whose theory of justice provides the foundation for ethical analysis given in "How Good Is Good Enough?".

Rousseau, Jean Jacques. Eighteenth-century French philosopher famous for his concept of the social contract.

Shneiderman, Ben. Computer scientist and leading expert on user interfaces and human factors. He developed eight "golden rules."

SEI. Software Engineering Institute. Leading institute for promoting software engineering. SEI developed the CMM process model discussed in text. It can be faulted for giving the killer robot its first break back in 1994.

Soloway, Elliot. Computer scientist who has long been interested in psychological foundations of programming. Now he is studying computers and children.

"Star Trek." Popular television series about the future.

Stoll, Clifford. Brilliant mathematician and astronomer, who has done a remarkable job of educating the public about computer systems and their limitations. Author of *The Cuckoo's Egg*.

Transactions on Software Engineering. Highly technical journal on software engineering published by ACM.

Waltz, Diane. First author of excellent paper on team dynamics. This inspired the fictitious Professor Milton's research of the same nature.

Weinberg, Gerald. Author of classic book *The Psychology of Computer Programming*.

Wiederhold, Gio. Database expert and first author of paper on megaprogramming.

Wilde, Norman. First author of paper on maintaining object-oriented systems, which helped to inspire the article on process visualization.

APPENDIX B

ENDNOTES AND REFERENCES

This appendix contains endnotes and references to the *Killer Robot Papers* stories. First we present general references that are relevant to the entire book. Then we present the story endnotes, which contain additional references for individual stories. Last, we present two "course packs" that could be organized around these references: one for a course on computers and society and a second for a course on software engineering.

GENERAL REFERENCES

This section contains the general references. The general references apply to most, if not all, of the stories in the book. These are organized into several categories, including fundamental concepts, software engineering, and computer ethics.

Fundamental Concepts

These papers present the philosophical questions that are at the heart of this book. These are the issues of accountability and responsibility when software systems fail, the fact that many hands are involved in building software systems, the complexity of software, and the fact that every software system has a penumbra that spreads out from the system and includes all those people whose lives are affected by that system. Collins et al. (3) used the term *software penumbra* in the manner that I have just described. However, in the discussion questions I used the term *penumbra* in a broader sense, viewing each ethical decision as having a penumbra. This is a nice, but not perfect, term. Perhaps I should be more optimistic and say that every ethical decision has a light cone emanating from it. I have also included a reference that includes the entire ACM Code of Ethics (1). Kitchenham and Pfleeger (4) discuss criteria for evaluating software quality.

1. Anderson, R. E.; Johnson, D. G.; Gotterbarn, D.; and Perrolle, J. "Using the New ACM Code of Ethics in Decision Making." *Communications of the ACM,* February 1993, 98–107. [The members of the Task Force for the Revision of the ACM Code of Ethics and Professional Conduct were Ronald Anderson, chair, Gerald Engel, Donald Gotterbarn, Grace C. Hertlein, Alex Hoffman, Bruce Jawer, Deborah G. Johnson, Doris K. Lidtke, Joyce Currie Little, Dianne Martin, Donn B. Parker, Judith A. Perrolle, and Richard S. Rosenberg.]

2. Brooks, F. P. "No Silver Bullet: Essence and Accidents of Software Engineering." *IEEE Computer,* April 1987, 10–19. [An oft-cited essay on software engineering. Brooks lists complexity, changeability, conformity, and nonvisualizability as four essential features of software.]

3. Collins, R. W.; Miller, K. W.; Spielman, B.J.; and Wherry, P. "How Good Is Good Enough?" *Communications of the ACM,* January 1994, 81–91. [This article presents a framework for deciding whether a computer system is ethical and for laying out in detail all obligations for the major parties involved.]

4. Kitchenham, B., and Pfleeger, S. L. "Software Quality: The Elusive Target." *IEEE Software,* January 1996, 12–21.

5. Nissenbaum, H. "Computing and Accountability." *Communications of the ACM,* January 1994, 73–80. [This paper discusses the issue of accountability and champions strict liability as a necessary starting point for holding software providers accountable. This paper introduced the "many hands" phrase that I have used throughout the *Killer Robot Papers* as a central theme.]

Software Engineering

The *Killer Robot Papers* presents many concepts from software engineering, including software process models, the life cycle stages, software maintenance, and configuration management. The following books cover software engineering from a variety of perspectives. A software engineering course could use one of these as the primary text, with this volume as a secondary text. Or a software engineering course pack can be organized to accompany this volume.

1. Booch, G. *Object-Oriented Analysis and Design with Applications.* Redwood City, CA: Benjamin/Cummings, 1994.

2. Conger, S. *The New Software Engineering.* Belmont, CA: Wadsworth, 1994.

3. Jacobson, I. *Object-Oriented Software Engineering: A Case Driven Approach.* Reading, MA: ACM Press and Addison-Wesley, 1992. [Considered one of the top books in the realm of object-orientedness by the *Journal of Object-Oriented Programming.*]

4. Mynatt, B. T. *Software Engineering with Student Project Guidance.* Englewood Cliffs, NJ: Prentice Hall, 1990.

5. Pfleeger, S. L. *Software Engineering: The Production of Quality Software.* New York: Macmillan, 1987.

6. Schach, S. R. *Practical Software Engineering.* Homewood, IL: Irwin, 1992. [Develops traditional software engineering topics using a detailed fictitious scenario.]

7. Sommerville, I. *Software Engineering.* 3rd ed. Reading, MA: Addison-Wesley, 1989. [Survey style.]

Computer Ethics

The following books show the evolution and development of computer ethics over the years. A course on ethics or social implications of computers could use one of these books as a primary text, with this volume as a secondary text. Or this volume could be used along with a computer ethics course pack. These books are listed in chronological order.

1. Johnson, D. *Computer Ethics.* 2nd ed. Englewood Cliffs, NJ: Prentice Hall, 1985. [The first edition was an early and influential book on computer ethics.]

2. Forrester, T., and Morrison, P. *Computer Ethics: Cautionary Tales and Ethical Dilemmas of Computing.* Cambridge, MA: MIT Press, 1990. [This book is weak on the formal analysis of ethics. It presents many incidents that will make novices sit up and take notice.]

3. Ermann, M. D.; Williams, M. B.; and Gutierrez, C., eds. *Computers, Ethics and Society.* New York: Oxford University Press, 1990. [A collection of papers presenting ethical theories and then applications to ethical and social problems.]

4. Kallman, E. A., and Grillo, J. P. *Ethical Decision Making and Information Technology.* New York: Mitchell McGraw-Hill, 1993. [This book has straightforward discussions of ethical decision making along with traditional case studies.]

5. Johnson, D., and Nissenbaum, H., eds. *Computers, Ethics and Society.* Englewood Cliffs, NJ: Prentice Hall, 1995. [A comprehensive collection of articles by some of the most influential authors in the areas of software reliability, computer security, legal issues, etc.]

Two Software Mishaps

These articles describe two major software mishaps in some detail. The Therac-25 article is becoming more and more popular as essential reading for computer science students. It is a wonderful article, and I recommend it highly. The essential killer robot scenario was written before I read the Therac-25 article, but some of the newer killer robot materials have used ideas from the Therac-25 paper. Specifically, the kind of user interface mishap described in "The Case of the Virtual Epidemic" is similar to a user interface feature that was described in the Therac-25 paper. The acknowledgment of the role of hardware safety features was influenced by my reading of the Therac-25 paper. Also, I rewrote some of my earlier materials on software reuse to reflect the fact that reusing software while changing the hardware may not work the way one would hope, and this idea came from the Therac-25 article. The killer robot, Therac-25, and CONFIRM share the common denominator of unethical and unprofessional behavior on the part of system providers.

1. Levenson, N. G., and Turner, C. S. "An Investigation of the Therac-25 Accidents." *IEEE Computer,* July 1993, 18–41. [Should be required reading for all computer science and technology students.]
2. Oz, E. "When Professional Standards Are Lax: The CONFIRM Failure and Its Lessons." *Communications of the ACM,* October 1994, 29–36.

ACM Special Interest Group on Computers and Society

Computer Ethics Bibliography

Professional Societies

The ACM Special Interest Group (SIG) on Computers and Society (CAS) publishes a newsletter, *Computers and Society,* which is a valuable source of information and case studies on matters of central concern to this book. The ACM SIGCAS home page is at http://www.acm.org/sig_hp/sigcas.html.

Herman Tavani has compiled a bibliography of sources on computer ethics and social issues. This appears beginning with the June 1995 issue of *Computers and Society.*

The ACM Special Interest Group on Software Engineering (SOFT) publishes a newsletter, *Software Engineering Notes,* which is a rich source of information on software mishaps and disasters.

You can get information about joining ACM, ACM SIGCAS, and ACM SIGSOFT by sending e-mail to ACMHELP@ACM.ORG. The ACM home page is at http://www.acm.org.

The *Communications of the ACM* has an excellent (perhaps definitive) series on the legal aspects of computing that is usually written by Pamela Samuelson of the University of Pittsburgh. The series is called "Legally Speaking." This is the place to go if you want information about intellectual property, legal implications of technology, liability, and so on. If you join the ACM, you will receive the monthly *Communications of the ACM.* The *Communications of the ACM* also includes the monthly feature "Software Risks," which is edited by Peter Neumann.

The IEEE Computer Society also has excellent publications, including *IEEE Computer* (with its own legal expert) and *IEEE Software.* The IEEE Computer Society home page is at http://www.computer.org. The IEEE (parent organization for the Computer Society) code of ethics is available at http://ww4.nscu.edu/users/j/jherkert/ethics.html.

The IEEE Society on Social Implications of Technology (SSIT) has a home page at http://www4.ncsu.edu/unity/users/j/jherkert/index.html. This home page has links to many other resources.

Of great interest is Computer Professionals for Social Responsibility (CPSR). Their home page is at http://www.cpsr.org/dox/home.html. This home page contains numerous links to other organizations whose activities relate to the social implications of computing, especially such things as privacy and First Amendment rights issues. The CPSR can also be reached via e-mail at cpsr@cpsr.org.

ENDNOTES AND REFERENCES
FOR INDIVIDUAL STORIES

New Generation of Robots Delivered
to CyberWidgets, Inc.

Robot Kills Operator in Grisly Accident

McMurdock Promises Justice in "Killer Robot" Case

Silicon Valley Programmer Indicted for Manslaughter

These newspaper articles introduce the basic background to the killer robot case. They also try to explain why Jane McMurdock wants to hold someone legally accountable for the death of Bart Matthews. The idea of having Randy Samuels misinterpret a mathematical formula was inspired by an actual software mishap that was reported in SIGSOFT's *Software Engineering Notes*. The real mishap resulted in the destruction of a missile upon launch in the 1960s. A robot killed its operator in an incident in Japan during the 1980s.

When the first killer robot articles were written in 1989, I had the prosecuting attorney indict Randy Samuels on the charge of manslaughter so that students could discuss the appropriateness of this indictment. If a program results in someone's death, is that the same as causing a death due to reckless behavior? Six years later I have decided to retain this implausible indictment, because I still want to ask the same question that I was asking back then. I do try to make the indictment more plausible by suggesting that the prosecuting attorney knows more than we do about the case. I hope that the implausible nature of the indictment does not make the reader too unhappy. Randy Samuels's legal situation is not really the central focus of this book. It serves as a point of departure for a more complete exploration into the nature of the incident.

Helen Nissenbaum's "Computing and Accountability" (general references, fundamental concepts) is good background reading for these articles.

"Killer Robot" Developers Worked
Under Enormous Stress

I learned about the "Ivory Snow theory" from a software developer in northern Virginia. It was actually the philosophy of his boss, and it makes a lot of sense for the kind of business systems that they were developing, as long as customers are aware of the philosophy and its implications.

This article is partly about the issue of forcing software out the door before its time. The article by Collins et al. ("How Good Is Good Enough?" general references, fundamental concepts) can provide an ethical underpinning to the discussion at this time. However, I think it is too early (in the course) to discuss the formal approaches. I think it is better for students to discover the need for a more systematic approach as the semester goes on.

The *mythical man-month* is introduced in the classic book by Fred Brooks listed here. The mythical man-month is the idea that adding more people to a late project will only delay that project further.

1. Brooks, F. P. *The Mythical Man-Month.* Reading, MA: Addison-Wesley, 1975.

"Killer Robot" Programmer Was Prima Donna, Co-Workers Claim

This article is about programmers and programmer psychology. Different aspects of programmer psychology will emerge when we discuss the ethics of speech in part II. Personality types (task-oriented, self-oriented, interaction-oriented) are discussed in many books on software engineering (e.g., Sommerville, general references, software engineering). Sommerville also discusses the research that established the superiority of heterogeneous teams over homogeneous teams. Most standard texts on software engineering also discuss team organization in some detail (e.g., Sommerville or Pfleeger, general references, software engineering).

The Weinberg book (2) is considered a classic on programmer psychology. It introduced and developed the idea of *egoless programming* that is discussed in the article. Ledgard (1) has an interesting discussion of programming teams and the problems that they face. Ledgard distinguishes between a *team* and a *group*. A group has failed to reach cohesion. He is especially graphic in describing problems a team might face. *Responsibility drift* is seen as a sign of imminent *team fragmentation* and failure.

1. Ledgard, H. *Professional Software.* Volume 1. New York: Addison-Wesley, 1987. [First of two volumes. This volume contains interesting essays on programmer psychology and teams.]
2. Weinberg, G. *The Psychology of Computer Programming.* New York: Van Nostrand Reinhold, 1971. [A standard reference; considered a classic in the field.]

"Killer Robot" Project Mired in Controversy Right from Start

All standard software engineering texts discuss software process models such as the waterfall model and prototyping. Sommerville (general references, software engineering) has a good discussion of these concepts. This might be a good time to read the Brooks paper "No Silver Bullet" (general references, fundamental concepts) because Brooks sees prototyping (or iterative development of software) as a possible silver bullet. Also, the "No Silver Bullet" paper introduces the intrinsically difficult nature of software engineering.

Fallen Project Director Accused of Conflict of Interest in Killer Robot Case

This article discusses the implications of introducing new technology into a project. The Jacobsen paper (2) discusses the promise of moving into the object-oriented realm and the pitfalls of doing so without proper planning.

Fichman and Kemerer (1) describe real methodologies and tools for doing object-oriented analysis and design. Software engineering students might like to look up the Fichman and Kemerer paper.

This article introduces some blatant ethical concerns. Did Cramer behave professionally and ethically in promoting SHEOL? This might be a good time to read the story "Ethics and Computing: The ACM Code of Ethics" in the *Killer Robot Papers,* or you might want to check out Anderson et al. (general references, fundamental concepts) for the complete text of the code.

1. Fichman, R. G., and Kemerer, C. G. "Object-Oriented and Conventional Analysis and Design Methodologies." *IEEE Computer,* October 1992, 22–39.

2. Jacobsen, I. "Is Object Technology Software's Industrial Platform?" *IEEE Software,* January 1993, 24–30. [Interesting discussion of object-oriented technology; its past, present, and future; and the need to move gradually.]

The "Killer Robot" Interface

User interfaces have been implicated in many software mishaps. This journal paper presents Horace Gritty's analysis of the killer robot interface based upon Shneiderman's eight golden rules. These came from Shneiderman's book on user interfaces (3). Another popular reference on user interface fundamentals (not the programming, but the design issues) is the Rubenstein and Hersch book (2). Rubenstein and Hersch describe interface design as "myth making." One of their human factors principles is "The perfect is the enemy of the good." This principle was distorted by Ray Johnson in the killer robot. For Rubenstein and Hersch this principle means that a perfect user interface may never get out the door. Brenda Laurel's book (1) is a wonderful compilation of essays by a bunch of creative people.

Please note that Jim Foley and Ben Shneiderman are real people (as indicated in our list of real people), and the books and papers ascribed to them in Professor Gritty's reference list are real references.

1. Laurel, B., ed. *The Art of Human-Computer Interface Design.* Reading, MA: Addison-Wesley, 1990.

2. Rubenstein, R., and Hersch, H. *The Human Factor.* Bedford, MA: Digital Press, 1984.

3. Shneiderman, B. *Designing the User Interface.* Reading, MA: Addison-Wesley, 1986.

Silicon Techchronics Promised to Deliver a Safe Robot

The issues of requirements analysis, systems requirements, and requirements specifications are discussed in standard software engineering textbooks. The

Samuelson article (1) describes lawsuits based upon breach of contract and implied warranty.

The theme of the July 1995 issue of the *Communications of the ACM* is "End-User Training and Learning," a major issue in this killer robot story.

1. Samuelson, P. "Liability for Defective Electronic Information." *Communications of the ACM,* January 1993, 36(1): 21–26.

Software Engineer Challenges Authenticity of "Killer Robot" Software Tests

Silicon Techchronics Employee Admits Faking Software Tests

The ACM is a real organization, but Turina Babbage is a fictitious character.

These articles discuss software testing and some ethical issues, including honesty, confidentiality, data privacy, codes of ethics, and intellectual property. Standard software engineering texts generally include a discussion of testing (for example, see Sommerville and Pfleeger under general references, software engineering).

A readable book about the problem of managing evolving versions of software is by Babich (1).

The actions of Silicon Techchronics employees can be analyzed using the ACM Code of Ethics (see Anderson et al., general references, fundamental concepts). Data privacy issues for organizations are discussed in great detail in the paper by Smith (2).

A brief treatment of privacy policies within organizations is also found in Wolensky and Sylvester (3).

1. Babich, W. A., *Software Configuration Management.* Reading, MA: Addison-Wesley, 1986.
2. Smith, J. "Privacy Policies and Practices: Inside the Organizational Maze." *Communications of the ACM,* December 1993, 36(12):104–122.
3. Wolensky, C., and Sylvester, J. "Privacy in the Telecommunications Age." *Communications of the ACM,* February 1992, 35(2):23–25.

A Conversation with Dr. Harry Yoder

The idea of sending Professor Yoder to Harvard Divinity School came from a book by Ari Goldman (1), who was a religion reporter for *The New York Times* at the time. Goldman's book is about an observant Jew encountering different religious traditions at the liberal Harvard Divinity School.

Kallman and Grillo (general references, computer ethics) are the real authors of a real text that is mentioned in this story. Clean-room software engineering is discussed in the paper by Mills et al. (2).

1. Goldman, A. *The Search for God at Harvard.* New York: Ballantine Books, 1991.

2. Mills, H. D.; Dyer, M.; and Linger, R. "Cleanroom Software Engineering." *IEEE Software,* 4(5):19–25.

Ethics and Computing: The ACM Code of Ethics

Software Developers Discuss
Ethics and Professionalism

These two articles present and discuss the ACM Code of Ethics. The ACM is a real organization, but Turina Babbage is a fictitious character. The ACM Code of Ethics appears in its entirety in Anderson et al. (general references, fundamental concepts). The IEEE and the IEEE Computer Society are also real organizations.

The computer professionals who met at the Angry Ostrich got around to discussing computer science education. An excellent meditation upon educational issues is contained in the paper by Denning (1). Two of the concerns in particular that Denning raises are raised in our discussion: the means of measuring competence and the meaning of grades.

The ACM self-assessment (2) is an excellent source of exercises that involve ethical dilemmas.

1. Denning, P. "Educating a New Engineer." *Communications of the ACM,* December 1992, 35(12):82–97.

2. Weiss, E. A., ed. "The XXII Self-Assessment: The Ethics of Computing." *Communications of the ACM,* November 1990, 33(11):110–132.

Long-Awaited Suits Filed in Killer Robot Case

The material in this article concerning warranties, negligence, and strict liability is based upon Pamela Samuelson's "Legally Speaking" column that is listed here. Helen Nissenbaum's article "Computing and Accountability" (general references, fundamental concepts) is also relevant at this point.

1. Samuelson, P. "Liability for Defective Electronic Information." *Communications of the ACM,* January 1993, 36(1):21–26.

Hacker Exposes "Process Maturity"
Controversy at Silicon Techchronics

Clifford Stoll is a brilliant astronomer and mathematician who helped to alert people to the problems of hacking and hackers. His 1988 *Communications of the ACM* paper (8) anticipates his best-selling book, *The Cuckoo's Egg* (7).

Both the article and the book discuss how he tracked down a hacker using some interesting stratagems.

Another source of information on the security of networks is the November 1994 issue of the *Communications of the ACM*. The focus of this issue is "Security Concerns Relating to Cyberspace."

SEI's capability maturity model is explained in Paulk et al. (5). The entire July 1993 issue of *IEEE Software* is devoted to the maturity movement. In addition to the paper by Paulk et al., there are papers on the cost-effectiveness of process improvement and the use of capability evaluations in selecting a software provider.

The paper by Saiedian and Kuzara (6) is an excellent introduction to CMM, the evaluation and assessment processes, and the implications for software providers and buyers.

Hutchings et al. (4) write not so much about a particular maturity model, but about process improvement itself. They describe a method for systematically improving the way that a software team works.

The July 1991 issue of *IEEE Software* has three articles on process improvement (1, 2, 3). These include a critique of CMM (1) and a response to that critique (2).

1. Bollinger, T. B., and McGowan, C. "A Critical Look at Software Capability Evaluation." *IEEE Software,* July 1991, 25–41.

2. Humphrey, W., and Curtis, B. "Comments on a 'Critical Look.'" *IEEE Software,* July 1991, 42–46.

3. Humphrey, W.; Snyder, T.; and Wilks, R. "Software Process Improvement at Hughes Aircraft." *IEEE Software,* July 1991, 11–23.

4. Hutchings, T.; Hyde, M. G.; Marca, D.; and Cohen, L. "Process Improvement that Lasts: An Integrating Training and Consulting Method." *Communications of the ACM,* October 1992, 36(10):104–113.

5. Paulk, M. C.; Curtis, B.; Chrissis, M. B.; and Weber, C. V. "Capability Maturity Model, Version 1.1." *IEEE Software,* July 1993, 18–27.

6. Saiedian, H., and Kuzara, R. "SEI Capability Maturity Model's Impact on Contractors." *IEEE Computer,* January 1995, 28(1):16–26.

7. Stoll, C. *The Cuckoo's Egg.* New York: Doubleday, 1990.

8. Stoll, C. "Stalking the Wily Hacker." *Communications of the ACM,* May 1988, 484–497.

The Unhealthy Workplace

A Tale of Two Cities

"The Unhealthy Workplace" is about repetitive strain injuries. It also discusses whether an employer has the obligation to provide a healthful work environment. Pascarelli and Quilter (5) is a comprehensive volume about repetitive strain injuries. I used this book as my source for information on symptoms and for preventive measures.

"A Tale of Two Cities" explores the issues of stress, the work environment, health, and happiness. I highly recommend the book by Karasek and Theorell (3) as providing strong empirical evidence that an unhealthy work environment is bad for one's health. This book discusses the pathways from a stressful job to poor health via drinking, overeating, smoking, and so on. I used Davis et al. (2) to construct my framework of a seven-dimensional analysis of job satisfaction and stress. My seven dimensions came from a list of ten factors in Davis et al.'s chapter on job stress management. I recommend this book especially because the *Killer Robot Papers* barely touches upon these important professional issues. Davis et al. also cover important issues such as time management and assertiveness training.

The ten suggestions for reducing stress come from a variety of sources. These include all the references in this section, especially Davis et al. (2) and Myers (4).

Myers's book, *The Pursuit of Happiness,* is a wonderful book that I heartily recommend. The epilogue of his book lists ten factors that enable happiness, based upon his research (he is a professor of psychology at Hope College in Michigan). Here are the ten enabling factors in Myers's list (p. 206):

- fit and healthy bodies,
- realistic goals and expectations,
- positive self-esteem,
- feelings of control,
- optimism,
- outgoingness,
- supportive friendships that enable companionship and confiding,
- a socially intimate, sexually warm, equitable marriage,
- challenging work and active leisure, punctuated by adequate rest and retreat,
- a faith that entails communal support, purpose, acceptance, outward focus, and hope

---

Williams and Williams (6) present clinical and experimental evidence that anger kills. The bulk of their book is devoted to techniques for controlling and overcoming anger.

Antonovsky (1) argues that a sense of coherence is a fundamental building block for good physical and mental health. He presents evidence for this premise being a reality. He defines a *sense of coherence* as follows (p. 19):

SENSE OF COHERENCE

The sense of coherence is a global orientation that expresses the extent to which one has a pervasive, enduring though dynamic feeling of confidence that (1) the stimuli deriving from one's internal and external environments in the course of living are structured, predictable and explicable; (2) the resources are available to one to meet the demands posed by these stimuli; and (3) these demands are challenges, worthy of investment and engagement.

Several of the general reference books on computer ethics also have chapters about computers in the workplace (e.g., Forrester and Morrison, Ermann et al.).

1. Antonovsky, A. *Unraveling the Mystery of Health.* San Francisco: Jossey-Bass, 1987.

2. Davis, M.; Eshelmal, E. R.; and McKay, M. *The Relaxation and Stress Reduction Workbook.* 3rd ed. Oakland, CA: New Harbinger, 1988.

3. Karasek, R., and Theorell, T. *Healthy Work: Stress, Productivity, and the Reconstruction of Working Life.* San Francisco: Basic Books, 1990.

4. Myers, D. G. *The Pursuit of Happiness.* New York: Avon Books, 1992.

5. Pascarelli, E., and Quilter, D. *Repetitive Strain Injury: A Computer User's Guide.* New York: John Wiley & Sons, 1994.

6. Williams, R., and Williams, V. *Anger Kills.* New York: Times Books, 1993.

Web of Deception

Krol (2) is a popular introduction to the Internet and World Wide Web. Numerous books are appearing in trade stores about World Wide Web, Mosaic, and Netscape. I have not seen Stoll's book (3) as yet, but according to a review in *U.S. News & World Report* it paints a very negative portrait of the Web and its implications.

An article in the *New York Times Magazine* on September 3, 1995, reported that all three home pages for presidential candidate Bob Dole on the Web were bogus, in other words, intended as satires rather than true representations of Senator Dole's positions.

The *Communications of the ACM* and *IEEE Computer* have had numerous articles on the Internet and World Wide Web from both the social and the technical points of view. The World Wide Web (specifically, digital libraries) is the focus of the April 1995 issue of the *Communications of the ACM*. The August 1994 issue of the *Communications* is devoted to Internet technology.

Other references on the World Wide Web and Mosaic are Berners-Lee et al. (1) and Vetter et al. (4).

1. Berners-Lee, T.; Cailliau, R.; Luotonen, A.; Nielsen, H. F.; and Secret, A. "The World Wide Web." *Communications of the ACM,* August 1994, 37(8): 76–82.

2. Krol, E. *The Whole Internet: User's Guide and Catalog.* 2nd ed. Sebastopol, CA: O'Reilly and Associates, 1992.

3. Stoll, C. *Silicon Snake Oil.* New York: Doubleday, 1995.

4. Vetter, R. J.; Spell, C.; and Ward, C. "Mosaic and the World Wide Web." *IEEE Computor,* October 1994, 27(10):49–57.

Visiting a Software Visualization Laboratory

This article refers to Brooks's "No Silver Bullet" paper (general references, fundamental concepts). Brooks claims that software is inherently unvisualizable.

The basic inspiration for this article was the paper by Wilde et al. (3). This is a very insightful and thought-provoking paper. It points out that object-oriented software has very difficult problems caused by the delocalization of plans. It describes some of these problems in detail and how they detract from the maintainability of the code. One of Wilde et al.'s first points is that if you can't understand the code, you won't be able to maintain it properly. Their paper suggests that visual tools, including animations, could be used to help make object-oriented systems more understandable and thus more maintainable. They give their Vahalla system as an example of such a tool.

Soloway's ideas about plans and program understanding are given in the second reference.

Professor Cleareye's laboratory is my attempt to suggest ways of visualizing software engineering concepts such as coupling, cohesion, and information hiding. These concepts are usually explained for non-object-oriented software in a standard software engineering text. For example, Pfleeger (general references, software engineering) does a very good job. Pfleeger also has a clear discussion of preventive, corrective, adaptive, and perfective maintenance. Our real-world data (as opposed to the made-up killer robot data) is based upon her book. One book that attempts to recast these concepts for object-oriented software is Lewis (1).

Booch (general references, software engineering) is a good source for finding out about the notation for classes described in this story.

1. Lewis, T. G. *CASE: Computer-Aided Software Engineering.* New York: Van Nostrand Reinhold, 1991.

2. Soloway, E. "Learning to Program = Learning to Construct Mechanisms and Explanations." *Communications of the ACM,* September 1986, 29(9):850–858.

3. Wilde, N.; Matthews, P.; and Huitt, R. "Maintaining Object-Oriented Software." *IEEE Software,* January 1993, 75–80.

AI Researcher Quits to Protest
System He Helped to Create

To the best of my knowledge, visual profiling as described in this article is still beyond the capabilities of those clever researchers in AI. I do believe that systems like this are possible in the not-too-distant future.

Martin's paper (2) is an interesting discussion of the public perception of computers as "electronic brains" in the 1940s and early 1950s, when the first computers were being made. People tended to credit computers with more capabilities than they actually had.

The idea for visual profiling was inspired by Clarke's (1) description of profiling as a form of data surveillance (dataveillance). Clarke's paper is a comprehensive accounting of data surveillance and the constitutional and ethical issues that it raises. Clarke's paper can be viewed as treating one aspect of the ethical implications of databases and database systems. Stonebraker (3) not only has been a leading influence in database technology, he also offers us a collection of seminal papers on database systems.

Wilkes (4) gives a brief description of where AI is heading as we approach the year 2000.

1. Clarke, R. "Information Technology and Dataveillance." *Communications of the ACM*, May 1988, 498–512.

2. Martin, D. "The Myth of the Awesome Thinking Machine." *Communications of the ACM*, April 1993, 120–133.

3. Stonebraker, M., ed. *Readings in Database Systems.* San Mateo, CA: Morgan Kaufman, 1988.

4. Wilkes, M. "Artificial Intelligence as the Year 2000 Approaches." *Communications of the ACM*, August 1992, 35(8):17–20.

Vision Quest: The Future of Computing

Letters to the *Sunday Sentinel-Observer Magazine*

"Vision Quest" is my attempt to communicate the idea that computer scientists and those who work with technology must be able to foresee future trends. Part of this involves the ability to anticipate the social and environmental impact of computer systems. In addition, computer scientists and those who are involved in the creation of new technologies must understand that creating something new is an awesome responsibility.

I do not consider a vision quest as belonging uniquely to Native Americans. I used a Native American setting because I felt that most readers would feel comfortable with and respectful toward this particular cultural setting. Certainly, in my own tradition, Moses' encounter with God at Mount Sinai was a vision quest, and I might have used a Jewish vocabulary, but that vocabulary would be less familiar to most readers. The historical evidence shows that Buddha, Christ, and Mohammed, as well as Moses, all went on vision quests of their own. Of course, Frank Kafka's vision quest is quite trivial by comparison to those of the great prophets and teachers of mankind, but this book, after all, is about computer technology and not about spirituality. I certainly hope that no reader feels that I have trivialized Native American spirituality or any other kind of spirituality with this story.

The global landscape was inspired by the megaprogramming concepts of Wiederhold et al. (4). I tried to use their basic ideas as a starting point for describing a global system based upon megaprogramming. My descriptions of intelligent autonomous agents are rather naive and intuitive. Intelligent agents are an important area of research. The July 1994 issue of the *Communications of the ACM* is devoted to this topic.

The theme of the July 1995 issue of *IEEE Computer* is "Virtual Environments." This issue contains startling descriptions of virtual reality systems that are not just games. The serious applications of virtual reality systems seem enormously promising.

Natural language processes play an important role in the computer system described in this story. The August 1990 issue of the *Communications of the ACM* has a special section on this topic.

In our story, the autonomous intelligent agents are seen being used in an educational setting. The May 1993 issue of the *Communications of the ACM* is devoted to educational technology. Sections include "Educational Systems and Designs," "Educational Tools," and "Educational Policies and Issues."

The September 1995 issue of *Scientific American* is a special issue devoted to "Key Technologies for the 21st Century." This issue has a large section devoted to information technologies, including articles on artificial intelligence, virtual reality, networks, and microprocessors. Another section on "Living with New Technologies" discusses the workplace, information technology, and digital literacy, among other things.

Stoll (3) and Negroponte (2) have recently written books (which I have not seen as of this writing) that sound like interesting explorations into the future of computing.

The *IEEE Computer* roundtable (1) presents industry and academic perspectives on the future of software and of the software industry.

1. Lewis, T., ed. "Where Is Software Headed? A Virtual Roundtable." *IEEE Computer,* August 1995, 20–32.

2. Negroponte, N., ed. *Being Digital.* New York: Knopf, 1995.

3. Stoll, C. *Silicon Snake Oil.* New York: Doubleday, 1995.

4. Wiederhold, G.; Wegner, P.; and Ceri, S. "Toward Megaprogramming." *Communications of the ACM,* November 1992, 89–99.

Varieties of Teamwork Experience

The paper "Inside a Software Development Team: Knowledge Acquisition, Sharing, and Integration" by Diane Waltz et al. (10) was really the inspiration behind this article on teamwork experience. The specific ideas that I have borrowed from that paper are (1) the idea of observing a software development team using video equipment; (2) the idea that conflict can play a positive role in team deliberations, but that conflict needs to be managed; (3) the idea of measuring and quantifying speech acts as a means of studying team dynamics and of surveying team members concerning their perceptions; and (4) the importance of maintaining an adequate team memory.

The idea for Milton type A diagrams comes from my friend Sally Ann Baynard Younes's doctoral dissertation in political science at the George Washington University. She used diagrams like these to explain how nations were evolving in their relationships to one another.

The various kinds of personalities that might participate in a team, as shown in the fictitious Milton diagrams, resemble those presented by Henry Ledgard in his two-volume series on software engineering (4).

In writing "Varieties of Teamwork Experience," I drew upon Jewish, Christian, and Islamic sources relating to the ethics of speech. Telushkin (9) has several simple chapters on the subject. His chapter on speech ethics begins like this (p. 65):

Do not go about as a talebearer among your people.

—Leviticus 19:16

Perhaps the least observed of the Torah's 613 commandments, this law posits that it is forbidden to say something negative about another person, *even if it is true,* unless the person to whom you are speaking vitally needs the information . . . .

The marvelous quote from the Epistle of James given in the article comes from the *Jerusalem Bible* (3).

The four sets of questions presented by Professor Yoder were based upon the first four sayings of the Prophet Mohammed in a collection of hadiths (sayings) that was edited by Abdullah and Al-Suhrawardy (1). These four sayings are (p. 49):

---

1. Actions will be judged according to intentions.
2. The proof of a Muslim's sincerity is that he payeth no heed to that which is not his business.
3. No man is a true believer unless he desireth for his brother that which he desireth for himself.
4. That which is lawful is clear, and that which is unlawful likewise, but there are certain doubtful things between the two from which it is well to abstain.

Thus, Professor Yoder's four sets of questions essentially advise

1. evaluating one's intentions,
2. avoiding gossip and minding one's own business,
3. using the Golden Rule to evaluate one's proposed course of action, and
4. avoiding ethically ambiguous actions and checking for better alternatives to the actions that you have planned.

Some of the general references on computer ethics also discuss ethical decision making.

The killer robot software development team is arguing about programming languages. Here are some references that could be used in order to discuss languages more intelligently. Goldberg and Robson (2) is the definitive reference on Smalltalk. Meyer (6) is a book about Eiffel and software engineering. Meyer (5) is presumably a book just about Eiffel (I have not seen this book as yet). Stroustrup (8) is a standard reference on C++. Sterling and Shapiro (7) is a popular book about Prolog. Wilkie (11) has a good chapter that compares various languages (including Eiffel, Smalltalk, C++, and Objective-C) from a software engineering point of view.

Another issue that is raised in this story is software reuse. This topic has been discussed a lot lately, especially in *IEEE Software*. The September 1994 issue of *IEEE Software* is devoted to software reuse, and the introductory article by Frakes and Isoda contains a software reuse reading list.

The final issue raised in this story is women in computing. Several issues of the *Communications of the ACM* have been devoted to this topic, the most recent being January 1995. The November 1990 *Communications* has two articles on this subject.

1. Abdullah, A. S., and Al-Suhrawardy, A. *The Sayings of Muhammad.* Foreword by Mahatma Gandhi. New York: Citadel Press, 1990 (originally published in 1938).

2. Goldberg, A., and Robson, D. *Smalltalk-80: The Language and Its Implementation.* Reading, MA: Addison-Wesley, 1983.

3. *Jerusalem Bible.* Garden City, NY: Doubleday, 1966.

4. Ledgard, H. *Professional Software.* Vol. 1. New York: Addison-Wesley, 1987. [The Milton diagrams were partly inspired by Ledgard's description of the personalities of teams and on teams.]

5. Meyer, B. *Eiffel: The Language.* Englewood Cliffs, NJ: Prentice-Hall, 1992.

6. Meyer, B. *Object-Oriented Software Construction.* Englewood Cliffs, NJ: Prentice-Hall, 1988.

7. Sterling, L., and Shapiro, E. *The Art of Prolog.* Cambridge, MA: MIT Press, 1986.

8. Stroustrup, B. *The C++ Programming Language.* 2nd ed. North Reading, MA: Addison-Wesley, 1991.

9. Telushkin, J. *Jewish Wisdom: Ethical, Spiritual, and Historical Lessons from the Great Works and Thinkers.* New York: Morrow, 1994.

10. Waltz, D. B.; Elam, J. J.; and Curtis, B. "Inside a Software Design Team: Knowledge Acquisition, Sharing, and Integration." *Communications of the ACM,* October 1993, 63–76.

11. Wilkie, G. *Object-Oriented Software Engineering.* Wokingham, UK: Addison-Wesley, 1993.

The Case of the Virtual Epidemic

The "many hands" issue that is raised by Nissenbaum (general references, fundamental concepts) appears here as Pam Pulitzer keeps asking her TV guests, "Who is inside DiaScribe?" Expert systems are described in the seminal book by Hayes-Roth et al. (1). The user interface peculiarity exposed by Professor Gritty was inspired by a related flaw in the Therac-25 operator console. This is described in the Levenson and Turner article on the Therac-25 accidents (general references, two software mishaps). "The Case of the Virtual Epidemic" also raises the issue of whether we can develop ethical guidelines for computer systems. This prefigures a discussion that comes up later in "Is Your Computer Stealing From You?"

1. Hayes-Roth, F.; Waterman, D. A.; and Lenat, D. B. *Building Expert Systems.* Reading, MA: Addison-Wesley, 1983.

The Case of the Deadly Data

The Smith paper (2) is a comprehensive study of data privacy issues at various companies within various industries. The paper by Clarke (1) explores the danger of databases yielding information about us that we might not want other people to know. Ethical decision making is discussed in most of the general reference books on computer ethics (e.g., Ermann et al., Kallman and Grillo).

1. Clarke, R. "Information Technology and Dataveillance." *Communications of the ACM,* May 1988, 498–512.

2. Smith, J. "Privacy Policies and Practices: Inside the Organizational Maze." *Communications of the ACM,* December 1993, 104–122.

Is Your Computer Stealing from You?

This article explores the question, What will be the impact of the computer on human abilities? This question is interrelated with the questions raised by Roger Clarke (1, 2) concerning ethical guidelines for computer systems. Roger Clarke starts with Asimov's laws and then develops ethical guidelines for information systems. It is interesting that Asimov's laws are really quite primitive. They were not written at a time when people were surrounded by computers day in and day out.

The paper by Collins et al. (general references, fundamental concepts) introduced the concept of the software penumbra.

1. Clarke, R. "Asimov's Laws of Robotics: Implications for Information Technology, Part I." *IEEE Computer,* December 1993, 53–61.

2. Clarke, R. "Asimov's Laws of Robotics: Implications for Information Technology, Part II." *IEEE Computer,* January 1994, 57–66.

Candid Professor

This television program is all about the paper by Collins et al. (general references, fundamental concepts).

A COMPUTERS AND SOCIETY COURSE PACK

One can easily organize a course or seminar around *The Case of the Killer Robot* by adding a course pack consisting of articles taken from the previously cited references. For the most part, I have only used articles from the ACM or the IEEE Computer Society. Articles from the *Communications of the ACM* can be reproduced freely for educational purposes. Articles from the IEEE Computer Society publications can be reprinted for a fee. Please consult the title page of each publication for precise copyright and permissions guidelines. Here is a sample of a computers and society course pack using the references given in this appendix. A software engineering course pack is also achievable from the references in this appendix.

Several new references, not previously cited, are listed in this course pack.

Software Disasters

1. Levenson, N. G., and Turner, C. S. "An Investigation of the Therac-25 Accidents." *IEEE Computer,* July 1993, 18–41. [Should be required reading for all computer science and technology students.]

2. Oz, E. "When Professional Standards Are Lax: The CONFIRM Failure and Its Lessons." *Communications of the ACM,* October 1994, 29–36.

Nature of Software Engineering

3. Brooks, F. P. "No Silver Bullet: Essence and Accidents of Software Engineering." *IEEE Computer,* April 1987, 10–19.

4. Wirth, N. "A Plea for Lean Software." *IEEE Computer,* February 1995, 28(2):64–68.

Ethical Issues, Guidelines, and Codes

5. Anderson, R. E.; Johnson, D. G.; Gotterbarn, D.; and Perrolle, J. "Using the New ACM Code of Ethics in Decision Making." *Communications of the ACM,* February 1993, 98–107.

6. Clarke, R. "Asimov's Laws of Robotics: Implications for Information Technology, Part I." *IEEE Computer,* December 1993, 53–61.

7. Clarke, R. "Asimov's Laws of Robotics: Implications for Information Technology, Part II." *IEEE Computer,* January 1994, 57–66.

8. Collins, R. W.; Miller, K. W.; Spielman, B. J.; and Wherry, P. "How Good Is Good Enough?" *Communications of the ACM,* January 1994, 81–91.

9. Nissenbaum, H., "Computing and Accountability." *Communications of the ACM,* January 1994, 73–80.

Data Privacy

10. Clarke, R. "Information Technology and Dataveillance." *Communications of the ACM,* May 1988, 498–512.

11. Smith, J. "Privacy Policies and Practices: Inside the Organizational Maze." *Communications of the ACM,* December 1993, 104–122.

Software Engineering Education

12. Denning, P. "Educating a New Engineer." *Communications of the ACM,* December 1992, 82–97.

Legal Issues

13. Samuelson, P. "Liability for Defective Electronic Information." *Communications of the ACM,* January 1993, 36(1):21–26. [Plus other articles in her column.]

Hacking

14. Stoll, C. "Stalking the Wily Hacker." *Communications of the ACM,* May 1988, 484–497.

Process Maturity

15. Saiedian, H., and Kuzara, R. "SEI Capability Maturity Model's Impact on Contractors." *IEEE Computer,* January 1995, 28(1):16–26.

Computer Culture and History

16. Fox, M. S. "AI and Expert System Myths, Legends and Facts." *IEEE Expert,* February 1990, 8–20. [AI from a practical point of view.]

17. Martin, D. "The Myth of the Awesome Thinking Machine." *Communications of the ACM,* April 1993, 120–133.

18. Turing, A. M. "Computing Machinery and Intelligence." *Mind,* 59(236).

A SOFTWARE ENGINEERING COURSE PACK

The following references were used as a software engineering course pack for an undergraduate software engineering course that I taught during the spring

1996 semester. This material borders on what might be appropriate for a graduate course on software engineering. My purpose was to use the course pack to introduce students to the literature of software engineering.

Software Quality

1. Brooks, F. P. "No Silver Bullet: Essence and Accidents of Software Engineering." *IEEE Computer,* April 1987, 10–19.
2. Kitchenham, B., and Pfleeger, S. L. "Software Quality: The Elusive Target." *IEEE Software,* January 1996, 12–21.

Working in Teams

3. Waltz, D. B.; Elam, J. J.; and Curtis, B. "Inside a Software Design Team: Knowledge Acquisition, Sharing, and Integration." *Communications of the ACM,* October 1993, 63–76.

Ethics for Software Developers

4. Anderson, R. E.; Johnson, D. G.; Gotterbarn, D.; and Perrolle, J. "Using the New ACM Code of Ethics in Decision Making." *Communications of the ACM,* February 1993, 98–107.
5. Collins, R. W.; Miller, K. W.; Spielman, B. J.; and Wherry, P. "How Good Is Good Enough?" *Communications of the ACM,* January 1994, 81–91.
6. Nissenbaum, H., "Computing and Accountability." *Communications of the ACM,* January 1994, 73–80.

Two Major Software Failures

7. Levenson, N. G., and Turner, C. S. "An Investigation of the Therac-25 Accidents." *IEEE Computer,* July 1993, 18–41. [Should be required reading for all computer science and technology students.]
8. Oz, E. "When Professional Standards Are Lax: The CONFIRM Failure and Its Lessons." *Communications of the ACM,* October 1994, 29–36.

Process Maturity

9. Paulk, M. C.; Curtis, B.; Chrissis, M. B.; and Weber, C. V. "Capability Maturity Model, Version 1.1." *IEEE Software,* July 1993, 18–27.
10. Saiedian, H., and Kuzara, R. "SEI Capability Maturity Model's Impact on Contractors." *IEEE Computer,* January 1995, 28(1):16–26.

Programming Languages and Software Engineering

11. Epstein, R. "What Every Pascal Programmer Should Know about Smalltalk." Lecture notes, tutorial presented at SIGCSE 1992. [I would be happy to make these available to instructors. Not listed among earlier references.]

12. Meyer, B. "Applying 'Design by Contract.'" *IEEE Computer,* October 1992, 40–51. [This is an excellent introduction to a disciplined approach to object-oriented design and programming. Not listed among earlier references.]

Analysis and Maintenance

13. Goldberg, K. S., and Goldberg, A. "Object Behavior Analysis." *Communications of the ACM,* September 1992, 48–62. [Not listed among earlier references.]

14. Wilde, N.; Matthews, P.; and Huitt, R. "Maintaining Object-Oriented Software." *IEEE Software,* January 1993, 75–80.

The Future of the Software Industry

15. Jacobsen, I. "Is Object Technology Software's Industrial Platform?" *IEEE Software,* January 1993, 24–30.

16. Lewis, T., ed. "Where Is Software Headed? A Virtual Roundtable." *IEEE Computer,* August 1995, 20–32.

APPENDIX C

DISCUSSION QUESTIONS

In retrospect, these questions are the *raison d'être* for this book. I am profoundly grateful to the reviewer who insisted that this book needed a section like this despite my initial belief that the *Killer Robot Papers* should be a standard work of fiction as much as possible.

In fact, the purpose of the killer robot material is to enable an exploration of the issues raised in these questions. I discovered in writing the questions that I was able to make some of the thematic threads in the killer robot materials more clear. I found that these questions express my fundamental concerns in a direct manner.

These questions are intended for all readers of this book, whether in a classroom situation or not. If you read the killer robot just for fun, there's more fun and insight (I hope) to be found in these questions.

These questions are intended to stimulate discussion and contemplation. Some questions suggest some kind of writing exercise, such as creating lists or writing an essay. Most questions, in fact, can be viewed as essay questions as well as discussion questions. No question is intended as a simple "yes or no" question, even if it appears to be such in form.

New Generation of Robots
Delivered to CyberWidgets, Inc.

1. How much input should an assembly line worker like Bart Matthews have into the process of designing a computer system with which he or she will eventually have to work?

2. Bart Matthews indicated that he "trusts" the robot. Where do you think this trust comes from?

Robot Kills Operator in Grisly Accident

1. Suppose you are charged with investigating the cause of the robot accident. Where would you begin? In other words, where would you expect to find the causes of the accident?

2. Generate a list of possible causes, such as operator incompetence, hardware failure, a software bug, and so on, for the killer robot accident.

3. Generate a list of possible suspects, that is, people who might have played a role in causing the accident. At this point identify these people by position or responsibility, such as "hardware manufacturer" or "software tester."

4. CyberWidgets wants to place the Robbie CX30 robot back on line as soon as possible. Give a list of conditions under which you would be comfortable with the Robbie CX30 being returned to service at Cyber-Widgets. In generating your list pretend that you are a part of CyberWidgets management.

5. Discuss the reasoning behind the list you generated for problem 4. In particular, how did you make your decision, and which party or parties were relevant to the decision you made? Later on in the book we introduce the idea of a software penumbra. This idea is introduced in Collins et al. (general references, fundamental concepts). We shall often define the penumbra more generally as the sum total of people influenced by a particular act or ethical decision. The penumbra can also include animals and the environment. Insofar as any decision to restore Robbie CX30 to service, who would be in the penumbra of your decision? Were there interested parties in the penumbra that you forgot to include in your decision making?

6. Who in the penumbra that you identified should have some say in whether Robbie CX30 is placed back on line? How do you propose to have those parties included in your decision-making process?

McMurdock Promises Justice in "Killer Robot" Case

Silicon Valley Programmer Indicted for Manslaughter

1. Develop a list of criteria that could be used to decide whether a programmer should be held accountable in a case such as the killer robot. These criteria, if completely or partially satisfied, would indicate that a particular programmer should be held accountable in some way. You will be asked to revise your list later in the book.

2. Should Randy Samuels be indicted for manslaughter in your opinion? Did he recklessly cause the death of another? Please observe that there is no legal precedent for a programmer being charged for manslaughter in a case like this.

3. Discuss the differences between "accidental death by firearm" and "accidental death by poorly programmed robot." Are the two circumstances fundamentally different? Should the law make a distinction between these two circumstances?

4. Should the law surrounding software accidents such as the killer robot incident stress punishment or prevention? If punishment, who should be punished if a software bug causes death, bodily harm, or financial loss? If prevention, what legal remedies would you suggest that might help to prevent accidents like this from happening?

"Killer Robot" Developers Worked Under Enormous Stress

1. Could there be a causal chain that starts with the hatred between Ray Johnson and George Cuzzins and ends up with the killer robot incident? Try to construct such a causal chain. That is, try to explain how the enmity between these two men could have led to the killer robot accident by means of a chain of incidents initially set off by their enmity. Is there something unique about this causal chain, or could other poor relationships have a causal connection to the accident? Another way of attacking this issue is to ask who is in the penumbra of their enmity.

2. Explain why it is not a good idea to add new programmers to a project that is already late (the mythical man-month).

3. Expanding upon question 2, consider the flow of information from the new members of the team to the old members and the flow of information from the old members to the new. What considerations might prevent a free flow of information between those who have been on the team all along and the new team members? How many new channels of communication exist because of the addition of the new team members?

4. Make a list of arguments for and against Ray Johnson's Ivory Snow theory. Are your points valid regardless of the kind of system being considered? Are there systems for which the Ivory Snow theory makes sense? Are there systems for which it does not make sense?

5. If you were pressured by your boss to get a product out before it was safe, reliable, or effective, what would you do?

"Killer Robot" Programmer Was Prima Donna, Co-Workers Claim

1. Consider the ideal of egoless programming. What facets of egoless programming would be easy for you to attain? What facets of egoless programming might be difficult for you to attain?

2. Make a list of the fundamental differences between solving a problem by oneself and solving a problem on a team. In what sense is working alone better? In what sense is working on a team better?

3. Is it possible for a team to have too little talent? (Obviously.) Is it possible for a team to have too much talent? How could a manager organize a team that would have the proper amount of talent and expertise?

4. List desirable traits of a programming team member. These traits should include talents and personality characteristics. Prioritize these as first, second, and so forth in importance. Consider a homogeneous team with five people such as you described. Does this team seem like a good team?

   Now shuffle the list of traits to create descriptions for five people with different characteristics. For example, the first person's list of traits might start like this: sociable, a good communicator, good writer, good planner, and so on. The second person might have a list like this: good programmer, good technical problem solver, and so on. Repeat for the other three team members. Would this heterogeneous team be better than the homogeneous team you derived in the first part of this problem. Why?

5. Is it a good idea to take on someone else's responsibilities on a team? What are the implications of doing so? What would happen if everyone on the team started to behave in this way?

"Killer Robot" Project Mired in Controversy Right from Start

1. Discuss the efficacy of the waterfall model versus the prototyping approach from the point of view of determining user needs.

2. Was Jan Anderson's behavior professional? Was her memo wisely worded? Was it nice of George Cuzzins to fire Jan Anderson on Christmas Eve? Does Silicon Techchronics sound like a nice place to work? If you were Jan Anderson, how would you have handled your disagreement with George Cuzzins?

3. Was it right for George Cuzzins to accept his appointment as Robbie CX30 project leader? Who is in the penumbra of this decision? Who is hurt? Who benefits? What are the possible implications of his lack of technical expertise for the team effort? Can he more than compensate with good leadership skills?

4. George Cuzzins dismisses many new technologies as fads, including user interface technology. What does this tell you about George Cuzzins? Is he just a cautious person who is suspicious of change, or is he trying to hide some deficiencies by attacking these technologies?

Fallen Project Director Accused
of Conflict of Interest in Killer Robot Case

1. Pretend you are on the Robbie CX30 development team. What questions would you raise at the meeting described in the text concerning the SHEOL CASE tool and Cramer's intentions for the project? How would you prepare for such a meeting if you knew it was going to happen?

2. Cramer's conflict of interest is clearly unethical. But why is it unethical? Discuss the penumbra of his decision to use the SHEOL CASE tool. Who is hurt? Who benefits? Consider the following ethical lapses: lying, stealing, cheating. Do these words apply to what John Cramer is trying to do?

3. Look up the ACM Code of Ethics (which is described in the *Killer Robot* article "Ethics and Computing: The ACM Code of Ethics" and also in Anderson et al. [general references, fundamental concepts]). List ways in which Cramer violated this code of ethics by forcing his SHEOL CASE tool upon the development team.

4. Who is in the penumbra of John Cramer's drinking problem? Who is being hurt by his drinking? (Presumably, no one benefits except for the liquor store and the liquor companies.) Discuss what various parties could or should be doing about Cramer's personal problems.

5. Generate a list of possible reasons for Cramer's disastrous management of project documents (i.e., his incompetence as project librarian). Discuss the implications of this function being performed so poorly. Suppose some of his reasons for doing such a poor job are deep personal complexes of which he is only dimly aware. Insofar as fixing the problem is concerned, are his personal reasons relevant? In other words, how relevant is it to the professional situation that John Cramer may have some difficult psychological problems?

The "Killer Robot" Interface

1. Make your own list of "golden rules" for user interface design. You may use some of Shneiderman's rules, but at least four of the rules must be your own. Discuss the Shneiderman rules that you deleted and the rules that you added.

2. List measures that can be taken during a software project to ensure a good user interface. Prioritize these as first in importance, second in importance, and so on. Classify each technique as belonging to the analysis, design, or implementation stage of the life cycle.

3. What aspects of the user interface do you think Bart Matthews complained about before his death? Would the measures you stipulated in problem 2 have identified these difficulties?

4. Are Shneiderman's golden rules technology-independent? Imagine a natural language interface or a virtual reality system. Do the golden rules still apply, or do new principles for user interface design emerge? For several of the new technologies that you might imagine, give the rules that no longer apply, and give new rules that are needed. Explain how existing rules might need to be redefined. For example, what would "maintain internal locus of control" mean in a natural language interface?

5. List ethical issues that might arise because of poor user interface design. Part of this question is to see the various ways in which users can be hurt by a poor user interface. Describe ways in which a user interface might lie or steal.

Silicon Techchronics Promised to Deliver a Safe Robot

1. The requirements document states explicit vendor obligations regarding the safety of the robot. Does this document clearly get Randy Samuels off the hook in terms of accountability, or is the contractual relationship between Silicon Techchronics and CyberWidgets a completely different issue? The legal aspects of accountability are not as relevant as your own perception of who should be held accountable. If these documents shift accountability, where is that accountability heading?

2. Who should be held accountable for the inadequate operator training?

3. Suppose you are in a position of responsibility at CyberWidgets, and you agree to cut back on operator training as a cost-cutting measure. Silicon Techchronics will give you a discount on the robots if the operator training can be pared back. Who is in the penumbra of your decision to cut back on operator training? Who is hurt by your decision? To what extent should those who have a stake in your decision (*stakeholders*) be allowed to participate in your decision-making process?

4. What difficulties do you see in making the user interface the last-ditch defense in case of dangerous exceptional conditions? What kind of questions should system designers ask about the robot, its behavior, and the user interface? What is the effect of not providing an on-off switch and relying entirely on the user interface to shut down the robot?

Software Engineer Challenges Authenticity of "Killer Robot" Software Tests

1. Do you believe that Mike Waterson acted in good faith when he asked Professor Silber to investigate software quality assurance at Silicon

Techchronics? List some of his possible motives for initiating this investigation.

2. Generate a new list of "suspects" you believe should be held accountable in some manner for the killer robot incident. This list may be the same as the one you made for question 3 under "Robot Kills Operator in Grisly Accident," except now you can name names.

Silicon Techchronics Employee
Admits Faking Software Tests

1. List ways in which Cindy Yardley's behavior was unethical. You can indicate the manner in which she lied, stole, or cheated. Identify the penumbra for her decision to fake the software tests. Who was hurt by her faking of the tests? Who benefited?

2. Consider the ACM Code of Ethics as summarized in the story, "Ethics and Computing: The ACM Code of Ethics." Which provisions of the code did Cindy violate?

3. Should life-critical software be subject to federal testing in the same manner as prescription drugs? Imagine someone faking the results of a drug test to get a drug out into the marketplace. Is that person a worse ethical offender than Cindy Yardley, or are their offenses similar in nature?

4. Discuss Ray Johnson's behavior in terms of ethics and propriety. Why do you think he chose Cindy Yardley to fake the tests? One student of mine thought there was some sexual politics going on here. Also, Cindy Yardley was probably known to be an ambitious person. Could these considerations have influenced Ray Johnson's choice of Cindy to fake the tests?

5. Why did Cindy Yardley send Ray Johnson an e-mail message concerning their "plot"? Was this wise?

6. Was it ethical, in your opinion, for Max Worthington to play the role of "whistle blower" by giving the press evidence of employee monitoring at Silicon Techchronics and by revealing who was responsible for the faked software tests? Look at this issue with who was hurt and who benefited from his decision in mind. Do you consider the documents that Worthington gave to the press stolen property?

7. Should corporations be allowed to monitor employees in the manner described in this article? If employees are informed of the monitoring, how likely is it to affect employee morale and quality of work? Who is hurt and who benefits from such a corporate policy?

8. If you were Cindy Yardley, what would you do if your boss asked you to fake a software test? Assuming that you have decided that faking a

software test is unethical, what alternative courses of action do you have at your disposal?

9. Randy Samuels's use of stolen software was both illegal and unethical. It also increases the "many hands" aspect of the killer robot software. How many hands are involved to this point as far as we know? Is this "many hands" aspect of software typical or atypical?

10. Suppose you are cruising along at 35,000 feet, flying in an airplane that uses software to control its aerodynamics (engine thrust, position of flaps, etc.). Does it make any difference to you whether that software has 200 hands in it or 20? Is the number of hands relevant to establishing the reliability of the software? To maintaining the software?

A Conversation with Dr. Harry Yoder

1. Consider this story as being a one-act play. Reenact or rewrite the play with yourself playing the role of Professor Yoder. Substitute your opinions and convictions concerning responsibility (i.e., the causal relationships) in the killer robot case. Try to use the *Sentinel-Observer* questions whenever possible, but give your own responses.

2. Do you think that ethics and religion are related, or are they two different things? To what extent are ethical values rooted in religion? Can an atheist be ethical? Can a religious person be unethical? Can standards for a profession be designed without explicit reference to a particular form of religious belief?

3. Do you agree that the ancient Jewish tradition concerning the shedding of innocent blood applies to the killer robot case? Is this a good model for adjudicating other computer accidents?

4. Do you agree with Professor Yoder that the immaturity of the discipline of computing is responsible for the fact that so many professional decisions introduce ethical considerations? In other words, do ethical issues enter into technical decisions because there are no standard practices? You might compare computing against the medical and legal professions. Are medical procedures devoid of ethical considerations because medicine is a mature profession?

5. Try to apply the mom test, the TV test, and so forth to one of the ethical dilemmas discussed thus far in the case of the killer robot. For example, should I steal the PACKSTAT 1-2-3 software? Should I fake the software test? Should I make the operator depend upon the user interface for his or her safety? Should I allow the robot out the door even though I know it is not working properly?

6. How did the people at CyberWidgets contribute to the killer robot incident?

7. Develop a list of criteria that could be used to decide whether a programmer should be held accountable in a case such as the killer robot. These criteria, if completely or partially satisfied, would indicate that a particular programmer should be held accountable in some way. (Reconsider the list you created in question 1 under "McMurdock Promises Justice in 'Killer Robot' Case.")

Ethics and Computing: The ACM Code of Ethics

1. Discuss the eight items listed under "general moral imperatives" in the ACM Code of Ethics. Do these seem appropriate for a professional code of ethics? Do you think that some of these imperatives are unnecessary? Can you think of an imperative that was left out but should be added?

2. Discuss each of the "more specific professional responsibilities" in the ACM Code of Ethics from this point of view: How do I, as a professional or as a student of computing, propose to satisfy these imperatives in my career? Or is it impossible to satisfy all of them?

3. Take an important character in the case of the killer robot, such as George Cuzzins, Randy Samuels, or Cindy Yardley, and evaluate his or her performance according to each of the "more specific professional responsibilities" listed in the ACM Code of Ethics.

4. Evaluate Ray Johnson and Mike Waterson on the basis of the code's "organizational leadership imperatives." Of course, you may not have enough information to evaluate them according to all of the imperatives listed.

5. Suppose you have been invited to serve on a task force to develop a code of ethics for your company. How would it differ from the ACM Code of Ethics, assuming that everyone thinks that everything you say is brilliant? Present a sketch of your code of ethics.

6. Support or refute the following proposition: "The ACM Code of Ethics should be made mandatory throughout the computer industry, and it should be enforced with appropriate disciplinary and legal sanctions."

Software Developers Discuss Ethics and Professionalism

1. Discuss the following proposition, either opposing it or supporting it: "It is important, for my own happiness, to work for a company whose values match my own."

2. Discuss the following proposition, either supporting it or opposing it: "It is better to work for a company with clear ethical guidelines than to work for a company with murky ethical guidelines."

3. Suppose you are at the Angry Ostrich Bar and Grill along with Bob, Sue, George, and the rest of the gang. What points would you like to make at various times in the discussion that no one else made?

4. Discuss the following issues regarding computer science (CS) education: Should the CS curriculum stress professional issues more than it currently does? How should professors measure competence? What are the most important qualities for a CS graduate to have? Should ethics be a part of the CS curriculum?

5. One point of departure for Peter Denning's essay, "On Educating a New Engineer" (see the references for this story in appendix B) is that faculty members have obligations of a contractual nature to students. This brings a new ethical dimension into the student-professor relationship, beyond what might be either implicit or explicit in university policies. You might want to read Denning's paper. Consider the student-professor relationship. Who is in the penumbra of that relationship? What is the impact of the quality of that relationship upon the larger society? In particular, how would you describe sensible mutual obligations involving students, professors, and stakeholders (e.g., employers) in the community? You might want to consider the Collins et al. paper (general references, fundamental concepts) because it will give you more information about the kind of obligations that parties might have toward one another.

6. Consider the following continuum of mental states (based on Antonovsky's "sense of coherence" concept; see the references for "A Tale of Two Cities"): "At one end of the continuum we have coherence, clarity, understanding, a sense of control and adequate means, a sense of orderliness and predictability. At the other end of the continuum we have confusion, a sense of not being in control, a sense of not being adequate to challenges, and a sense of chaos and unpredictability." Now suppose (and this is just a thought experiment!) that you can manipulate one variable in your workplace: the ethical environment. This variable can be manipulated using a slide (such as one finds in most modern Windows applications). You can slide that variable up to a highly ethical workplace with clear ethical guidance, or you can slide it down to maximal lying, cheating, backbiting, and so forth. As you manipulate the ethics "slide," what will be the impact upon the sense of coherence one experiences within that workplace? Please bear in mind that some people have maintained a sense of coherence even in the most hellish of environments. Still, we are trying to explore the relationship between ethics and this concept of a "sense of coherence." Were ethical rules formulated to preserve our "sense of coherence," which, as Antonovsky points out, is conducive to health?

7. On September 3, 1995, the *New York Times* reported that the navy is developing a new kind of naval vessel called an "arsenal ship," which represents a new step in the evolution toward automated warfare. Each

arsenal ship would contain a small crew who would be in charge of about 500 cruise missiles. These could attack enemy positions without any danger of the loss of American lives. In the next century ships such as this might replace the traditional aircraft carrier as the centerpiece of the naval fleet. What are some of the ethical implications of this trend toward automated and ever more impersonal warfare? Does this kind of automation and impersonalization of warfare make warfare more likely? More acceptable politically? To what extent does the person who works on the software for a cruise missile influence the deployment and use of that missile?

Long-Awaited Suits Filed in Killer Robot Case

1. Is strict liability, as described in the article, a good solution to the problem of how to hold organizations responsible for accidents like the killer robot? In other words, do you ascribe to the idea that organizations, as opposed to individuals, should be held financially responsible for damages that have been done?

2. Can you describe circumstances under which individual programmers should be held responsible, either financially or criminally, for software that does substantial harm?

3. Would you support the idea of software engineering becoming a true profession if that would mean that software engineers could be sued for negligence like doctors and lawyers? Is the state of software engineering such that software engineers should be held accountable in this way?

4. Is Sally Matthews making a good point when she says, "In my opinion, the programmer is in the robot, flailing those arms!" Who is embodied within the killer robot? If many people are embodied in the killer robot, what should be the legal implications of this observation? Or is the idea that there are people and institutions embodied within the robot a misleading one?

5. Do you see any substantial differences between the practice of software engineering and medicine from the point of view of the applicability of "negligence"? In principle, do you think software engineers should be held to a standard that is similar to the standard that physicians are held to?

Hacker Exposes "Process Maturity" Controversy at Silicon Techchronics

1. Suppose a hacker gets into a computer system. For several different hacking scenarios (destruction of data in a database, espionage into a military database, poking around in a university database), describe the

penumbra for each particular scenario. Who is the hacker hurting? What are some worst-case scenarios for such intrusions into sensitive computer systems?

2. Suppose you get an important personal e-mail communication. You respond in a personal way, but then you find out that the original message was a hoax and it was not sent by the person you thought. How do you think such an episode might change your view of electronic mail? How would you change your e-mail habits after such an experience? Would you consider the sending of false and misleading e-mail messages a serious ethical violation? What would happen if such messages became widespread? What would happen to your sense of coherence relative to electronic communications?

3. Why might programmers oppose process improvement? Give a list of valid concerns that they might have as well as a list of fallacious concerns.

4. Do you think process improvement will increase or decrease your enjoyment of your work as a programmer? If you work at a company that has begun process improvement, what has been the impact on programmers in terms of their enjoyment of their work?

5. Suppose you are a vice-president at Silicon Techchronics. Would you support the move to process improvement? If so, why? If you would oppose process improvement, on what grounds would you do so?

The Unhealthy Workplace

1. Did Silicon Techchronics act ethically in the way it set up its study of the cost effectiveness of establishing a healthful workplace? Who is in the penumbra of this decision? Who is hurt? Who benefits? Were the motives good ones?

2. How many people do you know who are suffering or have suffered from repetitive strain injuries (especially those relating to computer keyboard use)? How serious were their injuries, and to what extent have these people been able to return to a normal working life?

3. To what extent were you aware of repetitive strain injuries (RSIs) when you first began to work with computers? How much do you know now about such injuries? If you work with computers primarily at work or at school, how much information did your employer or your school give you about the risks of keyboard use? Was it their ethical obligation to inform you of these risks? To what extent should schools and employers be held responsible for informing students and employees about such injuries?

4. Do some research on how to prevent RSIs (for example, use the book by Pascarelli and Quilter cited as a reference for this article). Make a list

of specific work and exercise habits that you can practice so as to prevent a painful disability.

A Tale of Two Cities

1. For your current or a previous job or for your current situation at school, answer the seven questions that Pam Pulitzer asked of the workers at Chip Creek and at Silicon Valley. That is, discuss your job from the perspectives of

   a. being in control,
   b. knowing what needs to be known,
   c. social support,
   d. values conflict,
   e. work load,
   f. career advancement, and
   g. environment.

2. Now imagine a job in heaven. This is your ideal, dream job. (Maybe you already have this job!) Describe your dream job in terms of the same seven dimensions listed in question 1. Try to imagine and commit to writing as much detail as possible about this heavenly job. What makes it heavenly? What do you like about your co-workers? What do you like about yourself? What are your responsibilities? Discuss all seven issues in the list.

3. Now imagine the proverbial job from hell. (I hope this isn't your real job!) Describe it in terms of the same seven dimensions. Describe your job from hell in great detail, as painful as that might be. What are your co-workers like? What is your boss like? What are *you* like? What do you do? What is the environment like?

4. Now consider your heavenly job and your hellish job from the perspective of ethics. What is the status of ethical standards of behavior in the two workplaces that you imagined? Is there no difference between the two jobs in terms of the ethical environment?

5. Now consider your two jobs from the perspective of a sense of coherence, offered here again as a continuum with two extremes: "At one end of the continuum we have coherence, clarity, understanding, a sense of control and adequate means, a sense of orderliness and predictability. At the other end of the continuum we have confusion, a sense of not being in control, a sense of not being adequate to challenges, and a sense of chaos and unpredictability." Where is your dream job in terms of coherence? Where is your hellish job in terms of coherence?

6. Now list things a person might do to change a hellish job into a more acceptable one. To what extent can the individual change the circum-

stances within a job? To what extent is a hellish job one's own creation because of one's attitude toward others and toward oneself?

7. Make a list of whimsical and not-so-whimsical changes you might make in your life in order to reduce stress. For example, you might

   a. drop your calculus course,
   b. go on a two-week cruise in the middle of the semester,
   c. get more exercise, or
   d. develop better time management skills.

   Now analyze the penumbra of these decisions (not the four I listed, but your own list). Who is hurt? Who is helped? Obviously, some tactics for reducing stress hurt ourselves and others. Reducing stress is not a goal in itself. Stress at some level is helpful for growth.

8. Make your own (serious) list of resolutions to reduce stress (if stress is a problem for you). You might want to work with a book that offers comprehensive guidance on this issue (e.g., Davis et al., given as a reference for this article).

Web of Deception

1. Was Randy's use of his home page ethical? In other words, was it correct for him to use his employer's resources to post his manifestos and humorous essays?

2. Did Hoboken InfoSearch conduct its business in a professional and ethical manner? Did they have any obligation whatsoever to provide truthful, high-quality information in their home page? If the Web becomes a giant information shopping facility, are we back to "buyer beware," or should there be safeguards against information of poor quality? What about the First Amendment? Is the Web more like a giant book than a shopping mall? Who, if anyone, should be held accountable (e.g., liable for financial penalties) for Randy's satire on obscurity being offered as serious programming advice in the InfoSearch home page?

3. Support or refute Professor Clark's points about the Web point by point:

   a. Quality of information; lack of standards
   b. Ethics of speech
   c. Fragmentation of society; destruction of "public square"
   d. Loss of a standard language
   e. Cultural imperialism

4. Write a brief essay "The Web: The Promise and the Peril." This essay will give your own list of promises and perils of the World Wide Web.

5. Do you agree with Professor Denton that you just can't get enough information? We know that sensory deprivation can cause hallucinations. But what are the costs of information overload? Is there such a thing? Is it unhealthy to overstimulate the desire for information?

Visiting a Software Visualization Laboratory

1. Why do you think it is so difficult to visualize software in a comprehensive way? Or, if you disagree with Fred Brooks in his "No Silver Bullet" paper (general references, fundamental concepts), why do you disagree?

2. Discuss the relationship between global variables and coupling. Why will a system with tight coupling be difficult to maintain? Why are routines (functions) with global variables difficult to reuse?

3. Why are routines (functions) with poor cohesion difficult to maintain and reuse? Consider the maintenance or reuse of a routine with temporal, logical, or coincidental cohesion.

4. In what way are the concepts of coupling and information hiding related? Are failures to hide information a form of coupling, as Professor Cleareye claims?

5. Summarize the results discussed in the article relating to coupling, cohesion, and information hiding for object-oriented systems. Do you agree with Professor Cleareye's view that object-oriented systems present special problems in terms of maintenance due to "delocalized plans"?

6. Do visual systems such as those discussed in the story hold promise as tools for software engineers? Do you think visualizations can be developed to help software engineers just as X-rays and CAT scans help physicians? Can subtle problems with software design and functioning be captured visually?

7. Think about your own visual ideas for programming and program structure. Can you come up with any interesting tools and representations for programs that are visual in nature?

AI Researcher Quits to Protest System He Helped to Create

1. If visual profiling were possible with today's technology, would it be ethical? Should such systems be legal, or should the government constrain the use of such systems? Should the government itself be allowed to use such systems, for example, to prevent terrorist attacks? What about the Fourth Amendment's protections against unreasonable searches and seizures?

2. Is there any fundamental difference between visual profiling and profiling using databases as described in Clarke's paper "Dataveillance" (references for this story in appendix B)? Do you think the government can abuse its powers using dataveillance technologies?

3. Are we doomed to make computers in our own image? If we are bigoted, will our computers be bigoted? If we are violent, will our comput-

ers be violent? If we lie, will our computers lie? Is there any alternative? Can our computers be better than we are? Do we want them to be?

4. List and discuss new ethical shortcomings revealed about Silicon Techchronics's management.

Vision Quest: The Future of Computing

Letters to the *Sunday Sentinel-Observer* Magazine

1. Discuss the following proposition: "Creativity is a power that must be used responsibly." What is creativity? In what sense is it a power? Is creativity a driving force in the evolution of culture? Is creativity a central factor in the unfolding of future events? What was the purpose of the "rattlesnake test" described in the "Vision Quest" story?

2. Discuss the Global Landscape from the perspectives of

   a. programmer freedom and creativity,
   b. promotion of competition and free enterprise,
   c. providing an enjoyable applications development environment, and
   d. decentralization/centralization of power.

3. Discuss the Global Landscape from the perspective of its desirability and feasibility. Is this a desirable computing infrastructure for 2011? Is it feasible? Would you like to work in the environment being described?

4. Imagine that you are sent to see the future of computing in 2011 or thereabouts. What do you see? Describe it in as much detail as possible. Is it an inspiring vision, or is it a depressing vision?

5. Elaborate upon the Global Landscape features that were described by Whoopi Goldberg, virtual. List more completely the kinds of work you might give your slaves and servants to do. What kinds of threats might be lurking out there in the Global Landscape that Whoopi did not tell us about?

6. Describe worst-case and best-case scenarios for computer technology in 2011, 2026, and 2046. What can you do as an individual to encourage the best-case scenario and to discourage the worst-case scenario?

7. Write a letter to the *Sentinel-Observer* giving your opinion of Frank Kafka's vision quest story. Do not threaten to cancel your subscription. You don't have a subscription.

Varieties of Teamwork Experience

1. Do you agree with Professor Milton that conflict is inevitable in teamwork? Have you ever found yourself on a team in which there was

conflict? Did the conflict help the team to reach its goal, or was it hindering the team's progress? What did you learn from this experience?

2. Consider Professor Milton's discussion of "setting fire to the wheel of creation." Is it easier to start a fire or to put it out? Why?

3. Summarize the suggestions that Professor Milton made for running effective team meetings. Are there any important items that he left out? Based upon your experiences at work or at school, how many of Milton's suggestions are typically followed by software development teams?

4. Study the team transcripts given in the article. Make a list of people who are making a net positive contribution and another list of people who are making a net negative contribution. Of course, some characters may not make either list. For each character that you identified, indicate the nature of the net positive or net negative contribution made by that person.

5. What is wrong with the manner in which George Cuzzins is running these meetings? In what way is his lack of technical competence contributing to the way he runs the meetings and to his ineffectual leadership? Is this perhaps *the* decisive issue in his poor leadership?

6. Was it ethical for Worthington to point out a deficiency in Ambler's knowledge of C++? Of course, we do not know for sure that Ambler's knowledge is deficient. It could be that he is just slow on his feet. Try to analyze this situation from various ethical perspectives including

   a. the penumbra perspective (Who is affected by this speech act? Who is hurt? Who is helped?),
   b. the TV test, the smell test,
   c. Professor Yoder's ethics of speech question set (including the Golden Rule).

   If Ambler does not know C++, should he be supporting it? Should Ambler's knowledge or lack of knowledge have any bearing on your analysis of what Worthington did?

7. What do you think of George Cuzzins's remarks to Ruth Witherspoon about being "one of the boys"? Is this just innocent playfulness or the ignorant speech of a sexist? Can we use our analysis tools (i.e., Yoder's question sets) to decide whether this is ethical speech?

8. Imagine two cultures: one in which people are serious about the ethics of speech and about avoiding hurtful speech, the other in which anything goes as far as speech is concerned. In the second culture, lying, deception, gossip, and backbiting are pervasive. Which culture would you rather live in? Does this preference have any bearing on your own perception of what is right or wrong in matters of speech?

9. Compare the two cultures described in question 8 in terms of their sense of coherence. Sense of coherence is a concept affecting the individual, and we are talking about the overall sense of coherence of individuals in a culture. Here is the definition of *sense of coherence* that we have been using: "At one end of the continuum we have coherence, clarity, understanding, a sense of control and adequate means, a sense of orderliness and predictability. At the other end of the continuum we have confusion, a sense of not being in control, a sense of not being adequate to challenges, and a sense of chaos and unpredictability." Does unethical speech on a wide scale diminish the sense of coherence in a society?

10. Consider Professor Yoder's four question sets. Are these good tools for analyzing a decision that needs to be made concerning the ethics of a speech act? Are there any changes to these question sets (either deletions or insertions) that you would recommend?

11. Can you modify Professor Yoder's question sets so that they become a general set of rules for making ethical decisions? For example, one might generalize "speech acts" to "behavioral acts." The concept of the spread of information can be changed to the penumbra of an act. The basic outline for such a set of rules might be the following:

    a. Examine my motives.
    b. Identify the penumbra (Who is hurt? Who is helped?).
    c. Is my action consistent with Golden Rule and with professional ethical guidelines?
    d. Is the proposed action ethically ambiguous? If so, specify ethical alternatives.

12. Suppose you want to develop a set of ethical guidelines from first principles. List principles that you believe could be used as a foundation for an ethical system, for example, the idea of maximizing well-being for everyone. Explore the implications of your principles and their ability or inability to support ethical guidelines.

13. Defend or refute each of the following assertions:

    a. Not telling someone something that they do not need to know is an act of kindness.
    b. Everyone has the right to know everything.

14. The great religious teachers all warned against gossip and talebearing. Three quotes are given either in this story (the quote from the Epistle of James) or in the endnotes for this story (the quotes from the Torah and from the sayings of the Prophet Mohammed). Are these injunctions out of date and irrelevant to today's world, or is there some kind of ancient wisdom behind them that our culture is not acknowledging? In particular, can we understand these injunctions against talebearing as laws to protect the coherence of a society and the physical and emotional well-being of its people?

The Case of the Virtual Epidemic

1. You are a patient who is being diagnosed by the DiaScribe system. Do you want to know who is "inside" DiaScribe, or who DiaScribe embodies (using language that we have used to describe the killer robot situation)? What else might you want to know about DiaScribe? How do these questions differ from those you might ask a doctor about his or her background?

2. Do systems like DiaScribe represent a fair and ethical solution to the problem of health care for the poor? Consider the analysis given in Collins et al. (general references, fundamental concepts). Did the developers of DiaScribe take the least advantaged and most vulnerable into account?

3. Were adequate measures taken by John Blake to ensure the quality of knowledge being incorporated into DiaScribe? Would DiaScribe have been a better system if John Blake were himself a medical expert? Why do you think the DiaScribe developers paid so little attention to the user interface?

4. Do you find the test procedure described by Cynthia Ozark of the FDA convincing? Would such a test of DiaScribe convince you that it was indeed as good as a human doctor? Can you think of a more convincing test of the computer system short of making it go to medical school?

5. Discuss Professor Lowe-Tignoff's point that there are subtle differences between human and computer doctors. Human doctors can be true healers. Do you buy that? Do you accept his warning that computer systems have the potential to steal human capabilities?

The Case of the Deadly Data

1. Did Sally Smothers handle the information that she received from Ronald Knuth regarding Michael Keating in the correct way?

2. Which S.V.U. faculty and staff acted correctly and which incorrectly with respect to Michael Keating and his job application to Red Flag? I am referring to Ronald Knuth and Professors Benjamin and Krishna.

3. Should an organization that collects blood for use in blood products be allowed to profit from the information contained in the blood that it collects? To my knowledge, this is only a hypothetical question at this point. Should your DNA be considered your own private data (except for its use in a crime investigation)? What kind of control should you have over the information contained in your own blood and in your DNA?

4. Should data privacy policies be left to companies and organizations, or should federal law impose standards for data privacy on the national

level? Summarize deficiencies in data privacy policy at Red Flag as uncovered by Pam Pulitzer.

5. How was Red Flag deficient in protecting its sensitive data? How do programmers who develop applications fit into the equation of protecting the integrity and privacy of sensitive data?

Is Your Computer Stealing from You?

1. Do you agree that it is a meaningful exercise to discuss ethical guidelines for computer systems? Do you believe that these ethical guidelines should be codified in some form (for example, as a code of ethics from the ACM)? Regardless of whether you believe that such guidelines should be codified, sketch a set of first principles for the development of such guidelines.

2. Defend or refute Lowe-Tignoff's claim: "When you diminish another person, you always diminish yourself as well. When you diminish yourself, you diminish all others simultaneously."

3. Is stealing the most fundamental ethical lapse, as Lowe-Tignoff states, or is there some other, more fundamental ethical lapse? Review the ethical analysis question set you developed for "Varieties of Teamwork Experience," question 11. Can these questions be derived from the stealing concept? Is there some more fundamental principle behind your question set?

4. Is a judge-and-jury computer system as described by Lowe-Tignoff ethical? Analyze it in terms of

   a. its penumbra: the people it hurts or helps,
   b. the concept of stealing: Who is diminished by the system, who is increased?, and
   c. the ethical guidelines that you developed based on Yoder's question set (question 11, "Varieties of Teamwork Experience").

   In other words, for part c, pretend that you are the developer of the system, and ask yourself the question: Should I develop this system and release it to the public? Do your analysis questions give the result that this would be an ethical act (and thus that the judge-and-jury system is an ethical system)?

5. Perform a similar analysis for an ethics decision-making machine, a music composition machine, and a newspaper-generating machine.

6. List ways in which computers can augment Human Being. List ways in which computers can diminish Human Being. What can you do as an individual to prevent the creation of harmful systems and to promote the creation of beneficial systems?

Candid Professor

1. Study the four tables taken from the paper by Collins et al. given in the story. Each table describes obligations of parties involved in software development. Are you happy with these lists of obligations? Are there any obligations that you would like to add or delete?

2. Defend or refute Nate's point that the penumbra has important obligations to itself that were not listed. In particular, just as the provider has the obligation to itself to make a profit, the penumbra has the obligation to itself to protect its own happiness, health, and well-being. Relate this to Professor Lowe-Tignoff's ideas about not allowing computers to diminish Human Being.

3. Expand Collin et al.'s analysis to include the computer system itself. Is it helpful to list the obligations of the computer system to the provider (or developer), to the buyer, to the user, and to the penumbra?

4. Consider the manner in which CyberWidgets either succeeded or failed in its obligations as buyer, as outlined in table 2.

5. Make a list of obligations that a provider has to its employees and those that employees have to their employers. Analyze the killer robot scenario from the point of view of these obligations. Is a provider that does not fulfill its obligations to its employees likely to create a quality product?